DIVING INTO GLASS

Caro Llewellyn is the author of three previous works of nonfiction. She is the former director of several large-scale literary festivals and cultural events. She has hosted writers from every corner of the globe, including a number of Nobel Prize winners, and presented events at the Sydney Opera House, London's Southbank, the Louvre, and New York's Metropolitan Museum of Art, Town Hall, 92Y and historic Cooper Union. She is currently a director at Museums Victoria. *Diving into Glass* is her first work of autobiography.

DIVING INTO GLASS

CARO LLEWELLYN

HAMISH HAMILTON
an imprint of
PENGUIN BOOKS

HAMISH HAMILTON

UK | USA | Canada | Ireland | Australia
India | New Zealand | South Africa | China

Penguin Books is part of the Penguin Random House group of companies
whose addresses can be found at global.penguinrandomhouse.com.

First published by Penguin Random House Australia Pty Ltd, 2019

Cover design by Louisa Maggio © Penguin Random House Australia Pty Ltd
Cover photograph courtesy Shutterstock
Typeset in Adobe Caslon Pro by Midland Typesetters, Australia
Printed and bound in Australia by Griffin Press, an accredited ISO AS/NZS 14001 Environmental Management Systems printer.

A catalogue record for this
book is available from the
National Library of Australia

ISBN 978 0 14379 378 6

penguin.com.au

Life changes in the instant. The ordinary instant.
Joan Didion

Courage is being scared to death but saddling up anyway.
John Wayne

For Jack

Prologue

Shortly after my forty-fourth birthday, I was stopped in my tracks running in New York's Central Park.

Two days later, I wheeled a little overnight suitcase through the glass entrance of New York–Presbyterian Hospital in Washington Heights. I gave my name to a nurse, who checked me in and wrapped a plastic name and date-of-birth tag around my wrist. Soon I was lying in a narrow bed, naked except for a hospital gown tied underneath me with loose knots, as a neurologist scrawled a terrifying assessment of my condition on a chart, hung it unceremoniously at the end of my bed and left the room.

There was no denying I had been delusional. I'd lived my life like Lois Lane – taking risks and embarking on any number of shady pursuits in the name of truth and adventure, convinced that, just like the comic-book heroine, I had a caped superhero hovering at the ready to save me at the first sign of danger.

Worse still was the realisation that my hovering superhero was the same person who'd inspired my restlessness in the first place. My father always said, 'I'm your fall guy.' He'd taken a karmic hit big enough for the both of us and I'd assumed – counted on it, in fact – that this meant I'd skate through life unscathed.

It wasn't that I thought his pronouncement would get me through without heartbreak or the other upsets and disappointments that come upon a person. I knew I'd have my share of those disasters. But I did believe, on the strength of my father's say-so, that nothing *physically* would hurt me. His burden – not that he ever saw or talked about it that way – was heavy enough for the two of us. It wasn't anything I doubted or even thought about much.

From an early age, I very purposefully set out to do all the dancing my father could not. I made it my business to have adventures for two. I gave myself to fate and became well practised in turning around the ensuing chaos.

I'd survived my father's situation with humour and good cheer. Standing beside him in his wheelchair, I thought I'd learned everything I could ever want or need to know about humiliation and ardour.

Given all that, I thought I would be prepared for what happened when disaster snuck up and grabbed me like a thug in a dark alley. Yet when my moment came, cutting me loose from everything I thought I could depend on, it was as if I'd learned nothing at all. Grace was the very opposite of what I could conjure up.

But any gambler knows it's rarely just about the cards you hold. My father was an ace up my sleeve, but that was all I had. The rest of it – what was in my head – was messed up.

When the doctor who'd written on my chart came back to tell me I should consider moving into a home with no stairs, like the places I'd grown up in with my father, I wanted to get up and king-hit him across the ward. He couldn't know what was in my future just because I was lying in a hospital bed unable to feel my legs.

After everything my father said about being my fall guy, everything I'd seen him go through, there was no way a wheelchair could possibly be part of *my* life. He'd spoken. It was a given. I was invincible.

My father, Richard Dutton Llewellyn, was a twenty-year-old sailor when he was struck down by a debilitating fever. His temperature was so high, the ship's captain put him into a tiny boat and ordered two of my father's shipmates to row him to shore, a mile or so from where they were anchored off the coast of Adelaide. In the darkened spare room of his aunt Molly's home, in the quiet suburb of Fullarton, he convalesced.

My great-aunt Molly stood four-foot-ten, but what she lacked in height she made up for with understated grit. Molly had been a Red Cross nurse in World War II and, when my father fell ill, it was her diligent and intelligent care that brought him out of his delirium quicker than anyone expected.

One day, shortly after his temperature returned to normal, believing himself to be on the way to a full recovery, my father told his aunt he was leaving the house to run a short errand at the post office.

She warned him not to overexert himself and he said, 'I'll only be gone an hour.'

The following morning he tried to reach for the glass of water on his nightstand. But nothing moved. Not his arms; not his legs. He couldn't lift his head from the pillow.

'I can't move,' he called out to Aunt Molly, who ran to his bedside. Though he later claimed he wasn't afraid, I knew Molly, and she wouldn't have run unless she'd heard panic in his voice.

When Molly hooked her arms under the crook of his armpits and tried to hoist him into a sitting position, he was dead weight. Upright, he slumped like a rag doll and gasped for air. Whatever was happening was affecting his lungs, so Molly knew it was serious. She called an ambulance, which took him, sirens blaring, to the infectious diseases hospital.

By the time the orderlies hauled him onto a hospital bed, he was hardly breathing at all.

Incredibly, the key to the storeroom containing the hospital's mobile equipment, including respirators and iron lungs, was not to be found on its hook in the nurses' station. After frantic searching, a phone call was made to the matron, who'd overseen the night shift and had clocked out a few hours earlier.

The matron had lapsed in her own protocols and, after fetching something or other from the storeroom, put the key into her pocket and forgot about it until her home phone rang. Despite the emergency, she refused to return the key until her next shift, which was scheduled to begin later that day.

I always questioned my father about that part of the story. It's unimaginable that someone could be so monstrous, that a single person could have sealed my father's fate through such a wilful neglect of duty, but he never budged. The matron had the key. The matron refused to bring it back.

As a consequence, my father's life lay in the hands of a roster of nurses, doing whatever they could without the one thing they needed to keep him alive, a ventilator. Each time a lack of oxygen caused his eyes to roll back in his head, the nurses slapped his face and prised open his eyelids and shone a bright torch into his marine-blue eyes, pleading, 'Stay with us,' over and over.

My father was almost dead. By now he needed more than a ventilator to keep him breathing, he needed an iron lung. When the storeroom key finally returned, the door was unlocked and one of the long rocket-like machines was hurriedly pushed along corridors, wobbling and clattering on its little wheels, until it was parked beside my father's hospital bed. Four nurses used the bedsheet to hoist him inside. Sealing him in, they flicked the switch and listened as the machine's bellows slowly inflated and began breathing for him.

By the time the doctor arrived for his rounds the following morning, my father had been moved into a quarantine ward. There his parents had spent a sleepless night by his side, after the long drive to the hospital from their farm in Strathalbyn.

Once he read my father's chart and concluded a short examination, the doctor delivered his cruel verdict. Polio had rendered 95 per cent of the muscles in my father's body useless and collapsed his lungs. The chances of him surviving more than a few days were next to nothing. 'Don't get your hopes up,' he told my grandparents, and left the room.

I have always had a very particular image of my father lying in this metal contraption with only his head stuck out, as though he were looking up at the blade of a suspended guillotine, waiting for the drop.

My grandparents were practical people. At home they slept in single beds with two bedside tables between them. Their blankets stretched tight with perfect hospital corners, each of their flat pillows neatly propped up against the narrow headboard. My grandparents' room was still, as if nothing ever happened in it.

I never saw a touch between them, but in this moment my grandfather, standing beside my seated grandmother, might have placed his hand on her shoulder and given it a single pat.

A year later, my father was still alive. Locked inside the tin can that breathed for him, he longed for a lot of things, but mostly to be back out at sea. He even missed the rigour and fastidious routine of ship-bound life, where he'd once been ordered to clean a deck with a toothbrush.

With nothing to do but stare at the scuffed walls, the chipped paint and the cracked ceiling, he could not help but obsess over the ward's shabby state. Worst were the brass fittings – the doorhandles, light switches and plaques – blackened by use and time. 'Filthy,' he thought, and set his mind to scheming how to fix it.

It didn't matter that my father's new posting was aboard a single-occupancy 'vessel', he'd still be its commander. With the right co-conspirator, my father could bend just about anything to his will.

This is when he met a tall, good-looking trainee nurse from the country named Jill. She was in the final months of her apprenticeship, on one of the last rotations in her nursing education, when she was assigned to the infectious diseases hospital. He found her to be a willing participant in his ambitions and within days of her arrival she was cleaning the dirty fixtures with a soft cloth while he issued exacting instructions over the whooshing sound of the iron lung.

As she polished and scrubbed, and later as she administered his care, my mother and father told each other their life stories.

Everyone takes something different from their family's narrative. This was what I took: my father, still game and commanding despite paralysis, charmed a nurse from inside his iron lung. She was equally up for a challenge, determined to protect the weak, to preserve the dignity of this vital young man, so she took up his cause and made it her business to follow his instructions. Why not? They fell in love. Three years later they were married.

They had my brother. Then I was born. They opened a successful art gallery. My mother appeared in *Women's Weekly* magazine as Mother of the Year.

The message I took most to heart was: no matter how impossible it seems, how long the odds, words and a good story can help you overcome every single thing stacked up against you. A close second: do not dwell on your misfortunes, do not complain, do not feel sorry for yourself. No matter what befalls you, carry on like absolutely nothing's wrong. At the very least, there'll be a good story to tell at the end of it. Care for the weak wherever you find them, build an impenetrable wall around your own weakness so no one sees it. Grab each day as if it were your last.

They were irresistible ideas. Now I see not all of them were wise, but for a long time my parents' lives seemed to prove they were. I took up their mantle. I fell in love with literature and made that my career. I turned mishaps and embarrassments into good stories, and read books like my life depended on them. Sometimes it did.

But the day my legs went numb on the running track in Central Park, every one of those lessons evaporated. As if they'd never been spoken. As though I'd not witnessed or learned a single thing standing beside my father in his wheelchair.

Out of nowhere I found myself lying in a hospital bed, in a country that was not my own, with no good story to tell.

One

I was a runner all my life. At school in Adelaide, I was in the long-distance team, running long and hard for miles, my eyes set to the ground, one foot in front of the other until my legs shook and felt like they'd buckle from under me. Usually runners choose long or short distance and stick to one or the other, but I ran track too. Hurdles, relay, 800, 400, 200, 100 metres. It didn't matter what I ran, so long as I was spent when I crossed the finish line, bent over with my hands on my thighs, my chest heaving.

My life changed on a Sunday in 2009, a few weeks after my birthday. Heart-stopping, life-changing moments happen one ordinary instant after the other, until one instant is oddly not ordinary and then, sometimes, shockingly fast, the whole thing is irreversibly changed and you're faced with the very opposite of ordinary.

Just like there had been forewarning of my father's day of reckoning, there were signs for me too – but neither of us saw that day coming. Perhaps it's for the better that, as things unfolded, it was just one tiny incremental change after another, almost unnoticeable. Until it wasn't. Fifty years apart, we were both blindsided.

One ordinary instant after another until your life is no longer ordinary and your world lies in tiny shards at your feet and your next thought determines how well – or how badly – you will be able to piece those shards back together again.

Twenty minutes earlier, I'd been sitting on my bed in my Harlem apartment, bent over, chest on my thighs, tying the laces of my running shoes. Then I was down the stairs, out onto the stoop, where I stretched my calves against the tall steps. I walked to the corner of my street, took a left at Adam Clayton Powell Jr Boulevard and headed towards the park.

Even though I'd stretched, as I started up the hill at the northern end of the running track, I felt as though two ten-pound weights were strapped to my ankles.

Butter-yellow light flickered through the trees, which had just begun their slow burn into rusted fall colours. I loved the way the seasons in New York turned from one day to the next. There could be thick snow on the ground and the following day – or so it seemed – daffodils would magically push through the earth to announce spring.

At the top of the north-western hill I found myself increasingly unsure if my feet would land where they were meant to. I pressed on, steeling myself against the fear creeping over me, hoping the sensation would pass. After about a quarter of a mile, I couldn't feel my legs moving at all. It was as if I was disconnected from the ground, moving on two prosthetic limbs. Eventually I stopped, bent over and put my hands on my thighs like I'd done after crossing hundreds of finish lines in my life.

But I wasn't across any line. Certainly, I had run no marathon. I'd hardly begun, but my chest was heaving. When I straightened up, I held my palms open to the sky like a person receiving communion. They were completely wet.

I couldn't feel the wetness on my legs, only on my hands. It took me a moment to realise what had happened, but as soon as the confusion cleared, I walked into the bushes, gasping for air in panic and shame, tears streaming down my face, tramping through the foliage, deranged, looking at my hands like Lady Macbeth, wondering how on earth this had happened.

There are parts of Central Park – particularly at the northern end – where the foliage and trees are almost as thick as a wilderness. If someone blindfolded you and dropped you down in the middle of that thicket, once you navigated your way out you'd be amazed to find busy city streets only a few hundred metres away.

I pushed my way through scraggy bushes until I came across a huge tree felled by a recent storm and sat down on it. My track pants clung to my thighs and, when I stood up some minutes later, there was a large darkened wet patch where I'd been sitting. I hadn't just peed my pants a little bit.

I always listened to the same soundtrack when I ran and my iPod was strapped to my arm, ear pods in my ears. My flip-phone was in my pocket, but I was too embarrassed and too upset to call anyone. I wasn't even sure I'd be able to make myself understood through my heaving and tears. What would I say, anyway? None of it made any sense.

Eventually I pulled myself together enough to tie my sweatshirt around my waist to hide the wet patch between my legs and made my way out of the park. The great thing about New York City is that there's too much going on and too many people for anyone to notice much. Even so, I walked as fast as I could up Malcolm X Boulevard, my eyes down to the footpath, hoping I wouldn't see anyone I knew.

I undressed as soon as I got home, threw my clothes in the washer, put the plug in the bath, turned on the shower and sat in the tub clutching my knees to my chest while water, as hot as I could stand it, pummelled my shoulders. The dark cloud of realisation that there was no turning back from this moment bore down on me.

When the bathtub was filled with water up to my chest, I turned off the shower, put my head under the water and screamed as loud as I could.

Eventually my breathing returned to a steady rhythm, but I was still bewildered. Not only could I not understand what was happening, I was devastated by the idea that such a thing – whatever it was – could be happening to *me*.

I wasn't Athena, the ancient goddess of victory and wisdom, I was a snivelling Job, sitting in a bathtub demanding, 'Why me?'

I'd done everything I had been taught as dutifully as I knew how. I'd made a mantra of putting aside fear. The more frightening the task, the more strongly I believed it needed to be done. I rarely complained. I had leapt so many times, and the net had appeared so many times, that I relied on it without question. I had courted neither security nor stability, had made few demands on others, had kept myself free, and yet an hour earlier I had been looking down at my piss-soaked, numb legs, barely able to breathe.

What happened to my father's promise? Sitting in the tub in my apartment, I realised he had not protected me from anything. How could he? Promises like that can't be made. Even from the most well-meaning and protective parent. There are no superheroes waiting in the wings. We're on our own in life and fate will always deal exactly the cards it wishes, no matter the will or love of any human being. And yet I had believed my father, thinking the risks I took would never have consequences, the shaky, thin limbs I climbed out on without caution would never snap. But all my self-reliance and adaptability had failed me.

'Why me?' If I was ever going to get past that question I had to stop running. I had to work out how to take back control of the rudder that had been so dramatically snatched from my hand. It was time to look back.

Two

My parents were married in January of 1960 – a month when temperatures soared to a state record of 50° Celsius. It was, as the guests muttered, sweat soaking their prim clothes, 'stinking hot'.

Despite the relentless pelt of the sun, the photos of my parents on their wedding day are beautiful. They look radiantly happy. My mother wore a half-length veil with a white damask dress cut tight at the waist and hemmed below the knee.

My father looked distinguished in his black tuxedo despite needing to be pushed to the altar by his father. After the priest pronounced them husband and wife, my mother lifted her veil over her head herself and bent down to kiss her new husband. He kissed her back, and if either of them felt a hint of shame or embarrassment at having the traditional roles mixed up, no one saw it.

I often think back to that moment, and the many more like it I witnessed standing beside him, when he showed no sign of weakness or embarrassment. I might have been burning up with humiliation just by association, but he never wavered. I won't ever know whether he was a very good actor and underneath the facade of bravado and confidence he was really shaking in his boots, or if he truly believed he was just like everyone else and it was no big deal, despite the stares and whispers. He presented himself to the world with the confidence of a six-foot-two able-bodied man's man.

I called my grandmother on my mother's side Muttee. To her friends she was Tommy, although her real name was Ivy. Muttee made no mention of my father in her account of my parents' wedding day. In her self-published memoir *The Humble Folk*, which came out when she was eighty-nine, she recounted, 'I cooked each day for a week before the wedding. I also made Jill's three-tiered wedding cake. It was beautifully iced in a pale pink colour with tiny pink roses, tulle and ribbon in a very small basket on top of the cake.' A lot of detail; not a single mention of the groom.

All my mother's nursing friends were there and they were young women who knew how to have a good time. There was the same amount of drinking, dancing, bawdy speeches and good humour as at any wedding.

For many years that was how my parents lived. As though they were no different to anyone else. They flung style and bonhomie around like wedding bouquets. No one could tell how hard things were because the face they presented to the world was that of any young newlywed couple: deliriously happy, with a world of opportunity ahead of them. Perhaps others saw it differently. I know Muttee certainly did.

Many years later I discovered that, moments before my mother walked down the aisle, Muttee leaned in to her daughter's ear and gave her definitive verdict on my parents' wedding: 'I'd be happier if you were marrying a dog.'

My mother was the older sister to three brothers. She grew up in the small South Australian beach town of Tumby Bay, in the Spencer Gulf on the Eyre Peninsula. It was dry, tumbleweed land of brush and high skies.

As a girl, my mother wore her blonde hair in two long, plaited pigtails. Her name was Kathleen back then, but a neighbour called her Dooley Pegs and it stuck. Her father, Brink, turned the nickname into the rhyme 'Dooley Pegs, pickled eggs, lolly legs'.

'Nothing but the best for our Dooley Pegs,' he used to say.

Muttee said she was a 'precocious' child. In *The Humble Folk*, she described her as 'quick as lightning' and 'always into something', which was genteel code for my mother being smart, naughty and strong-willed.

I'm not exactly sure how old she was when she developed a habit of biting other children – perhaps she was five or six. She only bit the nice ones. By her own admission, she wanted to know how these good little boys and girls tasted.

Already she knew she was different from others, and somehow knew that difference ran deep – as deep as the taste of a person. After numerous attempts to make her stop taking her incisors to the flesh of other little boys and girls, and complaints from their parents, Muttee grabbed her daughter's arm firmly and warned her, 'I will tie you up.'

Muttee was not one for hollow threats and after the next offence my mother found herself in the backyard, chained to a post and with the dog's collar around her neck. Despite Brink's protests, Muttee left my mother in the sun long enough to break her biting habit.

Brink was a well-liked stock and station agent who eventually bought his own farm. He set chickens on it. There were tragedies along the way as he learned the life of the land, but once he got the hang of it, he did well enough.

But chicken farming wasn't my mother's dream. Her favourite thing was going to the local country dances. She loved waiting for the sound of the engine purr of a dusty beat-up ute pulling up to her house, announcing the handsome son of one of the local farmers, and from there they'd drive to the church hall and shimmy away.

My mother often came home with the Best Dressed trophy. Muttee was a very skilled seamstress and made all the ball gowns my mother wore. She fidgeted when Muttee made her stand on an old wooden box to measure and fit the expensive taffeta and shot silk material to my mother's slender body. The annoyance of the fitting was far surpassed by the delight of the dance.

She was a teenager when Muttee took her out of school and ordered her to start work at the local sewing factory. My mother left school but refused the factory. She had bigger plans than to be bent over a whirling Singer sewing machine all day with a hundred other poor, uneducated girls. Nursing, she thought, would use her mind as well as earn her an income and independence. She began planning her move to the city.

Three

My father's parents lived outside Strathalbyn, a small town on the south coast of South Australia, in an old settlers' house made of local stone. Their home consisted of three low-ceilinged rooms, whose mud floors were polished smooth and hard by my grandmother's incessant sweeping and the footfalls of the family of four. Outside the flywire doors and windows were 440 acres of drought-prone land where they farmed wheat, peas, hay, barley, flax and sheep, with most of their meagre income coming from chickens and a small herd of dairy cows.

My grandmother kept track of the comings and goings on their property in a small leather-bound diary. At the end of each day she sat at the kitchen table entering the price of stock, money they'd received for crops and other routine farm matters. Only occasionally did she comment on anything personal.

The entry for 28 December 1936, written in blue ink from a fountain pen, recorded the birth of her second child, my father. 'Baby boy born. Hot today.' My father's birth was noted with as much fuss as the arrival of a new calf in the back paddock.

My father, Richard, was a quiet boy. He was born a farmer's son, but could never get acclimatised. He escaped his environment, made the best of his harsh rural life, by steeping himself in books. In the pages of a beaten-up *Boy's Own* adventure novel he could travel wherever he wanted.

His older brother, Jim, often found him skiving off from farm chores, lying down in a dried-out creek bed at the edge of their property, reading novels or comics. He'd quickly read every book in his school's library and looked forward to a monthly trip to visit family friends, not to enjoy their children's company or to take an outing, but so he could borrow the latest edition of Arthur Mee's *Children's Encyclopædia*.

My ancestors on my father's side were free settlers, which meant they'd come to Australia of their own accord, not as convicts. They were enticed to this strange, far-off place, sixteen years after South Australia was first colonised, by the promise of a new start.

In 1837, an advertisement appeared in London's Exeter Hall encouraging people to emigrate to South Australia with the promise:

> *This is the country for a small capitalist, with sober and industrious habits: his family, which in England is often times an encumbrance, will be a fortune here; and he will attain a rank in society, which in England is rarely attainable.*

Another commented on the prospects of those willing to make the treacherous journey across the seas:

> *In Adelaide, all the comforts and luxuries of life may be attained; and an individual who is pining in the cold-catching and uncertain climate of Great Britain – struggling to keep up the necessary appearances of fashionable life, and to be a 'somebody', upon a very limited income – may be changing his abode to the genial climate of South Australia, live like a little prince and become a 'somebody', with the same amount of income upon which he could barely exist in England.*

My father's ancestors bought the promise, packed their modest belongings in large trunks and set sail, clinging to the belief that this colony would offer them the best of the Empire, without the poverty and injustice.

When my father wasn't reading, he would lie in his small cot bed at night with the light off and imagine the adventures of his great-great-grandfather, Captain Jamieson. He had been a private contractor who transported convicts from England to the penal colonies of Van Diemen's Land or New South Wales. Captain Jamieson received a flat rate per registered ton of cargo, along with an allowance of 14 pence per convict per lunar month. It was in his interest that the human cargo arrived in good health, but even so, others with the same incentive didn't boast as good a record as Jamieson.

It was 1852 when Captain Jamieson decided to pack up his home in Aberdeen to start a new life for himself. With his third wife and ten of his twenty children aboard the 100-ton wooden schooner *Rosebud*, Captain Jamieson, now a passenger, set sail with his large flock to try their luck in Adelaide.

Despite the harsh realities of beginning anew in a rugged, dry climate in a fledgling settlement at the bottom of the world, the family thrived. Half a century later my grandfather's father was headmaster of a large school in the then highly prosperous mining town of Moonta.

The town's name comes from 'Moontera', which means 'impenetrable scrub' in the language of the area's Narungga people. Below the thick bracken, in the hard, dry land underneath, lay rich veins of copper. Despite the inhospitable setting, it was a prestigious posting where he presided over the welfare of 3000 children.

Given my grandfather's circumstances – the son of an esteemed headmaster with a good posting – it seemed likely that he was set for a life in academia or some other professional field. But as it did for so many of his generation, World War I changed the trajectory of his life.

My grandfather was a very athletic seventeen-year-old when he enlisted along with some 400 000 Australian men, at a time when the country's population was less than five million. Shortly after, he travelled halfway across the world to the battlefields of Europe.

He was a dispatch runner, a human courier who ran messages across no-man's-land and behind enemy lines, one of the war's most treacherous assignments. For three years he navigated his way through the mud, rats and corpses of battlefields on the Western Front, including at the last campaign of Ypres, one of the war's final and most bloody clashes.

My grandfather never spoke to me about the war despite my incessant questioning. Standing with his back so close to the gas heater I thought the legs of his pants might catch on fire, he told me war wasn't to be glorified with stories. He was always in front of that heater; it seemed my grandfather could never get warm enough.

While my grandfather remained silent on the subject, my father fuelled my curiosity by recounting the story of my grandfather's escape from the infamous Red Baron. I never tired of hearing it.

'One day,' he used to tell me from his wheelchair, speaking in his most serious voice, 'your grandfather was running a message through a large open field of no-man's-land, when a small biplane came thundering down upon him. Grandfather looked up and could clearly see he was being lined up in the crosshairs of the pilot's machine gun, which hung out over the side of the plane. Your grandfather thought, "This is it."'

My father always paused for effect at this point in the story and I felt sick to my stomach even though I knew the ending.

'He waited for a stream of bullets to rain down upon him. But the little plane just kept coming towards him until it got so close Grandfather threw himself down on the muddy ground. He could feel a whoosh of hot air run across his body and the engine's roar was loud in his ears, but the plane's shadow rushed over him. When he lifted his head and got to his knees, he realised he'd been let go by the infamous Red Baron, who flew away without firing a single shot.'

My grandfather never knew whether the Baron had taken pity on him, alone in the middle of that open field, or simply run out of ammunition. I wanted to believe that the Baron made a decision not to kill my grandfather. So I didn't like it when my father finished off the story with details of how, not long after that incident, just before the war's end the Red Baron was shot down and died.

I knew the Baron was no angel, but it didn't seem right that the man who'd spared my grandfather's life could not have been spared himself. I used to imagine scenarios of the two of them meeting after the war, discovering they'd 'met' previously. What different interpretations they'd have of that encounter – one my grandfather never forgot but one the Baron likely dismissed the moment he lifted up and flew away. Moments can be like that. Significant for one person, utterly forgettable to the other.

There's still a long way to go in rehabilitating veterans with PTSD, but back in Grandfather's day there wasn't any help at all. I never saw signs of distress or trauma in him, but my father, all through his youth, woke to the screams of my grandfather's nightmares.

My grandfather may not have wanted to talk about the war, but my father was hell-bent on drilling our family history into me and my brother. I thought Grandfather was bald from old age, but my father told me his hair fell out when he was twenty from exposure to mustard gas. After the war, he only ever had a thin strip of light-coloured wisps curving from his nape to his temple. His pate was so shiny it looked like someone had painted it with varnish.

My grandfather couldn't settle after he returned home from the war; he got a job at the local bank but quit after a few months – he couldn't stand to be indoors after all the open air of those battlefields. Shortly after, he set sail for Siam, where he invested in a tin mine that went bust not long after he sank all his money into it. He returned home broke but with a white gibbon called Mickey, which he gave to the local zoo.

One of my father's favourite holiday outings was to go see Mickey, by then hanging from a dead branch behind thick, muted glass in the South Australian Museum. But I could never take my eyes off the places where Mickey's hair had fallen out, making his skin look cruelly bare. The last time I went to the museum with my father, I was surprised to find Mickey still there in his dark and dingy exhibit, just as I remembered him from my childhood.

My father's enthusiasm for Mickey and the stories he told us about the monkey's journey to Australia, even though they were pretty funny, couldn't win me over. Poor Mickey just looked neglected and sad. Even as a child it seemed like I was looking into an open coffin.

Four

As he sat on the shore gazing at the horizon, my father, under the trance of his Captain Jamieson, dreamed of endless skies, unknown ports and peoples. He wanted to be taken somewhere very far away and have experiences very different from those he knew. From an early age, he strapped his buggy to his pony and set out along the rocky path from the farm to the ocean's edge.

It turns out my parents shared a common dream for escape and rebellion. My father's day of freedom finally came when he was sixteen. He took a job with the Adelaide Steamship Company, working his way up and down the coast of Australia on large cargo ships. Hauling goods from one end of Australia to the other was not for the faint-hearted. The crew was small and each of them a lot older than my father, who was really still just a boy. He was the rookie but he loved it.

Despite the modesty of the family's home and life on the farm, when it came time for my father to go to school he had been sent to one of Adelaide's most expensive boarding schools, Scotch College. There he learned to speak like a stuck-up mummy's boy. The other members of his crew, hardened sailors vehemently on the side of the working class, quickly beat out any sense of entitlement my father may have brought aboard.

It wasn't long before my father was rolling his own cigarettes. He stopped introducing himself as Richard – he was now Dick.

In 1953, aged eighteen, he joined the Royal Australian Navy. The navy claimed his heart even before he set sail, outfitting him with his white dress uniforms and blue work ones, along with all his other gear, for free. He couldn't believe it.

'Free' never stopped being my father's favourite word. 'Discounted', 'reduced' and 'bargain' were others, surpassed only by 'fire sale', which opened up in his mind the opportunity for bartering. He loved almost nothing better than feeling like he'd got the upper hand in a negotiation, and he was very good at it. Of course, within a few years he would have an unfair advantage in any transaction. Usually he refused to play that card, but when it came to a deal, who could fleece a cripple?

In the navy he took on the specialties of navigation, demolition and diving. When he went diving, he wore an old-fashioned diving suit with a big round metal helmet that I imagined made him look like he'd stuck his head in a fishbowl. More than being in the water, he loved the demolition work. What eighteen-year-old boy wouldn't? Sometimes they came ashore and he got to blow up railway lines with dynamite to practise derailing enemy trains. I thought that sounded like a lot of fun when he told me about it.

My father's happiest days were at sea. He never stopped telling me and my brother that. We spent many weekends going to visit old ports and looking at beat-up, rusty boats. Our father wasn't into shiny and new; he liked old things with good stories to tell. He certainly had one.

He was two years at sea when that fever and lethargy struck, the captain sending him ashore, where he was looked after by his mother's sister, his aunt Molly. What happened that day he felt recovered enough to go on a short errand became part of our family's folklore.

After he called over his shoulder, 'I'll only be gone an hour,' he walked out into the bright light. He filled his lungs with air. After weeks of delirium, he could sense he'd be back at sea soon. He felt good.

He didn't go far from the house. Just as he'd promised, he was returning from his trip to the post office less than an hour later. Even so, after so long in bed he felt tired from the simple exertion of walking and planned to go straight back to resting.

However, just before he reached the corner of his aunt's street, he saw a woman struggling up a flight of stairs with two heavy suitcases. He called out, offering to help. She put down her bags and said, 'Thank you. That's very kind of you. I've packed too much.'

My father bent over to lift the bags and struggled to carry them up the stairs to her door. The moment he put them down and they said goodbye, he knew he'd made a mistake. He felt faint and nauseated. He gripped the railing tight as he walked back down the stairs.

The following morning, when he went to reach for the glass of water on his nightstand, he could not move.

It's a particularly cruel twist to my father's story that polio got him on its way out. As far as everyone was concerned, the disease had been beaten after the introduction of the Salk polio vaccine. A national immunisation effort had been rolled out the year before but since polio usually only affects children, my father, past the danger years, hadn't been given the vaccine.

As he slept, in eight quietly vicious hours, polio took all movement from my father's long legs, his arms, his hands and then – the final blow on the list of devastations – it collapsed his lungs.

It wasn't just one thing that went wrong that day when he arrived at the hospital. As is often the way, a number of factors came together to shape my father's destiny. He was a sailor ashore, caught in the middle of a perfect storm.

In 1928, Philip Drinker and Louis Agassiz Shaw invented the iron lung, which was initially called a 'tank respirator' or 'Drinker respirator'. Drinker and Shaw's first machine used air pumps from two vacuum cleaners, powered by an electric motor. The pumps changed the pressure inside an airtight metal box, pushing and sucking oxygen in and out of the lungs of the person lying inside, breathing for them. It was originally designed as treatment for coal-gas poisoning but was quickly identified as life-saving for polio victims as well.

When the ambulance men handed over my father on a stretcher, the hospital's machines were in the locked storeroom. Why they hadn't been more insistent that the matron bring the key before her next shift, or didn't send someone to her house to get the key, or simply hatchet the door down themselves, I never understood.

Instead, the nurses held their vigil that first night. Without them, there is no doubt my father would have died.

Surprisingly, considering the havoc it wreaked on so many young lives during its three decades of epidemic, polio is not a very efficient disease. It is rapidly killed by heat, formaldehyde, chlorine and ultraviolet light. Ninety per cent of polio infections cause no symptoms at all, with the rest experiencing nothing much more than fever and lethargy. Only about 1 per cent of infected individuals will suffer any lasting manifestation of the disease, such as the wasting of limbs.

My father, however, had such a severe presentation of polio, nobody thought he could survive it. I had never heard of the medical term for his condition, bulbospinal polio. My father certainly never described it that way to me. When my brother and I were growing up, he rarely discussed his condition or mentioned the word polio. But now I know bulbospinal polio describes patients who present with both brainstem (bulbar) and spinal cord symptoms.

My father always believed that it was carrying that woman's suitcases up the stairs that did him in. He surmised that the strain of lifting such a heavy weight when his immune system was still so weakened and vulnerable allowed the lurking virus to take hold.

My father's story, as he always told it to me, had it that if that simple series of events had not taken place he would have been one of the 99 per cent in whom the disease leaves no lasting mark.

Whether it was his act of kindness that tipped him over the edge, I will never know. But my father, like anyone whose sense of meaning in the world is suddenly and seemingly inexplicably devastated, needed a narrative. He needed to explain to himself what had happened. The story of the suitcases helped him go on but it also shielded him, and all of us, from the more painful reality.

This story, so large in my mind from the day it was first told to me, set me to thinking that my father believed he had brought his fate upon himself. No matter how subtle he intended it to be, that was the message I took away. He did something and there were consequences.

Sometimes when I walked along the footpath beside my father, I imagined the woman with the suitcases walking behind us, feeling sorry for the children of the cripple, oblivious of her role in putting him in that chair.

Having someone to hold accountable makes it easier to comprehend life's surprises than if they're random strikes. In the beginning, I didn't have a narrative for the numbness in my legs. I swirled around in a dizzying frenzy of unanswered questions. The doctors didn't know what was wrong with me. It didn't look exactly like anything they had seen before, so any question I asked was met with an indefinite answer.

It was easy, then, to adopt my father's way of thinking about what had happened to me. Over time the idea settled in that I, too, had brought whatever this was upon myself. Deep inside I felt that I was paying for my choices in life, that this affliction was entirely of my own making. Had I lived a more traditional life, a stress-free one, less on-the-edge, none of this would have happened. Just like him, I was to blame.

Five

During the initial weeks of his hospitalisation, my father was in and out of consciousness. No one but his mother thought he'd come through it. Even so, those young nurses opened the lid of his iron lung and stared down reality to give my father his daily physical therapy.

Every few hours they diligently moved his limbs, which had been put into plasters to avoid deformity. They pushed and pulled any way they could in the hope that his arms, legs and hands might maintain some movement. When he was conscious to feel it, he described the pain as the worst he'd ever had. In the early stages of polio, when the virus is active and on the attack, it inflames the entire nervous system, turning each nerve ending into a red-raw transmitter of agony.

The valiant efforts of those nurses saved my father's fingers from claw-hand deformity and preserved some movement in them. I always thought my father had beautiful hands, even if they didn't work very well.

He was fed through a tube. Nurses sometimes asked what he thought about the future. It couldn't have looked bright from where anyone stood. The doctors never hid or sugar-coated their prognosis. He couldn't and wouldn't survive. They told my grandparents he'd be dead within the year. But that was not my father. He was a fighter and he gave this battle all he had.

As he explained it, his recovery was in large part down to the fact that he saw the whole thing as an adventure, some new challenge to experience fully, no matter its horrors. Instead of asking himself 'Why me?' he thought, 'Why *not* me?'

It turns out 'Why *not* me?' is the very best question to ask yourself at the worst moment in your life. With that question on your lips and in your head, your eyes are set to the horizon and, before you've even made your first move, you have taken a step to clawing your way back to life.

'Why not me?' means you can live. You can be happy. Most importantly, in my father's case, it meant he could seduce a nurse, no matter how unlikely that might be in the circumstances.

'Why not me?' means you have curiosity, and that's the same thing that had drawn my father to the sea four years earlier – a new port every few days, different horizons, each demanding reorientation. My father liked change and he liked challenges, and polio gave him a large dose of both. When he was told he'd never walk again he told us his second thought was 'This will be interesting.'

It's ironic that, in the end, it wasn't the open seas that took my father on his life's biggest adventure, it was the disease that constrained and stilled him.

What prepares us for life's defining moments? When mine arrived, I wasn't prepared at all, despite my father's example. What had he taught me if not the knowledge that you can think your way out of anything? How could I not know that I had two choices: sit and wallow or stand up and fight?

Yet facing my own catastrophe, I just wanted to give up. When I found myself in hospital, I knew the question to ask was 'Why not me?', but it didn't make me any more accepting or dull my rage. I didn't want to fight. I'd been fighting all my life. I wanted to surrender.

I took up smoking and lied on the doctor's questionnaires about my daily consumption of alcohol. I'd always been an athlete, but I refused to do even the daily stretching exercises they recommended to stop 'spasticity' in my legs. I locked myself away in my apartment, wilfully turning all my stubbornness into making myself sicker, repeating the question 'Why me?' over and over, with each utterance burying any hope of grace deeper in the ground.

When my brother found out that I'd been hospitalised because I couldn't feel my legs, he rang me from Australia. I could hear he was crying. 'We're cursed,' he said. 'First Dad and now you.'

I wanted to correct my brother. *He* wasn't part of the *we*. My father and I were the cursed. As far as I could tell, my brother still had a bright, wheelchair-free future. But I kept my mouth shut.

After about half an hour into our call, something jolted a memory in him. 'Do you remember that Dad always said polio was the best thing that happened to him?' he asked.

I remembered. How could I forget that?

'He honestly thought he wouldn't have amounted to much had he lived life as an able-bodied person,' he said, trying to get me to see the bright side. I remained silent. 'He believed it, you know.'

In my father's case, it was an incident he observed as a young boy that taught him not to indulge in self-pity, no matter how brutal the blow.

It's a fact known among farmers that a standing crop of barley can be fatal for livestock if consumed in large quantities. The animals can't digest the fibres, so most farms don't cultivate both barley and livestock. But barley was one of the few crops that thrived on my grandparent's rugged and sandy land, so my grandfather hatched a plan to have the two.

My grandfather was an excellent fencer and his idea was to construct a sheep-proof, double-rung wire and wooden-post fence around a large field and plough it with barley seeds. My grandmother – being the true farmer of the household – was not convinced it was a good idea, but when she couldn't dissuade him, she urged him to at least leave an extra-wide strip of unsown dirt alongside the fence. He could see her wisdom and did as she said before setting a modest flock of sheep in the adjoining paddock, confident the two were securely separated.

Despite his diligent fencing, one night, when the barley had fully matured, its thick sweet scent proved too tempting for the animals. They broke through the wires, gorged themselves on the plump grains and were discovered at dawn by my grandfather, tipped on their sides, bellies bloated, with their legs out as straight and stiff as blow-up dolls'.

My grandfather looked over the field long enough to take stock of his loss and then went to tend the cows. Once all the cows were milked and set out to pasture, he picked up his butchering knife from a dusty ledge in the shed and my father overheard him say with resignation, 'Well, I'd better get to it, then.'

He walked back to the barley field and spent the rest of the day at back- and heartbreaking work, skinning his dead flock.

The incident wasn't spoken about at dinner that night – that was not my grandparents' way. But the air was full of recrimination and guilt. My grandmother seething with 'I told you so'; my grandfather's usually rod-straight shoulders slumped. His pride was hurt, but he loved his flock and losing them is what took the wind out of him.

The next morning, while his brother Jim was in town selling the bloated, skinned carcasses for dog meat, my father counted 150 sheepskins. They were hung out on the wire fences, which my grandfather had already restrung.

Losing that number of sheep was devastating financially, but it was the emotional hit of that day that never left my father. Something small but significant had shifted in my grandfather. He'd been humiliated and, although most wouldn't have noticed the small change, my father could tell the waft of it clung to him.

It wasn't until years later – facing his own catastrophe – that the lesson really hit home for my father. When tragedy strikes, 'you can cuss and have words, but in the end, you simply have to get on with it, salvage what you can to the best of your ability and make the most of it. No matter how poor your options.' He told me the story of the sheep every few years, just to make sure that the lesson stayed front of mind: we think the opposite is true, but life's foundations are flimsy.

As a child visiting my grandparent's house, I loved to make enormous two- or three-deck houses of cards. The story about my grandfather reminded me of how, when I was building them, one wrong move, one gust of wind, one bad card placement, sent the whole lot tumbling down. And when it did, particularly when my brother walked into the room and started flapping his arms and jumping up and down, I grumbled and tried to punch him, but then I picked up each and every card and began resolutely building a different kind of house.

I guessed that's what my father did. After polio, he picked up what he could and built himself a different kind of house. As strange as it seems, what was happening to him as he lay inside that iron lung was more interesting to him than it was terrifying.

But if you are born into a situation, you think it's normal, no matter how strange and intriguing it is to the rest of the world. My father's condition was so everyday that I wasn't curious at all. He was what he was. So what if he was different to everyone else? To me, he was simply my father, wheelchair, contraptions and all.

Six

The shameful truth was that it wasn't until my early thirties that I found out about iron lungs, quite accidentally, flipping through a fifties end-of-year-recap issue of *Time* magazine I'd picked up from a second-hand bookstore. It had never occurred to me to ask my father about the machine. When I was growing up we were all too busy getting on with life and acting like things were normal.

The issue of *Time* featured a double-page black-and-white photograph showing rows and rows of what looked like metal coffins in a stark room – the single adornment on the walls a cheap oil painting of the Queen. The only thing that distinguished the metal boxes from coffins was that each had a child's head sticking out of one end, supported by a headrest the size of a small chopping block. A nurse in a starched white uniform and hat, which reminded me of a nun's habit, stood at the door with her hands clasped in front of her.

I didn't have to read the caption. Polio. The only thing that stopped me searching those boys' faces to see if my father was among them was that I knew he was one of the last people in Australia to contract the virus. By the time he joined the ranks of polio victims, all the children in the photograph I was staring at were long dead or had gone home to live the rest of their lives with calipers strapped to their wasted and deformed legs.

I remember thinking the iron lungs resembled not only coffins, they looked like rocket ships. If you tipped one up vertically and set a match to it, you could shoot the kid inside right up to the stars. I bet many of those kids wished to be shot into the stars. I knew that's what I'd want. My father said being in one was like being underwater in one of the old-fashioned diving suits he'd worn in the navy.

It's often surprising what we actually want to know about the unimaginable. There were so many questions I could have asked him, but what mattered most to me was whether he had a blanket over him underneath all that cold hard steel. Of all the things I could have worried about – his devastation, his anger, his pain, his terrible fear – I was worried about my father being cold. Even as an adult the rest was too big for me to comprehend. Who wants to think of their father like that? The thought of him being cold was bad enough.

He was in ward C4. At the far end of a large room of about thirty metal hospital beds, two iron lungs breathed life into my father and another young man, who had also come late to the disease. I imagined the action of the iron lungs to be like the old wood and cloth bellows we used in winter to blow air on the newspapers and twigs in our fireplace. When I pumped the handles, the little flames grew. Air is fire and life.

My father always believed that the long delay in getting into the iron lung caused his extreme paralysis. He thought lifting the suitcase had weakened him to the virus, but it was the delay in his treatment that sealed his fate. It is easy to be destroyed by moments like these, by the idea that things could have gone differently. That it was mere chance that led my healthy young father, full of life and in love with the sea, into the last wave of polio victims.

Instead he learned – and taught me – never to languish in the what ifs, never to look back. But there was a contradiction in this that I didn't see at the time: while he resolved never to dwell on how things might have been different, he ascribed the utmost meaning to these small moments of agency, these small turning points. That emphasis seemed to suggest that things *could* have been different: if he hadn't carried the suitcase, if the matron hadn't delayed, he might have been back on the water within weeks.

In this telling, his paralysis was not mere chance, not the result of mysterious cellular changes that no one could predict; it was the result of a few identifiable errors and transgressions. Though he vowed never to ask himself 'Why me?' he had, in fact, already answered that question with a few definitive, unscientific conclusions: that by lifting that lady's suitcases, he'd somehow brought this upon himself. That being true, he could never question his fate, and he certainly couldn't ever complain.

Visitors were rarely permitted at the infectious diseases hospital, although close family were allowed to come during specified times for short visits. Inevitably, friendships dropped away. Who except the most loving and devoted would put themselves at risk of infection from a disease that had terrorised a generation?

For an entire year, my father's twenty-year-old life revolved almost exclusively around the repetitive routine of his medical care, the nurses' attention and daily visits from his mother and father, who drove an hour each way to sit at their son's bedside.

Once visiting time was over and his parents had retreated through the heavy swinging doors at the end of the ward, there was little he could do but stare at the ceiling and study its cracks. Under the strict watch of the ward's matron, staff were discouraged from interacting with patients, so mostly he had to be content with the distant fragments of conversations from the nurses' station or monitoring their comings and goings by the squeak of their rubber-soled shoes along the corridors.

Treating patients in the infectious diseases hospital was part of nursing training, so every few months there was an influx of young women in white uniforms working through their medical education. These young women in my father's ward – still teenagers in most cases – faced a room of male patients with leprosy, scarlet fever and tuberculosis. Then, at the end of the room, there was my father, tucked away inside his metal box.

One of those young nurses caught my father's eye. Rumour had it my mother didn't behave like most people thought nurses should. She was tall and good-looking and had a reputation for standing up to her superiors. 'The fact that she was unaffected by authority at this point interested me greatly,' my father remembered one day, sitting with me in the sunroom of his beachfront home, looking at the sea.

Once she brought him a bunch of long-stemmed roses, which she arranged in a vase and set on his metal bedside table. 'I hope these will cheer you up,' she said, smiling.

But when the matron caught a glimpse of what she was doing and recognised the roses from the hospital grounds, she bellowed across the ward, 'Those are my roses you have stolen, Nurse. I will put you on detention for this.'

My mother wasn't fazed at all. 'Surely, Matron,' she replied sweetly, 'since I picked them from the grounds, they are public property.'

On her birth certificate, my mother was Kathleen Jill Brinkworth, but she never liked her first name so everyone called her Jill. When she married my father she became Jill Llewellyn. Decades later, after my father left, she changed her name officially – she dropped Kathleen for Katherine, moved Jill back to being her second name, added Sky (it cost the same amount of money to add another name) and became Katherine Jill Sky Llewellyn. When she became a poet, that all changed again. She became Kate Llewellyn.

One of her closest nursing friends remembers the first time she met my mother. 'There was a nurse who everyone had ganged up on. You know, the group has to find its scapegoat. Well, one night we were sitting around and the most popular girl among our group started up about nurse X and just as everyone began to chime in, your mother called her out. "Stop being so nasty," she said, and we were all taken aback. I never forgot it.' All the other nurses, wanting to be accepted as part of the group, followed the leader, but my mother didn't care for it, not if acceptance came at someone else's expense. She made that very clear and the taunting stopped.

Lying in his iron lung, my father couldn't believe his luck. Here was a beautiful young woman who treated him like any other young man. She didn't handle him with kid gloves – she handled him, that's for sure – but she never treated him like he was sick. What a blessing for a young man who was very, very sick to have a beautiful girl flirting with him, trying to make him feel every bit as hot-blooded as he had been before his hospitalisation.

The other blessing they had in their favour – the greatest and most miraculous blessing of my father's illness – was that as his nurse, my mother had occasion to notice early on that the polio had not interfered with his sexual function.

If she was in the ward alone at night, they fooled around. And when she was assigned to bathe him, they'd do the same. It was their own special kind of courting. Being strictly forbidden and against the rules, it played to their rebellious natures, giving their dalliance all the more allure. But it gave my father more than just sensual relief and release. Crucially, it gave him back some of his former sense of agency. Here he was, immobilised yet still able to get a pretty girl to do what he wanted.

As luck or circumstance would have it, he happened upon the right girl, enlisting charm and charisma to do the work his body couldn't, and it worked.

That's not to say that he lied or misrepresented himself to my mother. There wasn't much about the truth to be denied or ignored, and she was anything but stupid. It's simply that with two options in front of him – anger on the one hand and 'let's salvage what we can of this' on the other – he decidedly chose the latter.

It was only after spending a week in a hospital, unable to feel my legs, that I looked back at these scenes of my parents together. For the first time in my life, I actually wondered how it could have happened. Some days I was unable to even drag myself out of my state-of-the-art hospital bed or face visitors. The thought of trying to seduce anyone was the furthest thing from my mind. In fact, I had already decided that part of my life – seducing or being seduced – was irrevocably over.

And I wasn't even lying in an iron lung. My body – from the outside at least – still looked more or less like it always had. My father's body on the other hand, inside and out, showed every sign of the massacre that had besieged him.

It was only then, facing my own calamity, that I found myself unable to live out my father's example of constantly moving forward. I looked again at that scene in the hospital, nine years before my birth, and wondered: what gets a game, beautiful young nurse on her knees, polishing brass at the command of a patient in an iron lung? How could it be that a young woman with many other suitors chose to visit him regularly, even when she was no longer assigned to his ward? A man who would never walk, who would never be able to hold her or their children, or protect them from physical danger. What did he say and do to draw her in?

It is hard to know, but shortly after her time in the infectious diseases hospital, she told her nursing buddies back in the dorms that she'd met the love of her life.

On my father's twenty-first birthday, recently out of the iron lung but still hospitalised, my grandparents arrived at his bedside with a neatly tied-up box. My grandfather had tried to tell the girl at the department store not to bother with the bows but she paid him no heed.

With the box perched in my grandfather's lap, he undid the satin ribbons and lifted its contents – a Philips portable radio – above my father's weak chest so he could see it.

The radio had a battery, a power cable and a set of headphones so my father could listen to it privately. The headphones were a ploy to get around the matron's decree that he couldn't have a radio because it would disturb the other patients. As if they'd have cared. My father can't have been the only one who needed some intellectual stimulation and fun.

'I wish I had kept it,' he said decades later, like a man proudly describing his first car. He often said he thought it'd be a collector's piece if only he'd hung on to it. More likely, and perhaps only one of a handful of moments when sentimentality outstripped his devotion to commerce, it was for its emotional significance that he wished he'd kept it. What my mother was giving him was private and strictly between them; the radio was the first taste of *public* freedom he had.

With the nurses' help, he worked out that if they wedged the radio between his upper arm and the metal railing of his bed, and they bent and positioned his arm to the right spot, he could turn it off and on and change the station himself. It's only when you've lost everything that these simple, absolutely unremarkable daily activities take on huge significance. That being able to change the station on a radio is a pleasure and a success that a young man will remember for the rest of his life.

'The other thing about that radio,' he said, laughing at the memory, 'was that as soon as the matron left the ward, the nurses pulled out the plug on the earphones and turned it up full blast and everyone who could jumped around dancing.'

One of those dancing nurses, of course, was my mother. 'I got to know her quite well and when she finished her term in my hospital, she came back to visit me and we developed a relationship, which became very important in my game of being able to go home,' he said, sounding more ruthless than he may have intended.

He knew back then that marriage was the only way for a person with a disability to get independence. Before the days of caregivers and support workers, wives or husbands were the only alternative to mothers or institutionalisation. My father knew, if he ever got out of hospital, he was destined for the Home for Incurables or being cared for by his parents. Neither of those options pleased him.

My mother was fun and clever but, more importantly, he knew she was defiant. He could see that she was the kind of woman who *would* throw it all to the wind – every sensible reason there was to *not* be with a man in his situation – to be with someone she loved. She didn't care about the odds. In fact, I think he could see she quite liked them stacked up against her.

My mother was the most reckless person you'd ever meet, but in this instance, that was the best thing my father could have wished for.

It's one thing to be struck by polio after you're married and have the vows 'in sickness and in health' to tie you together. The chances of finding someone when you are in the eye of the storm of an illness like my father's? Well, that was simply miraculous.

For a long time, I didn't ask myself if benevolence was enough to account for *her* choice.

Seven

A few weeks after getting out of the iron lung and being transferred to a standard hospital bed, my father was moved to the male geriatric ward. There he lay awake at night, unable to sleep with the snoring of thirty old men and the scent of death. He was a 95 per cent paralysed 21-year-old seaman, lying in a geriatric ward, plotting his future.

He was now in a wing of the hospital called C3, which was a completely different environment to C4, where he'd been during his time in the iron lung. The matron here was happy for the nurses to chat with the patients when they had time. Under these new conditions my father's health began to improve further and he put on weight.

His principal carer was a Czechoslovakian nurse he called Mother Checky. When he was finally well enough, she determined they should try to sit him up. Mother Checky spoke to my father of her plan and involved him in the decision-making about how they could best take this big step. After more than a year lying down, this was going to be no small thing, and my father was grateful for the warning. Even so, it didn't go well.

On Mother Checky's count of three, she and two nurses lifted my father's head and limp torso up off the pillows. Then the nurses each scooped one of his thin legs over their forearms and swivelled him around on his bottom so his legs dangled over the side of the bed.

'I can still remember the shock of it. It was one time when I thought I really should give up hope,' he told me. 'There I was thinking to myself that sitting up meant I was about to take a huge step forward in my recovery, but when they swung my legs over the bed and sat me up straight for the first time, I looked down to see I had an enormous, distended and sagging stomach. It was grotesque. I was devastated.'

All the muscles in his stomach had dissolved during his hospitalisation and there was nothing to support his organs, which felt like they wanted to fall out of his body. The pain was excruciating. Breathing was so difficult he couldn't stay upright for more than a few seconds. The moment he was laid down again, and the nurses left to continue their work, the aftershock and realisation of all that he'd lost finally struck him. He wept. My fearless father was terrified.

They bound his waist tightly in bandages before they tried sitting him up again. The wrappings held his innards in place and, over many days, they incrementally increased the time he was able to remain upright. Eventually he was strong enough that a nurse who lived very close to the hospital pushed him in a wheelchair to her home, to see her pet cockatoo.

But if he was to sit upright for any length of time, he needed to have his legs held straight out in front of him so his weakened heart could pump blood to his feet. No wheelchair existed that enabled this. When the doctors told him that he'd be able to go home for weekends if he could sit upright, my father petitioned hard to have a custom chair made. Along with a change of scenery and a return to some normalcy, most importantly going home would afford him time with my mother 'on private territory', as he discreetly put it.

That special chair was six months in the making.

When it finally arrived, a weekend at home was arranged and carefully orchestrated. My father was delivered by ambulance to my grandparents' place on a stretcher like a dead body. The orderlies carried him into the house and laid him down in one of the two single beds in the back bedroom. It was the same room where my brother and I slept during our visits, many years later. There he stayed until the designated time the following Monday morning when two other men with a stretcher came to take him back to hospital.

My father had the customised wheelchair, but my grandfather was not strong enough to lift him on his own, or he was too scared. Each of these weekends the chair sat parked in the corner and my father spent the entire time flat on his back.

There's nothing like necessity to fuel invention. During one of these weekends at home my father got the idea for a lifting machine. An old friend of his brother, who lived across the street, came from a long family of engineers. Bob Todd could make anything he set his mind to and my father happened to know Bob also had a functioning workshop in his backyard.

It was perfect. My father sent his brother to Bob with a message asking him to visit. When Bob arrived, my father didn't bother with too many niceties before explaining the reason for the invitation. When my father needed something, he wasn't shy in asking for it. Nor did he ever expect his demands to be refused. On the rare occasion they were, he either dug in deeper and became more insistent or he simply moved on to ask the next person. Bob didn't need convincing. He agreed immediately.

Over the following days, Bob sat beside my father and together they worked up a design for a machine that could operate in both directions – get him out of bed and into his chair and then the reverse, out of his chair and back into bed.

After years of polio epidemic, just as there wasn't an appropriate wheelchair for him, no such machine existed to help my father in even the most basic of ways. We'd invented locomotives, cars, heavy automated machinery. At the time we were on the way to putting a man on the moon. But a lifting machine?

Bob sketched images of all kinds of contraptions in a notebook, making large and small modifications as they discussed mechanics, hydraulics and design. Bob and my father didn't care what the machine might look like, they were only interested in functionality. Finally they settled upon a simple sketch, which Bob took to his workshop.

A week later, he wheeled in a prototype made of thick metal pipes welded together with lead, producing seams that always reminded me of lumpy veins. Attached to the pipes were the hydraulics of an old Holden carjack, which worked as the hoist. My father was elated. He insisted they immediately try it out.

'It's going to work, Bob,' he said. 'Come on, hoist me up!'

Bob was a little reluctant at first. 'Ah, I'm not sure it's a good idea just yet, Dick. I should do some more testing.'

It wasn't really that Bob was worried about the durability or safety of his machine – he'd taken good care with all the joints, and the pipes were an inch thick – but he'd never dealt physically with a crippled person.

'Don't be scared, Bob, you're not going to break me,' my father said, sensing the real source of Bob's anxiety. 'Just grab them and move them into place,' he said, indicating his legs with his chin. 'You don't have to be gentle.'

Even with instruction, it took a little while for Bob to get my father strapped in. But once he was in place, Bob took to the lever and our father lifted off the bed. It was like a magic trick. Had I been there, I would have jumped up and down and cheered.

That prototype was in our family for more than forty years. It went up and down at least twice a day and never once malfunctioned. When my father died, we gave the lifting machine to another family taking care of someone with paralysis.

Sometimes my brother hooked himself into the straps and tried to convince me to pump on the handle to hoist him up and down, but I didn't think that was very funny and never agreed. The worst thing I could imagine was both my brother and father being in chairs. It wasn't something to even joke about and whenever he suggested it I got mad and slammed the door behind me. He could work out how to pump it from where he was on his own.

After these first weekends of freedom, my father was even more determined to get out of hospital permanently. With his custom wheelchair and his homemade lifting machine, at the age of twenty-two, his legs still in plaster, my father was released into the care of his parents.

During the hospitalisation, my grandparents left the farm in the care of my father's brother and moved into my grandmother's family home, about fifteen minutes from the city centre. It was a large estate, big enough that Aunt Molly had built her own house in what used to be the family's orchard. Gran's father, my great-grandfather, had been a successful brewer, running beer up and down the Murray River. When his paddleboat caught fire, he decided that incident, and the unpredictability of the river's capacity during droughts and floods, was a sign for change. He sold Dutton Breweries and took up farming.

When they realised my father would never recover from polio, they bulldozed the grand colonial home of Gran and Aunt Molly's childhood and built a modern blond-brick one with a block of six apartments at the back. The old house wouldn't be practical for my father, who they assumed would live with them the rest of their lives; the new house was built with no steps. The apartment block at the back of the property supplemented the meagre profits from the farm, which had been given over to my uncle to manage, and gave them an assured and easy income while they tended to their youngest son.

During the week, while my mother worked at the hospital, Gran and Aunt Molly looked after my father, but on the weekends my mother visited and took over his care. This was the next step in my parents' courtship – my mother learning how to look after my father outside the structure and support of the hospital.

One day my father was picked up in a government car and taken to the St Margaret's Rehabilitation Centre for an assessment. The specialist there wheeled him in front of a manual typewriter and told him to hold his hands up above the machine and press the clunky keys. My father explained that he couldn't lift his hands that high, let alone type. Then he explained that even if he could type, he had absolutely no wish to become a typist.

My 22-year-old, unemployed – and seemingly unemployable – paralysed father had loftier ideas for his future.

'Well, then,' said the stunned doctor, 'we simply can't rehabilitate you!'

My father argued that he should be given the £500 they would have spent on his rehabilitation so he could invest in a business. The doctor laughed.

'I'm really grateful they refused me that money,' he said when I expressed my outrage at the injustice of their denial. 'It taught me immediately that if I wanted to do anything, I was going to have to do it myself.'

Polio made my father an entrepreneur. In the late fifties and early sixties nobody dreamed that paid employment was possible for disabled people. It was unthinkable. History's shameful truth is that disabled people were kept out of sight. They were not even called 'people with a disability', they were 'cripples', to be shunned. The idea that these cripples could contribute to society, or even that they had equal rights, was decades away.

Then and there my father decided to change all that.

He began by making tablemats and coasters using cork offcuts from Bob Todd's workshop. My grandfather had a collection of old bank calendars featuring watercolour and pencil reproductions of South Australian historic buildings. After convincing my grandfather to hand over his prized collection, my father began the first of many business ventures.

My brother and I got frustrated watching our father cutting carrots – even slicing an apple took him forever. So we were glad we weren't there to watch as he sliced out the image from one of grandfather's old calendars with a box cutter and a metal-edged wooden ruler.

But he persevered and, once the picture was cut, he pasted it onto the cork base he'd had Bob Todd cut to size in his workshop. When the glue dried he varnished over the thick paper with a small brush. Then he called Gran to lift the tablemat off his tray and set it aside to dry. He applied five more coats of varnish to each.

When the varnishing was finished, he had Gran place each mat facedown on his tray and painted the underside with glue. Then Gran helped him lay down green felt, which he smoothed out flat with his forearm so there were no air bubbles. Once they had dried, Grandfather trimmed the fabric tightly along the rim of the cork with Gran's sewing shears, which were too heavy for my father to hold and he couldn't have manoeuvred anyway.

When he described the process to me and my brother one day, we rolled our eyes. 'That must have taken *forever*!' I exclaimed.

My brother said, 'I'm bored just listening to the story.'

Perfection had been drilled into our father by the navy, but it was never more important than in those days after his release from hospital. He knew his life depended on whether the tablemats looked professional, not handmade by a cripple and bought only out of pity. So my childish declaration that it must have taken forever was right: each one took days to complete.

The mats were sold in sets of six, so whatever he earned was a pittance for the time taken. But time was something he had a lot of and it was important to keep himself busy. Every such menial task served a bigger purpose. Freedom.

My brother and I used to be tasked with setting out those mats for formal dinner parties. I can still remember the feel of them in my hand. Sometimes we took to either end of the long dining table and flicked the mats to each other – felt side down – so they skimmed fast across the shiny surface in our own game of air hockey.

As my father wished he'd hung on to his radio, I wish I still had a set of those placemats. With every single mat, he was clawing his way out of dependency. He sent his mother out to department stores with the samples. She took orders, which he filled, and eventually he earned enough cash that he felt ready to propose to my mother.

Eight

The story of my parents' early years together is almost a caricature of resilience and pluck. With a start-up loan from Gran and Grandfather, they bought what was then commonly called a 'mixed business', the Swan Library. Run out of a small shopfront on the busy King William Road, it included a deli, library and dry-cleaning service. It had a comic and magazine exchange as well as a more formal library, from which people borrowed books for sixpence each. Newer titles went out at a shilling apiece.

They lived in a single room adjoining the shop with two old doors bolted together to separate the kitchen from the bedroom. On their third night they woke to an enormous crashing, which they thought was an earthquake. My father said their bed dropped through the floor on account of white ants, which had eaten through the floorboards. I don't doubt there were white ants since my father had clearly bought a dump, but I do wonder if they were actually asleep.

The backyard had a couple of dead cars in it, which my grandfather eventually cleared. They planted a good lawn and in time had quite a nice garden.

There was no 'caregiver's support', no electric wheelchairs, no fancy equipment beyond Bob's homemade lifting machine and my father's special pushchair. Apart from those two items, all they had was their wits, guts, good humour and love for each other. For quite a while that was enough.

The business opened at 7.30 in the morning and closed at 9.30 at night. My father had been out of hospital for less than a year, so he was still weak, but each morning my mother bathed, dressed and fed him before pushing him into the shop. There he stayed until closing time, his legs in plasters sticking out straight in front of him, covered by a mohair rug. In between serving customers, my father read through the entire library, minus the Mills & Boon romances.

Books again became his world, as much later they would become mine. His sea days may have been over but, with a book in hand, he could be out there aboard the *Pequod*, chasing down the great white whale, Moby Dick. His imagination took him places his body could no longer go. It saved his life.

Even with the reading, he recalled, 'It was still a long day. But this was freedom, so life was sweet for me.'

He was fascinated by the customers who came to the store. Sitting in his chair, immobilised, he was a ready listener and, even if he hadn't been, he was a captive audience. He knew all the gossip, along with the woes and infidelities of many marriages. He loved it. It passed the time and he learned the nuances of other people's lives and psychologies.

They say that people who lose their eyesight or hearing develop their other senses to help make up for the deficit. Our father couldn't move but, in movement's absence, he learned to watch and truly notice. He could read a person just by the way they walked. Often he'd ask me and my brother what we observed about a person who happened to be walking towards us.

'What can you tell me about that man in the blue vest?' he'd say, pointing with his chin.

'I don't know,' my brother would say. 'He's got brown hair?' When he sensed my father saw something more, he'd object, 'I don't know anything about him.'

Of course, our father then enjoyed telling us all he'd garnered. 'They come across as arrogant, but that's hiding a deep insecurity,' he'd say, and we'd wonder how on earth you could tell that from a distance. However, sure enough, if we ever did get the opportunity to discover more about one of the people he'd sized up, we quickly came to realise our father had nailed it. As kids, it seemed to us that he had magical powers.

One day, one of their regular customers asked if he could put a notice for a home he wanted to rent out in the shop window. My father agreed. When a prospective tenant came in to inquire about the advertisement, my father described the house and its owner, and arranged for them to meet. When the owner came in to report the successful leasing of his property, my father saw an opportunity.

Shortly after, he began Llewellyn Letting Agency. In time it gained hundreds of clients. My father supplied index cards for handwritten property advertisements that were stuck to a noticeboard in the shop.

He also placed formal ads in the local newspaper and kept a shoebox filled with corresponding cards describing the properties he managed, without ever having been inside them. He charged the homeowner a flat fee of five pounds, guaranteeing that he would find them a suitable tenant or give their money back.

It was the early sixties when my mother became pregnant with my brother, Hugh. They held a 'fire sale' of all the books in the library, converting that room into a nursery.

My father was sick with worry that the baby would be born with a deformity on account of his polio, even though doctors assured him that wasn't possible. Still, he worried he was taking a huge risk. I'm sure he wasn't the only one.

To everyone's quiet relief – none more than my father's – as medically predicted, my brother was born with all his fingers and toes where they were meant to be.

They bought what they thought was a 'childproof' cot, to be sure my brother would be secure when my mother was busy with my father or they were working in the shop together. One day she went for a short errand while my brother was asleep. She left the door of my brother's room ajar and positioned my father's chair so he could watch over him while he slept. The idea was that he'd be able to entertain Hugh from afar if he woke.

Wake he did, but not as expected. About ten minutes after my mother's departure, my brother appeared in his nappy at the foot of my father's chair, having somehow escaped the cot.

At this point of the story I always punched my brother in the arm, because I knew how embarrassed he was that it involved him being in a nappy.

Particularly when it was just my father in the shop, my parents kept the store's front door open to attract customers. Of course, after showing himself to my father, my brother headed straight for the open door.

My father only had his voice to stop my brother from toddling out onto the main road, where trucks roared past and a car had recently killed their dog, Jordie, who'd escaped his leash. My father had been powerless to stop the dog running into traffic even though he'd been right there when it happened. Now the same fate was about to befall his son.

No one passed by on the footpath or came into the shop. My father desperately tried to keep Hugh amused by talking to him. He even sang. But his chatter was no match for the draw of the stream of cars, buses and trucks thundering along the busy street, just steps away from the shop's front door. My terrified father sat helpless as he watched his son wander out towards the footpath. He yelled, but that alone was unlikely to stop an eighteen-month-old boy whose eye had been caught by all the colour and movement just across the threshold.

Perhaps it was the fear in my father's voice, but for some reason Hugh stopped in the doorway and sat down on the step. He seemed perfectly happy watching the cars go by from there. My father kept up a constant stream of conversation, desperate to keep Hugh in his spot.

There they sat at their posts, my brother in his nappy on the step, my father in his chair about ten feet away, until a stranger came by. She scooped Hugh up in her arms and offered to take him home to her house until my mother returned. So relieved to see my brother safe, my father didn't think to ask the woman's name or get her address before she walked out of the store holding my brother over her shoulder.

When my mother returned home and my father told her what had happened, and admitted he had no idea where their son was or whom he was with, my mother became hysterical. Two hours later, Hugh was returned, bathed and outfitted in brand-new clothes from a fancy store. That woman, Greta Begley, became my parents' lifelong friend.

Nine

As I understood it, my mother's anguish began with my birth. By now, they'd sold the shop and moved to a large family home in the quiet suburb of Dulwich.

The often-told story was that my mother's father had a fatal heart attack on 5 September 1965, hours before I was born. I was told that my grandfather's last breath was snuffed out just before I took my first screaming gasp of air. Given the coincidence, my birthday was always both a celebration and a mourning.

Muttee said losing her husband, Brink, was like losing her spine. But she found comfort imagining that her husband slipped his gentle soul into mine as our paths into being and oblivion crossed.

My mother didn't see it that way. She was never the same after his funeral.

A poem written by my mother titled 'Washing Up' appears at the end of Muttee's memoir, *The Humble Folk*. It describes Brink's adoring love of Muttee, and how he looked at his wife longingly as she went about her daily chores. It's a beautiful description of a man simply, truly and deeply in love with his wife. But the twist comes when, in parentheses, my mother writes that even then, forty years prior, in her very early teens, she was envious of that love, of that 'dog's eyes' look.

Perhaps it was combined with postpartum depression and a breakdown, but it was in the days following her father's death that my mother swiftly and resolutely fell out of love with my father. Brink's death was my parents' end game.

For forty-nine years I believed my grandfather died on my birthday. I had to read the passage about Brink's death in Muttee's memoir three times before I could fully take it in. According to Muttee, Brink died on 8 September – three days after I was born.

Three days doesn't seem like much, not until you have to revise the meaning of your start in the world. All my life I have celebrated my birthday and mourned the grandfather I never knew on the same day.

Even more than discovering that Brink didn't die on my birthday, it shook me when I re-read my mother's poem, 'Theatre', in which she says that having pushed out her baby she felt relief, but beyond that all she had was a sense of everything falling away from her. She describes a bottle of whisky beside her bed, ten depressed days later, and Brink weighing the child like a lump of butter on Muttee's kitchen scales.

I'm sure I'd read or heard her read that poem in public before, but I had never realised its true significance. Since I had always believed my grandfather and I never met, I had always assumed the poem was about my brother, since it's Brink weighing the baby on the scales.

But now I understand I had it all wrong. That baby was me. What's also suddenly clear is that she has the bottle of whisky beside the bed *before* Brink was dead. The whisky is not there because of her father's death; it's there because of me.

Children love to hear the story of their first days and descriptions of their baby selves. It's how we form narratives about ourselves and begin the record of who we are. When it came to my birth, though, everyone had a different version. At least in my mother's poem my sense of my start in life holds true, which is that from my birth my mother was depressed and drank to dull the pain.

Yet, in fact, none of these versions of Brink's death is true. Not the one in Muttee's memoir, not the version I'd believed throughout my life, not the account in her poem.

According to a transcript of Ronald Brinkworth's death certificate he died of coronary thrombosis on 9 September 1965, four days after my birth. Listed as a 'retired poultry farmer', he was buried at Willaston Cemetery on 10 September.

As life begins, so it continues. Mine began with competing realities. What hope did I have? Apart from the question of what day my grandfather died, my life has often felt as though I was stood in front of a funhouse mirror and ordered to trust the distorted version that was reflected back at me. I became a questioning and suspicious child, hardwired to detect deceit.

My mother kept the whisky bottle beside her bed. Anything to black out the three of us – me, my brother and my father. When the whisky was no longer enough, she swallowed a bottle of pills and lay down to sleep for good.

What was that morning like for her? I never asked her directly, but it must have been premeditated. She pushed my father into another room. She put the phone on his tray, just like she did every day. Did he suspect something was darker in her mood than on other mornings? Did she give anything away, give him a hint of her plan? After she left him, she laid me down in my cot and put a bottle of formula in my fat hands. Did she kiss me? Where was my brother?

Whatever resolution she had come to beforehand, in the drug's daze something switched, sending her stumbling out of her room. Perhaps the bottle of formula fell from my hands and I cried out, perhaps my brother came in to rouse her. When she reached my father, sliding along the walls to keep her legs from buckling under her, she slurred the words, 'Call an ambulance.' I doubt my father had to ask why.

My mother was released from the hospital into the care of the Begleys. Gran moved in to look after us.

My mother saw a therapist for a while, but it didn't stick. She preferred to take matters into her own hands. As with many of us, her way was to *not* think about it.

I'm not sure how long she was away but, eventually, she did return and home life resumed its rhythm. But I can only imagine she must have been in a stunned haze. After all, in her absence nothing had fundamentally changed for the better. If anything, it had got worse, because now *the incident* hung in the air like a threat.

She was in no state to nurse me, and our father wasn't strong enough to hold me and manoeuvre a bottle, so I was fed in my cot with the bottle of formula wedged between the legs of a crocheted toy donkey my Aunty Babs gave me at my christening. Later my father told me it was Hugh who really watched over me.

I think it must have been different for my brother. When he was born, our parents were very much in love. But in the midst of their unhappiness I learned to fend for myself and not make a fuss. He quickly caught up. We learned to stay out of the way; better still, to be invisible. We made the best of what we had and tried our hardest not to rely on the people who were really meant to look after us.

For a long time, I thought misery was the norm. My brother and I learned to rely on each other. But he was older than me, so he took on most of that responsibility.

Even though my mother wasn't coping, or maybe because she wasn't coping and my father thought it would help lift her spirits, he decided to enter her in the *Women's Weekly* Mother of the Year competition. He filled out the forms, wrote a short essay about all my mother's best qualities and had Gran post it.

On the strength of his entry, she made it into the finals. A beautiful young woman looking after two small children and a man in a wheelchair. It was perfect *Women's Weekly* material. If Oprah or Ellen had been on television back then, my mother would have come home with a new car and a sponsorship deal.

Being chosen as one of the finalists meant a home visit by the panel of judges. They arrived unannounced early one Saturday morning. My mother had moved into the spare room by this time and when the doorbell rang my parents were in their separate beds. My mother opened the door to the strangers in her nightgown. The small group explained their visit, whereupon she invited them in to see me sleeping in my cot and my brother in his bed.

They went first into my brother's room but found him missing. Then they stood in my doorway, finding my cot empty. My mother began frantically calling out for us. Eventually she and the stunned judges found me, perhaps six months old, in my pram under the mandarin tree with my brother, not yet four, sitting on the lawn beside me. Apparently I'd woken up and my brother had taken me outside so my parents could sleep. We were quietly and happily passing the time on our own.

Even despite the incident of the missing children – or perhaps because of it, since the judges surely considered us extraordinarily good and independent children able to amuse ourselves at such young ages – the judges awarded my mother first prize, which came with a bag of loot including a string of pearls and an electric carving knife.

Whatever reprieve the excitement of winning the prize gave them didn't last long. My mother was not faring well from the strain of home life and what had become a loveless marriage. Why would she? Tending to the needs of two small children and a man in a wheelchair would take its toll on anyone, even if there was all the love in the world.

Each morning she woke up, brought my father tea and a piece of toast, hoisted him out of bed with the hand-operated lifting machine onto a commode in the bedroom. When he was done she washed him with a washcloth, dressed him, put him in his chair, brought him his toothbrush and toothpaste. Then she attended to a baby girl and a small boy before getting herself dressed and ready for the day's run of activities. Just those few hours' tasks would be enough to send most of us back to bed for the day, or turn to a bottle or pills. Or both.

It was around this time that my mother started writing poetry, handwritten on scraps of paper and left lying around the house. Perhaps she hoped someone would read them and appreciate her pain. But my father couldn't search them out from his wheelchair, and my brother and I were oblivious.

So my mother's poems lay around the house unread and my father clung to what he could take control of: the letting business. He soon had the market so cornered, influential members of the real estate industry felt the pressure and decided to put an end to his venture. They lobbied for new legislation requiring local agents to be licensed. The examination to obtain a licence was held on the second floor of a building with no elevator. My father was stymied.

Ever since he left hospital, my father knew that if he didn't have money to make free choices, he'd end up institutionalised in the local Home for Incurables. If my mother decided to leave, he knew that's where he'd end up.

Then there was the question of me and my brother. He had a string of mighty incentives to maintain the facade that theirs was a happy marriage and to keep working.

After being banned from the real estate business, he had my mother wheel him out into the backyard every day for two weeks. There in the sunshine he thought about other work he could do from home in his chair.

My father did this whenever he had to make a big decision. Someone pushed him out into the sunlight and he sat there all day, thinking out a solution. We knew to leave him alone. It might take just a few days or it might take a number of weeks, but when he was done, not only would his face and hands be tanned, our life's course would swiftly change direction.

Ten

The home in Dulwich they moved into after selling the shop on King William Road was a large colonial-style house with a red-tiled verandah, white guttering and a corrugated-tin roof. The large front door was framed on three sides by red, blue and yellow stained glass, surrounding a central motif of a blood-red banksia. From the outside, our home looked like everything was as it should be.

The stained glass let red and blue shards of light into the hallway on sunny days. The entrance made onto a long corridor with three rooms off to either side. On the left, as you entered, was my father's bedroom, my mother having taken up residence in the spare room directly across from his. Next on the left was my brother's room and then mine. Opposite my brother's room was a large sitting parlour with upholstered lounge chairs and a stereo on which my mother played Joan Baez, *Flutes of the Andes* and Nana Mouskouri records.

Most of the records were badly scratched or buckled, because my mother and her friends rarely put them back in their sleeves after being played; they just stacked one on top of the other, often on the hot amplifier, which melted and warped the wax. Some were bent beyond playable. I hated it when the needle got stuck and repeated the same moment again and again, until someone lifted the arm and repositioned the diamond stylus past the scratch. For that reason I didn't mind sorting through the stack of records every now and then, reading the round labels in the middle of each and sliding them into their plastic sleeves and correct jacket.

I was my father's daughter. He believed if you had something, you took care of it. You kept it until you could no longer wring another use out of it. I still cut the bottoms off bottles of moisturiser so I can scrape out every drop. Waste not, want not.

Across the wide hallway from my bedroom there was a formal dining room with ivy wallpaper and a small fireplace. Most of the space was taken up by a large, heavy adjustable table of dark wood that seated ten people in its fully extended setting, but could fit fifteen or more if you found extra chairs and the guests touched elbows. There was a swinging door from the dining room into the kitchen, which opened onto a large porch with slat windows. Black and white linoleum flooring ran along the end of the house from the kitchen to the bathroom and laundry.

In the backyard, there was a mature mandarin tree. In season it was laden with sweet, juicy fruit that I later took to high school to share with friends and throw at teachers we didn't like when their backs were turned to write on the blackboard.

There was also a fixed metal swing under a long trellis outside our back door. The trellis was covered in grapevines, which shaded us in the summer and in winter shrivelled up into knots of dead twigs. In the middle of the coldest months, I could never believe that the vines would bear fruit again – the thick grey trunk looked dried up and lifeless.

On either side of the back door, under the shade of the grapevine, were two enormous white pots, each with a large pink camellia bush. My mother did well with the camellias, which thrived on the tea-leaves discarded from her teapot each morning. We had a seemingly never-ending supply of pretty pink camellias in glass vases through the house.

We lived on a quiet jacaranda-lined suburban street called Swift Avenue, about a ten-minute drive from the city centre. At the time, Adelaide was a few hundred thousand people shy of a million inhabitants. As the government-sponsored water awareness advertisements on television taught me, I was born in the driest state of the driest continent.

Adelaide was designed on a grid of right angles and straight lines. Wide boulevards, intersected by smaller streets and laneways, crisscrossed the city. Surrounding this were thick ribbons of parkland, and one of these parks was across a four-lane road at the end of our street. Sometimes it was lushly green, but most of the year it was brittle-dry twigs and dead grasses that snapped and cracked under my feet as I walked.

Unlike the other parks, though, ours had a horseracing track. On race days, my brother and I spent a lot of time there.

Hugh was often instructed by one or both of our parents, or he just instinctively knew, to 'look after your sister!' This signalled we needed to make ourselves scarce, which we did. We rode our bikes for hours on end and no one seemed bothered when we were gone for most of the day.

Our favourite place was the racetrack. One day we misjudged the fast-moving traffic and only got halfway across the four-lane road before another train of cars and trucks came driving at us. Traffic thundered in front and behind us. I was a tomboy and tried to never let my fear show – particularly in front of Hugh – but I was terrified. He didn't say anything, but he took my tiny hand as we waited on the small strip of white paint in the middle of the road as cars roared past on either side of us. People yelled through the open windows of their cars. 'Stupid bloody kids!' 'Get off the damn road!' Finally, when the coast was clear, we dashed across the road, our arms outstretched like planes.

On race days we often lay down on the grass, right underneath the white wooden fence of the track's inner border, with our ears to the ground. The rumble of hoofs pulsed through my small five-year-old body. I could feel the horses through the earth long before they took the last turn onto the straight in front of the old wooden members' stand. It was exhilarating. The thunderous sound as the horses galloped around the corner – almost upon us – the smell of horse sweat mixed with the loamy track kicked up under the horses' hoofs, the sounds of men shouting, the crack of whips on rumps, the guttural sounds of the horses outstretched at full pelt.

I liked the horses, and wanted one of my own. I loved their smell and how the scent clung to my hands after I reached across the fence when the trainers let me pat one. I could feel the power through my fingers: horses spoke freedom. When I got home I lied about washing my hands before dinner so I could sleep with the scent.

Hugh didn't care for the animals so much. He liked them okay, and he always let me have time in the area where they brushed and prepared them for the track, but he was more drawn to the gamblers, the men inside. Everyone believed they'd backed a winner and my brother seemed entranced by the menace, liked seeing the broken fates of men whose loss had just hit home. We'd had our own share of disappointments and I think he liked to see that same look in other people's faces, to know we weren't alone in that feeling.

My brother would somehow manage to coax my pocket money out of me and then coach me on how to talk our way into the members' stand so he could place a bet. If I was ever reluctant, he'd push me in the back between my shoulderblades to get me to tell the man policing the entrance that we'd lost track of our parents, who were somewhere in the stands. I pretended to look upset and my brother did the best he could to seem like he was consoling me. Of course, they let us through.

The bookies weren't allowed to take money from children but, occasionally, if my brother was convincing enough and I nodded along in agreement to his assurances that we were under instructions from our parents and placing a bet on their behalf, they would sheepishly take our money, glancing over their shoulders.

Our bets placed, we ran, ducking and weaving, saying, 'Excuse me, excuse me,' through the well-heeled throng. Adults always made way for us to stand right at the front so we could see the race. We yelled and shook our small fists in the air at whatever nag my brother had bet on, usually because he liked the horse's name. If we won, which surprisingly we sometimes did, he took me to the corner store and I got to pick out all my favourite lollies.

When it wasn't a race day and our parents were busy, we caught yabbies with old meat we set out in the sun until it smelled high. We tied the stinking offcuts to long pieces of twine and dangled them in the cold water of the small creek, which ran along the outskirts of the park. We put our catch into dried-out paint cans filled with murky water from the stream. Once we had a good number we carried them home, sloshing water along the way.

I helped to snap the dry sticks we collected as we walked. When we got to the backyard Hugh positioned the sticks crisscross atop scrunched-up newspaper to make a little fire in a small hibachi barbeque on the concrete slab under the grapevine.

Over his fire he boiled water in an old aluminium saucepan blackened by flames and dropped the snapping creatures into the bubbling liquid. I watched the yabbies' shells change colour from brown to orange. Eventually their big claws stopped clenching and their bodies floated lifeless to the water's surface, at which point Hugh plucked them out with metal tongs and put them on a plate.

As soon as they were cool enough to pick up we snapped open their shells with our fingers or crushed the thick claws with our teeth. Those we couldn't open that way we placed on the concrete ground and hit with a hammer. The meat we sucked out was sweet and tender and their crabby smell lingered on our skin well into the evening, even if we were instructed to use soap to clean ourselves up after the feast.

Eleven

After two weeks sitting in the sun, my father re-entered our world to tell us he'd thought of a new way to make money. My mother did not drive and electric motorised chairs had yet to be invented, so whatever my parents did next, it had to involve customers coming to them. To the disbelief and dismay of friends and family, the sailor and his nurse became art gallery owners.

My father called in an advertisement in the newspaper for artists to have their work exhibited and sold in our house. It was pretty weird – even by our standards – when my parents suddenly had strangers wandering through our home, looking at paintings and sculptures.

Our bedrooms were off limits to the arrangements and the dark-green ivy wallpaper in the dining room made that space unsuitable for anything but the boldest art so it was usually only the hallway and sitting room that were used for exhibits.

As unlikely as it was, the experiment worked. A few years later they opened one of the most successful art galleries in the state in a purpose-built gallery in our suburban backyard. Neither of my parents had known the first thing about art. They grew up counting sheep and heads of cattle, collecting eggs, living by the seasons. I'm pretty sure neither of them had stepped inside an art gallery of any repute before they decided to open one in our home, but my mother learned to hang paintings and my father was a convincing salesman.

Opening in 1968, Llewellyn Galleries turned my parents into hipsters; my mother took to wearing miniskirts and tight poloneck sweaters. By 1973 – the year I turned eight – the gallery had had eighty-three professional exhibitions. That amounted to a new show every three weeks, each one involving negotiating with the artists, hanging, marketing and publicising, opening, selling and closing. Straight after one exhibition closed, another opened. The schedule didn't let up and I think they both liked it that way. The busier they were, the less they had to think about their misery. I learned early how to lose myself in work.

My mother was very good at 'flipping the switch'. She could be dark and gloomy with us but, when it was needed, she transformed into a great hostess and bon vivant. She was the life of the party. Her moods were sometimes hard to keep track of, but it was good for us all that she could summon that up when required.

My father could sit in the gallery all day, waiting for customers. He started reading books on art history and a few young, up-and-coming artists gave him crash courses in art appreciation. The exhibitions and the artists often made the papers and my parents became celebrities in the burgeoning Australian art world of the seventies.

Artists such as Bert Flugelman became family friends. Bert's elegant stainless-steel sculptures made Rundle Mall and the plaza of the Adelaide Festival Centre bright spots in a dreary cultural landscape. He had a withered arm from polio that hung like a dead branch from his shoulder and I could never work out how he made those beautiful, perfectly formed reflective sculptures with one arm, but he did.

Franz Kempf, Annie Newmarch, Robert Boynes, Sydney Ball – all were regular guests at dinner parties that went long into the night. My brother and I often woke up to scores of empty wine and beer bottles, overflowing ashtrays and other detritus littering the dining and sitting rooms. Usually the dining table was left as it was the moment everyone finished their meals, pushed back their chairs and went to the sitting room to smoke and drink more, listening to James Taylor records and talking about art and politics until the very early hours.

My mother made it into the papers on her own when she saved our local parklands from becoming a commuter car park. She organised rallies and my brother and I helped her paint placards to wave. We had a bucket of eggs thrown at us once, but the petition she initiated got 10 000 signatures, which she delivered to the local council's general meeting in a large wheelbarrow she bought for the occasion. Having alerted the media to her plans, she dumped the hundreds and hundreds of pages of signatures on the front steps of the council building. The next day, it was on the front page of every paper in town. A couple of days later, the council's plans for the car park were abandoned.

At this point my parents were a charismatic and complementary pair in business, if not in life. Their talents far exceeded their origins or station. My father, given his love of command and order, would no doubt have gone on to have a decent naval career had he not been struck by polio. My mother, given her defiance, may not have done so well within the nursing hierarchy. Maybe she would have found something she was better suited to, or got an earlier run on her life as the poet she was about to become.

What they achieved, where they were so clearly and forcefully heading, was counterintuitive. It was extraordinary how my mother and father forged something better. My father's disability didn't hold them back, it spurred them on. It pushed them both into achieving more and living more interesting lives.

The nurse and the seaman became real players in Australia's vibrant cultural scene of the sixties and seventies.

For me, the myth that misfortune begets meaning was being solidified.

Twelve

Trouble was brewing between my parents, but the dinner parties, openings and picnics, which were happy times, continued. With other people around there was relief in the pretence that they were a team and we were a functioning family.

My parents carefully secreted their true feelings but the reality was that they were trapped together in an ugly vice of need and unhappiness, which was laid bare when it was just the four of us. The fights intensified.

Even so, we never missed our annual family beach holiday. I'm not sure which of them insisted on keeping to this ritual – it could have been either one of them, because they were similarly strange like that. One moment they could overlook our needs, verging on neglect, the next they'd insist that we take a family holiday 'for the benefit of the children'. It was dizzying.

Grandfather drove an old blue and white Holden station wagon that he never took over 25 miles per hour. I often teased him that I could ride my bike faster than he drove, but my taunts never persuaded him to put his foot down. He was a steady-as-you-go man and a steady-as-you-go driver.

He often ferried us around the city from one outing to another, and holiday time was no different. By now my father had a collapsible wheelchair, and Grandfather packed it into the back of his car alongside our little cases and drove us out of the city. Back then, long before the freeways, the road to the South Coast was narrow and potholed. The journey was marked by lush green vineyards, enormous fields of wheat and windswept barren hills that curved down and dropped into the ocean.

Each year we stayed in the same rented house in the small seaside village of Aldinga. The house was on a wide street, lined with low, scrubby bushes, a few blocks from the beach. Every morning my brother and I ran with empty saucepans in our hands to meet the milkman, who arrived on a horse-drawn cart. The milkman ladled still-warm milk from a huge metal canister into our containers. As hard as I tried, I could never walk back up the uneven stone path as fast as my brother without leaving a trail of white splotches in my wake.

At the end of the street was a reserve of dry, sandy scrubland, which we walked through to get to the beach. My father's wheelchair crackled over the sticks as we pushed him along the rocky path to the edge of the sand, where he watched on from a distance as my mother, brother and I swam in the cold blue ocean.

I would like to think I waved at him from the water and ran back up along the sand every so often to tell him about the fish I'd seen or the crab that bit my toe, but I'm not sure I did. He made it easy for my brother and me to get on and not worry too much about him, never complaining, asking lots of interested questions about our antics when we did eventually return to the side of his chair.

One day, on our way back from swimming, our wet towels dragging along in the dirt as we walked, we came upon a thick black snake lying perfectly still across the path. It looked dead. My father yelled for us all to stop in our tracks, but my brother walked into the shrubbery to find a stick. My father kept yelling, telling my brother to leave it alone, but he couldn't be stopped.

'Don't be stupid, Dad,' he said. 'It's dead. It's not going to bite me.'

My brother walked up close and started prodding until the snake's top half raised up. It opened its mouth to show its large fangs and started hissing. My brother jumped back and my father began banging his hand on his tray, but of course he made almost no sound at all. My mother stamped her feet and started screaming, and the snake slithered away in the dust.

At the house, a large wooden chest was filled with children's dress-ups. I loved putting on the pirate or cowboy outfits and performing little scenes with my brother for our parents. Our acting almost always included me dying in some catastrophe or other, after which my brother, who for many years declared he wanted to be an undertaker, laid me out and delivered the news of my death to our bereaved parents.

There were many variations of this scene over the years. Whether I was a slain pirate or had been shot down in a cowboy duel, I was told to lie on the nearest table. There my brother crossed my little arms on my chest and draped a sheet over me with instructions to keep my eyes closed when our parents came to identify the corpse.

'Yes, that's her,' they said, solemnly identifying my tiny body through pretend tears. My brother said how sorry he was for their loss and lowered the sheet back over me. They'd all keep up the game, my brother asking whether they wanted me cremated or buried. They mixed it up – sometimes they discussed a small wooden coffin and a beautiful headstone with poignant words about my short life, other times they decided to have me cremated. The minute I heard the word cremation, I got sick of being dead and jumped off the table. I didn't like the idea of going up in flames.

When my mother shone her light on you, there was nothing better. She was fun and funny. When she was feeling good, she was full of energy and did her best to make our lives normal. They both did, but the heavy lifting fell to her.

I was often frustrated that my mother resisted learning to drive, when it would have saved us so much time and given us all more independence. As it was, either I did the shopping from the local delicatessen at the end of our street or she rode her bike to the supermarket and piled the groceries into a large wicker basket she had strapped to the back. We had to rely on friends and my father's parents if we wanted to go anywhere further. If I wanted to go to a friend's house, I had to ride my bike or get their parents to pick me up if they lived too far away.

Now I understand why she resisted. I think she recognised she didn't have the temperament or concentration for getting behind the wheel. More importantly, if she added driving us all around to her daily to-do list, she'd have had even less time to herself. Driving would just be another responsibility, even if it had made some tasks easier.

But that choice also meant that if ever my father were to be included in our outings, we had to call on others. My father could telephone people to organise that, but even then one of us had to put the phone and the address book on his tray so he could dial the number. Usually it wasn't worth all the bother, so he just stayed behind, in bed or minding the gallery.

When we went on picnics with other families, they picked us up from our jacaranda-lined street on a Sunday morning, when the gallery was closed, and drove us up the narrow winding roads to the Belair National Park, a beautiful nature reserve in the hills. There my brother, the other kids and I ran around in gumboots, climbed trees and played hide and seek, while the adults lay on blankets and my father sat in his chair on some piece of relatively flat terrain.

My mother packed a picnic basket and there were always flagons of wine for the adults. Those were fun days. We often brought our kites, but they usually got caught in the trees unless we walked to the large oval, where we could launch them unfettered high into the sky if there wasn't a football match in progress. If there wasn't enough wind to pick it up, our mother would run fast to give the kite the lift off the ground it needed.

In those moments, it was as if the darkness and trouble had never existed. I often felt like I had two mothers. Or that I had dreamed the messy version she could be. One was lively, caring and hilarious, the other was someone to be very careful around.

Thirteen

My father was an early riser, even if there was no actual rising without my mother's help. He was usually already awake when I wandered from my bedroom to the edge of his high bed to say good morning and crawl in beside him. The bed was raised by four three-inch-high wooden blocks to allow room for his lifting machine to wheel into the gap. My father slept motionless on a mountain of specially cut foam, a sheepskin rug to stop him from getting bedsores, and pillows to elevate his legs and lungs so they could drain of fluid during the night.

My father's side of the bed seemed like a mountain range because of the peaks and valleys made by the oddly cut foam wedges and pillows at both ends. In the middle was a steep dip. The other side of the bed – no longer slept in by my mother – was as flat and smooth as a plain.

On account of the blocks under its legs, the bed was hard for me to get into, but I soon worked out a method of hoisting myself up by clutching the blankets on what had been my mother's side and pushing off the wall. It took some effort but it was worth it, because it was that or talk to him while sitting on the floor.

Beside him in bed, we'd often watch *Sesame Street* together, counting the numbers and waiting for Cookie Monster to appear or for Oscar the Grouch to come out of his trashcan.

If it was early, before *Sesame Street*, we often played snap or go fish. My father's chest was the table and, when it was his turn, I handed him each card from the pack without looking at it. We made up a set of our own rules for snap so my father could play; I still had to slap down my hand on the cards on his chest – gently – but he was allowed to simply say 'Snap!' to make a play for the stack. I learned to shuffle even though the pack was big for my hands.

But mostly he read to me. It was his job to read the words and mine to hold the book steady and turn the thick, cream-coloured pages of my favourite book, Oscar Wilde's *The Happy Prince*, which my mother gave me for my fifth birthday. Sometimes I jigged the book up and down to make it hard for him to keep track of his place on the page. He never got mad at me or told me to quit fooling around. Polio taught my father patience, and he had a ton of it where I was concerned.

I made him read that book so often, he must have known some of it by heart.

High above the city, on a tall column, stood the statue of the Happy Prince. He was gilded all over with leaves of fine gold, for eyes he had two bright sapphires, and a large red ruby glowed on his sword-hilt.

It's an unlikely love story of a statue named the Happy Prince and a swallow who fall in love on the eve of a cold winter, somewhere in Europe. I still have that book, the pages of which I turned time and again for my father to read to me. The cover is ripped and curled, and the pages are stained, but it remains one of my most treasured possessions.

Just as my father's polio meant my parents got to be hipster gallery owners, his condition meant I had a relationship with him that was very different from most of my friends' relationships with their working and largely absent fathers. My father was around all the time. I took for granted playing cards with him in the morning, watching *Sesame Street*, having him read to me and hanging out with him all day in the gallery.

If my father's door was closed in the morning, it meant he was getting up. I'd knock to let him know I was there and he'd either yell 'Hang on!' or whistle, depending on where he was in the process of getting dressed. If he wasn't ready, I sat on the hallway floor and waited. When he was respectable – when he had on his trousers, his corset and a singlet – he whistled, which was the all-clear signal that I could come in.

My father never regained the muscles in his stomach and couldn't sit up straight without a seventeen-inch-long whalebone corset, which he wore every day despite the long drill of putting it on. Each morning my mother rolled him over onto his side and lay the corset flat on the bed. Then she pulled at his stomach and shoulders like she was unfurling a heavy carpet and rolled him back on top of it. Then she fastened twenty-five hook-and-eye clasps down the front, pulled three straps tight and buckled them.

For years he wore corsets bought from the women's undergarments section of Myer. The corsets came in pink and flesh tone, and he had both.

My parents repeated the daily steps of their routine like a pair of synchronised swimmers. It was efficient, effective and fast, considering all the manoeuvres.

I realise how unbelievable it is that it only occurred to me in my forties that we didn't have an accessible bathroom in our home. Sure, I was young, but it just shows how little I thought about the logistics of my father's situation, even well into adulthood.

Children live and accept their reality, even if it entails a pot in the bedroom and a wife carrying her husband's waste through the house every morning, which is what I now understand she must have done.

At first, the only thing that came to mind was that, for close to a decade, my father never felt the joy of water cascading over his body. Before I thought about him using the toilet, I thought about him showering.

Some practicalities, though, I remember as clearly as if I'd witnessed them yesterday.

To brush his teeth he was brought a glass of water, his toothbrush and toothpaste in a small kidney-shaped metal container. He couldn't lift his elbows from their resting place, but could raise his forearms off the wooden surface of his tray, which was always on the front of his wheelchair whenever he was in it. The tray was a polished piece of plywood and attached to a chrome bracket at the front of his chair. I didn't ever do much to assist in my father's getting dressed, but I did sometimes bring him the little bowl so he could clean his teeth.

Later, when I was big enough to carry it, I learned to secure his tray. The tray helped him sit upright and kept him from tipping forward.

He wrote letters on his tray, ate meals on it. He cradled, carried and sat his children on it and, much later, his grandchildren.

Some of my father's physical restrictions were masked by a few 'tricks'. His tray helped him a lot with these. With his left forearm flat on the wooden surface, his wrist bent back and hand extended, he could use his fingers as a cradle to support the weight of his other arm. From there he was able to complete simple tasks on his own, like brushing his teeth, eating meals, holding up flat-bottomed glasses to drink and rolling his own cigarettes and smoking.

He was stubborn about his independence, but he was happy to let go of some things. He brushed his teeth, but preferred someone else to brush his hair. The extra effort needed to lift his hand just those few inches higher to his head could be better used elsewhere.

He made peace with his mobility limitations, accepting what he could and couldn't do physically. He decided what really mattered was how he presented himself to the world. He worked hard at not letting himself go, at not *looking* disabled despite the undeniable reality of his chair.

Fourteen

There were good reasons for our double life. It was important for all of us that the outside world didn't see the fissures. I don't remember my brother or me ever being explicitly asked or told, but we knew never to let on that anything was other than how our parents said it was.

That silent directive (yet as loud, to me at least, as if they'd screamed in my ear) did not concern only the emotional underpinnings of our lives, but the physical ones too. I'm sure that no one other than my father's parents knew just how hard it was for him to participate in even the simplest activities. When my parents turned up to a party, they made it seem like they'd walked there, arm in arm, just like every other couple in the room. They ate and drank and smoked cigarettes along with the rest. My father's motto: no matter what, turn up smiling.

But the reality was very different. The preparations and logistics of doing something as simple as turning up to a party were hugely time-consuming and complex. If any single step was missed the consequences were never as small as they might appear in isolation. No wonder I found myself in a career managing complex logistics – I'd been groomed for that work from birth.

In public we were a happy family and the facade worked. We were all complicit in the ruse. We played perfect hosts to friends and visitors to the gallery. From the age of about five, I learned to stick cheddar cheese cubes with toothpicks for the exhibition openings. It felt like there could be hundreds of them to stake for a single opening and I did them all as patiently and carefully as a child could. Hugh was an old hand and showed me how to politely offer the snacks to the guests on a platter. A bit later, he taught me to pour a glass of wine from a flagon without spilling too much. We were our parents' miniature hosts – cute additions to the already infamous openings at their hip gallery.

Inside, though, when the doors were closed and we were just the four of us, everything changed. Sweetness left the moment the visitors did.

From the age of five, I developed chronic croup and often woke in the night, gasping for air as desperately as if someone had their hands tightly around my throat. Croup is a common childhood affliction, which manifests as difficulty breathing and a cough that sounds like a barking seal. Many children have mild or one-off episodes of croup, but mine was regular and alarming.

Some years ago, I read asthma is called 'the silent scream'. That the disease represents not only a physical condition but an emotional one too. Since croup is the childhood version of asthma, I immediately recognised that this was what my illness had really been about. Being sick was a way for me to check out from the situation at home. I may not have said in words or actions that our life was hard, or that I needed attention, but I was screaming it with croup.

When I got sick, I usually went to hospital and stayed for days in a special bed that had a clear plastic tent over it. The tent had a large zipper – like the entrance to a camping tent – except that this zipper only had a tab on the outside, so there was no escaping. My tent also came with a wide plastic pipe stitched into the side that attached to a pump, which sprayed a vile chemical mist into my afflicted lungs and throat.

My tent was totally different to my father's iron lung, but there I was, locked in my own breathing machine with lungs that didn't work properly.

No matter how sick, I begged not to have to go to hospital, not to be put in the awful tent. To try to ward off the emergency room, my mother carried me into my father's bed, placed me beside him, pulled his upper arm underneath my neck to rest my head in the crook of his right elbow, and he 'jigged' me – a small jerky back-and-forth motion of his forearm that was as soothing to me as rocking.

I gasped and barked in his arm while my mother prepared 'the towel'. The towel was actually a towel, but drenched in a concoction of vinegar, methylated spirits and hot water. She wound the sodden, stinking cloth loosely around my neck. There I lay through the long night, in my father's arm, inhaling the cutting fumes until my breathing settled and I was lulled into sleep by his jig.

Sometimes this routine saved me from the hospital, as did sitting on my mother's lap on the closed lid of the toilet after she shut the door and filled the bathroom with hot steam from the shower. But more often, she called a cab to take me to the emergency room, leaving my father and brother in their beds.

On the occasions I was in hospital, my mother must have called my father's parents, a neighbour or a friend to come over and look after my father and brother. Either that or she left me with the doctors and nurses, returning to see me during visiting hours. I do remember often lying in my hospital bed wondering where everybody was. My illness was exhausting and terrifying for everyone, including me.

My childhood croup turned into asthma. I was about twenty-seven when I had a particularly dramatic attack in a doctor's surgery. I'd been bedridden and coughing blood for about a week before my boyfriend insisted I see a doctor and drove me to a clinic not far from our house despite my protests that I'd be okay. We'd been waiting about an hour to see the doctor when one of my hacking coughs turned into gasps for air. I felt like I was drowning.

The receptionist ran to the doctor in the examination room. He excused himself from his patient and rushed me, blue by this stage, into an adjacent room. By the time he got the syringe full of adrenalin out of the mini-refrigerator, my veins had collapsed. My boyfriend almost passed out as medics arrived in an ambulance, put cardiac monitors on my chest and wheeled me out on a stretcher. I spent a week in hospital being injected with morphine and steroids for severe asthma and pneumonia in both lungs.

The morning I was discharged, the doctor gave me a list of prescriptions along with two fistfuls of pill bottles.

'How long do I take these?' I asked, staring down at the medications in my hands.

'Every day for the rest of your life,' he said.

I couldn't stop crying after that. It was not the last time I heard those words from a doctor, and not the last time I ignored them.

I had similar episodes in various hospital emergency rooms throughout my twenties and early thirties. That first attack had been in August, which was the month in which my parents had finally separated, years earlier. It sounds like magic foo-foo, but I'm sure it was no coincidence. For more than two decades I could count on spending most of August sick in bed – or hospital, more likely – wheezing and coughing.

Some scientific-minded people may wince at the idea that a body can manifest emotional illness, but I believe it to be true. My body bore the scars of my parents' miserable marriage.

I never learned to register or express my own needs, because compared with my father's physical needs and my mother's emotional ones, mine were so far down the totem pole they were insignificant.

My father was the sick one. He never said it or intentionally made me feel this way, but to my mind his polio trumped anything I could possibly be going through, even when my croup was actually very serious. He'd gone through all the life-threatening stages of polio when he was first hospitalised. All I ever thought was, 'He can't walk, what can I possibly complain about?'

It's something I still struggle with. I have to be very, very sick before I take myself to a doctor. Even then, I might just opt to stay in bed taking over-the-counter drugs when what I really need is steroids, morphine and someone to look after me.

A few years ago, I went to an exhibition of the artist Ed Ruscha at the Whitney Museum in New York City, where I stood transfixed in front of his painting:

I WAS
GASPING
FOR
CONTACT

The text was written on an angle in large white capital letters across a hazy orange circle. It looked as if the words were on top of a whirlpool, on their way down a drain. I couldn't move from where I stood.

My croup and asthma were the silent scream, but air wasn't the only thing I needed inside that plastic tent. I was screaming for someone to hold me. I needed contact.

My childhood bedroom had blue floral wallpaper with curtains of the same soft hue. A large, framed window looked out on an overgrown strip of garden that around the time of my birthday bloomed with generous cascades of white flowers. In the winter, when the flowers were stripped bare, I could see through to the neighbour's house. My curtains had matching sashes of thick blue cotton trimmed in pink piping. On either side of the room was a brass single bed, painted white, with blue bedcovers also with pink piping that matched the curtain sashes. The curtains draped open perfectly, so when I put my toys away and made my bed the room looked like a picture in *Home Style* magazine.

I loved my bedroom, but at the height of our parents' trouble, when I was about five, I began to notice where the sheets of wallpaper didn't line up properly, making jagged, disjointed flowers. It seemed like sloppy work.

I lay in bed one morning before anyone else was awake and picked away at one of the misshapen flowers until I got enough of it under my fingernail to lift it off. The paper didn't come entirely away from the wall; the backing clung fast to the plaster underneath, but two or three flowers ripped off and the room felt a little more honest.

It was a small act of rebellion on my part, hardly worth noting, except that it mattered greatly to me to have evidence that my home wasn't as perfect as we were pretending. When I told my brother about it and showed him what I'd done, he grabbed at a loose edge and pulled it further so my rebellion would have been obvious if anyone had cared to look. Our tiny mutiny accomplished, we went out to the kitchen to make ourselves breakfast.

Apart from these small acts of defiance, my brother and I tried to be on our best behaviour. Sometimes it was hard to know what was our best behaviour, even harder to know why we were in trouble or people were screaming.

We tried to help as much as we could. I wasn't big enough to push our father in his chair, but as well as doing most of the shopping from the little deli at the end of our street, I did the family's laundry once I'd run out of clean clothes. For a long time we had a semi-automatic washing machine, but it only had manual rollers to wring out the water at the end of the cycle. The wet washing was too heavy for me to lift out of the machine so I devised a way to catch and twist the sopping wet laundry around a broom handle, hoist it up into the air and then feed it through the rollers, the squeezed towels, sheets and clothes spat out on the other side flat like a biscuit.

My father enjoyed watering the garden at the end of the day, after the gallery closed. I helped him with the hose and took over when the spray of the water couldn't reach into an inaccessible nook from where he sat. Best of all, no one bothered us when we were watering the garden. It was quiet time.

He couldn't get close enough to the thick bed of nasturtiums we had on the far side of the garden, so I always took over to drench them. I couldn't fathom how the water didn't wet their leaves at all, it pooled into balls – like iron solder does when it heats up – and rolled off into the dirt. The nasturtiums gave off a different scent to the rest of the flowers, too. They had a sweet and sour smell.

My brother, bigger and stronger than me, pushed my father's wheelchair and did a lot of the other chores. Even so, we were no shortage of work ourselves, and my father wasn't much of a sweet-talker just for the sake of it. If you were in his good books, there was no end of praise, but he didn't abide bad behaviour.

By now his firm assessment was that my mother was behaving badly most of the time, so she can't have been getting a lot of joy or encouragement from him. What self-esteem my mother had, or what empathy she received, she had to make for herself. Or find from other sources.

She could have left the usual way, packed up her bags and probably her children as well. Although I suspect we were just part of her entrapment at this stage – I think she would have been quite happy closing the door on the lot of us. Instead she used other exits – pills, booze and then other men – in a desperate attempt to blank out our miserable home.

When she joined a book club, my father knew it was a hollow alibi for infidelity. Sometimes if I got croup in the night my father would call her friends, trying to locate her. When she couldn't be reached, Grandfather was the one who delivered me to the doctors in her stead. I'm not sure how my father admonished her when she returned, or if he did at all. By this stage, he may have just decided to turn a blind eye. He was at her mercy, after all.

Fifteen

Miraculously, my father got a second chance at happiness and my mother got the opportunity for a guilt-free escape. Although in the end only one of them embraced the gift beyond the first rush of freedom, at least for a moment, light returned to our troubled home.

Surely neither of my parents believed their silent – and not so silent – dreams could ever come true. From anyone's perspective it seemed highly unlikely that either of them would find happiness again. Yet it did happen, for my father at least, in 1972, shortly before my seventh birthday.

Rebecca – Becky – Roberts was a beautiful young American drama student in her early twenties. My mother employed her as a housekeeper and nanny while she went on an art-buying trip to Sydney. Here was her saviour, in knee-high boots, a miniskirt and a poncho. 'You are my sister,' she told Becky, holding her shoulders and kissing her cheek before her trip.

What happened in the weeks she was away was that my father and Becky fell in love.

It would be easy to think that my father somehow manipulated a seemingly bright-eyed, naive and trusting young woman from America's Midwest. How else would he be able to escape his misery? He was in a desperate situation, in an unhappy marriage with two small children, and who could blame a desperate man resorting to desperate measures and all kinds of trickery?

Since Becky was the closest thing to a lifeline my father was likely to find, it's not difficult to imagine him doing anything he could to interest her. But the truth is, quite separate from all the mess, he fell for Becky and she fell for him. That he got to escape his situation was an incidental bonus.

My father was still a relatively young man. Being in a wheelchair didn't change that. Suddenly he had a twenty-something-year-old dressing and undressing him. Someone who didn't resent and despise him. My 95 per cent paralysed father did what any young man in a miserable marriage would do: he seduced her.

At first my mother was as happy as my father. When he told her what had happened in her absence, she told Becky, 'You are my way out.' She went interstate to celebrate her new freedom. All of a sudden, the leash binding her to that backyard post of her childhood was severed. She couldn't have been happier.

Becky moved in and continued to care for the three of us,

except that she was now openly sleeping in my father's room. My brother and I missed our mother, but she wrote us lots of postcards and letters and we spoke on the phone every now and then. Life went on. Becky was good to us and our father was happy, so we were happy too.

One night after my brother and I had been put to bed, my father asked her, 'Do you want to come on an adventure with me?' At the time, I think they both thought it would be a short adventure, that my father wouldn't live all that much longer, given his polio. She said yes, and that's exactly what they did.

I don't remember how long my mother was away. Children have a very different sense of time to adults, but it didn't feel like a small amount of time. Perhaps a couple of months?

Why she returned when she did is unknown to me, but one day she suddenly appeared. Now we were five. She told me and my brother that she wouldn't be staying in the house. She asked Hugh to help her carry the mattress from the spare bed in my room out through the back door and across the lawn to the gallery. That's where she stayed. On a single mattress on the floor of the art gallery. The rest of us slept in the house.

In the morning, before the gallery opened, she and Hugh hauled the mattress into the woodshed. Like a modern-day GPS gone off course, we all recalibrated. I'm not sure whose idea this set-up was, but it was a bad one. Anyone could see it was a kerosene-soaked bonfire ready for a match.

Who wouldn't make themselves scarce in this arrangement, if you can even call it that. I don't remember all five of us being in the house together, except for one night. There was something in the air all that day. Some kind of shimmering expectation. I have no idea why, but the day was different.

My brother and I were told to set the dining table. We got our father's placemats from the cupboard and set five places at one end. We placed the cutlery as neatly as we could, setting each fork on our best linen napkins.

Our mother was fastidious about manners and etiquette, and my brother and I were taught early how to set the table properly, with the starter and main course forks on the left, knives on the right, the soup spoon to the right of the knife, the dessert spoon to the left of it. 'You eat your way in,' my mother told us. Glasses were to be placed above the knife. Bread and butter plates to the left of the forks. Knives turned with their serrated edge towards the plate.

Sometimes my mother's rules were hard to keep track of, since it often felt like our family lived like there were no rules. Ironing was for idiots who didn't have anything better to do with their time, but if we didn't put our knife and fork together at the end of a meal, our mother would say sharply, ' Excuse me,' with a rise of her chin to point to our plates.

This evening's setting had all of that as perfectly straight and correct as we could.

The whole thing was weird. Even I knew it. My mother had cooked a lamb roast. We never ate together as a family – usually my brother and I ate our meals lying on the floor flat on our stomachs, in front of the television, watching *Bewitched* or *The Brady Bunch*. So what was this about?

If the dining table were narrower, and we could have reached, my brother and I would have been kicking each other underneath it, but as it was we sat in our high-backed chairs and watched wide-eyed as the tension brewed. I remember worried looks between Becky and my father. At some point she put her hand on my father's tray and he manoeuvred his palm onto the back of her hand. Right then, with that gesture, I saw something snap in my mother.

I knew she could turn on a dime. We were in for trouble.

I looked over at my brother and opened my eyes wide and lifted my eyebrows as high on my forehead as they would go so he knew something was about to go very wrong. By now we were both trained to our mother's moods, but even though I was younger, I seemed to have a better sense of when she was about to unravel. Perhaps because he knew her before the trouble, my brother was more inclined to ignore and forgive these switches.

When he signalled back that I was overreacting, an annoyed look and shake of his head like he had a fly buzzing in his face, I got mad. I knew this as clearly as if she'd made an announcement about what was in store for the happy couple.

I started counting the ivy leaves on the wallpaper above my brother's head, trying to distract myself from the coming storm. I used many such techniques to escape the fights clouding those years. They were like drinking a glass of water backwards when you have the hiccups or counting sheep when you can't sleep. I taught myself to concentrate hard on something, on this occasion not losing track of my place in the pattern. For a moment, the tension faded out.

Our father was at the head of the table, sitting in front of a recently hung, life-sized portrait of himself, which had been painted by one of the artists he and my mother represented. With the painting positioned against the dark green foliage of the wallpaper, I liked to imagine he'd been painted in a wild jungle, on safari.

Becky sat to his right. Our mother, playing hostess, was seated to his left, in front of the swinging door to the kitchen.

I wonder whom the happy-family charade was aimed at? In any event, the charade was over when our mother got up, leaned across the table, gathered everything in a sweep of her arm, and smashed it to the floor.

Our mother's next move reminded me of a schoolyard game of dare we used to play. She picked up the carving knife and began stabbing it down onto our father's wheelchair tray. I watched as she gouged holes in the wood, waiting for the knife to go into the back of his hand. It seemed to take place in slow motion, but when she was done stabbing his tray, she took the knife to the canvas of our father's portrait. When she finished slashing it, the corners draped down like the sails of a boat becalmed at sea.

All this can't have lasted very long at all, but when it was over the dining room looked like the cage of a crazed animal. The lamb bone seeped its juice into the carpet amidst the broken glass and crockery. The silverware we'd so carefully placed was strewn over the floor. Even my brother was screaming. I wanted to tell him, 'I told you so,' but I was screaming too.

Someone called the police. I'm not sure if it was Becky or a neighbour who heard the trouble. It was certainly not our father, who could only sit in his chair yelling at everyone to stop screaming. I don't remember the exact sequence of events, but I do remember my mother paying us no heed once she knew the police were coming. She got busy trying to put the room back together, presumably so it was in some kind of order before law enforcement turned up asking questions.

Our father told my brother, 'Take your sister to her room,' and that's what he did, holding me by the shoulders and ushering me out like I was a feeble patient in a hospital being taken to have a nasty procedure. When we got there, I told him I wanted him to sleep in my room that night. There was no mattress on the spare bed, since it was out in the gallery for my mother, so we untucked the sheet and blankets from the end of my bed and he climbed in there. Head to toe.

It wasn't long before we heard sirens out in the street. Shortly after a young officer from the local precinct knocked on my bedroom door.

'You kids okay in there?' she asked, poking her head in. 'Do you mind if I come in?'

Hugh said she could come in and then the light went on and she was standing next to my bed.

'Can you tell me what happened tonight?' she said gently. 'Are you two sure you're okay?'

We told her that our mother lost her temper but we were fine and it wasn't all that bad. She asked us if we were scared.

'No,' we said in unison, like the trained puppets we were.

A family friend arrived while the officer was talking to us and it seemed as though they'd come to an agreement about what would happen next without even speaking. It was like a baton handover. As soon as our family friend arrived, the officer left. The next thing Hugh and I knew we had blankets around our shoulders and we were in the back of a car driving to our family friend's house. Once we got there, we were shown to freshly made beds in the spare room.

We stayed there for a few days. The family had two girls, one my age, the other a bit closer to my brother's age. They had a pool and we swam and dive-bombed for hours on end. We played out endless re-enactments of *Bonnie and Clyde*, which we watched on the big television in their rumpus room. The idea of a rumpus room was new to me and my brother. It was amazing to be allowed to take over an entire space with toys and games and not have to clear the floor to make way for a wheelchair.

The adults tried to act like everything was normal and we were just having a sleepover. No doubt they discussed our situation in worried tones when we were out of earshot or had gone to bed.

If anyone asked how I was doing, I said, 'I'm fine.' I was at the time. We were with friends, swimming in their pool and playing games in a rumpus room. No one was yelling. That was more than fine to me.

Becky and our father moved out. I'm not sure where they went to first, maybe they stayed with Gran and Grandfather, but eventually they ended up in North Adelaide, right near another large area of parkland. Our mother moved back into the house and took over our father's room, and for the most part we lived with her.

My brother and I went back to being not so fine, not that we'd have told anyone even if they'd asked. We were a couple of co-conspirators in our parents' game. A child's loyalty to a parent is a given. It's a sacred rule at the core of being a kid. We were still of the age that our sense of self and security was so tied up with our parents', we couldn't possibly have separated the two.

But a parent's loyalty, it turns out, is not a given. It felt like my father had a whole new life to look forward to with Becky and, when they left, it wasn't just us they left behind. The gallery was in our backyard, so there was no more work for him there. He and Becky had to build a new life for themselves.

Our mother's initial joy about the situation never returned. Soon it was presented to the world that Becky had broken up their happy marriage. The saviour became the homewrecker.

Many years later, when I asked my mother what happened that night when everything went sideways at dinner, she said, 'Everyone loves their jailer.' I didn't know what that was supposed to mean, but my mother acted like it made perfect sense.

It turns out Muttee's declaration on my parents' wedding day that she'd have been happier if my mother were marrying a dog was not so misguided. She knew my mother wasn't cut out for the life of a long-term caregiver.

My father was consistent even in his faults. He was hard to categorise, but he was pretty predictable, or at least I knew what to expect from him. If I cleaned the windows but left even one smudge, he'd point it out. It didn't matter if I'd already packed the newspaper and vinegar away and was on my way out the door to play, I'd have to bring it all back to rid the window of its blemish. Everything was to be done properly. 'If you just did it right the first time,' he'd say to my protests.

But my mother was not so easy to predict or surmise. You could make a truthful statement about her one moment, then she'd turn around and the exact opposite would be true the next.

Becky had the personality for life with my father. That's not to say she was meek or subservient, she was neither of those things. But she was malleable, in a way my mother never was, and, most importantly, Becky didn't need to compete for attention.

My mother was empathetic. No matter what else in her psychology drove her to it, she could never have married my father were she not. She often helped people in the street who were down on their luck, or sent my brother or me with meals to a neighbour who was going through a difficult time.

She once helped a blind man who'd got lost on his way home and they struck up a friendship. She sometimes cooked for him and in return asked him to help her with odd jobs around the house. She understood it would be valuable for him to feel like the help-*giver* sometimes.

My mother found out that he could see brightness, so when he came over to mow her lawn, she laid white tea towels at the edges of the grass. She then guided him to the mower, which he powered up with three strong pulls of the starter cord once she'd placed it in his hand. When the mower started humming, he made his way slowly forward in a straight line until he saw the light reflected from the first white cloth. The tea towel was his cue to make a turn. Once he completed the fourth edge, my mother moved the tea towels into smaller concentric squares until the entire lawn was clipped short.

Sixteen

Despite all the proof to the contrary – the wheelchair, the lifting machine by the bed, the fact that I had not once in my life been picked up by my father – I didn't really believe he couldn't walk. I thought he was being lazy, that he simply liked all the attention and us doing everything for him.

My daytime suspicions were fuelled by recurring dreams of him running. These night-time visions of my father's long legs running towards me, his arms outstretched, were so vivid that not only was I disappointed and genuinely surprised when in the morning I found him lying perfectly still in his bed, I was *mad.*

I was eight when I came to the firm conclusion that my father wasn't a cripple, he was a fake. I devised a plan to get to the truth. Even then, I was not one to *not* take action. It seemed perfectly clear that someone had to take charge and, since everyone else was too busy with their own business, I took matters into my own hands.

I decided the only thing to be done was to set my father on fire.

The idea came after someone at school told me about a man in a wheelchair who was miraculously cured of a spinal cord injury when a fire engulfed his home. The tale had it that when the rubber tyres of his wheelchair began to melt and the chrome buckled, and he couldn't wheel himself any further, he simply got up from his wheelchair and walked out of the house to escape the flames. It was my call to action. I figured my father would be able to do the same thing; he only needed sufficient motivation.

When I told him the story about the man in the fire, and how I planned to set his new home with Becky alight so he'd walk again, he made her hide all the matchboxes. He knew I was deadly serious. Meanwhile, I searched for matches, dreaming of roaring heat so hot that my father would have no choice but to stand up and walk away from that damn chair.

If Becky was worried about me setting the house on fire, she never let on. She was not a disciplinarian, nor was she ever critical. She grew up with the American idea that everyone deserves a ribbon, so even if she was mad, she somehow managed to turn her criticism into praise.

Becky was the eldest of three brothers and a sister. Her parents moved to Australia from Minnesota at the height of Nixon's presidency, when Becky was nineteen. Becky's father was a softly spoken social worker who loved to sing. Her parents were disgusted by the war in Vietnam and the assassinations of Martin Luther King and

Bobby Kennedy, and wanted to be as far away from Nixon's mess as possible. Adelaide was about as far away as you could get.

Her mother was a pianist and the children grew up singing together around the piano. They were religious progressives. My father couldn't tolerate religion. He thought it was the cause of a lot of the world's ills and didn't dampen his arguments on Becky's account. In the end Becky stopped going to church, but she never lost her faith.

My father was ruthless in that regard. Rather than accommodating Becky's beliefs, he argued. Some of it may have been for his love of a good debate, but I think it was also about controlling what she did with her Sunday mornings and whether it was appropriate to leave him behind to do something on her own. My father was done with being left behind. He'd learned his lesson from his first family, who left him behind almost as a matter of course.

For Becky, it wasn't about leaving him behind, it was about nourishing her soul. But he couldn't see it like that and Becky didn't push back. She'd been appalled by how we all treated our father. She was right. We were shameful.

Early on in their relationship, Becky worked at a school for disabled children. There encouragement and reward, rather than discipline and smacking, were the guiding interventions. She dealt with me that way too.

One day I went to the school where she worked. I'd never seen anything like it. My father may have been in a chair like many of the kids in the room, but he did not dribble, or scream, or rock himself furiously back and forth. You'd think I would have been ready for it, but I wasn't, and I was very glad when the end of the day came.

Becky taught me to ice skate at a local rink. She enrolled me in gymnastics at the nearby YWCA and drove me there in her little

VW Beetle every Saturday morning, cheering me on as I jumped and somersaulted my way through the class. When it was just the two of us, she let me steer the car and change the gears. She could sew and mend my clothes and made me outfits from patterns she had sent over from America. She tried to teach me to sew, but I had no knack for it, so we made popcorn balls with butterscotch syrup instead.

All the while, my mother's blinding hatred for Becky and my father grew. Eventually, some of her judgements wore off. When I was at their place, rather than spending time with them, I took to tending an old horse that had been abandoned by its owner in the parkland near their new home. I bought hay for it with my pocket money, brushed its matted coat and pretended it was mine, until the park sent it off to the knacker's yard because its fees hadn't been paid.

I really liked spending time with Becky, but I couldn't tell my mother that. I believed I had to take sides, so I never told my mother about all the fun things we did at Dad and Becky's. It would have been treachery.

At Christmas, Becky wanted to take us carolling. In America, it was a Midwestern tradition, but in Adelaide, it was unheard of. When my brother and I complained to our father that we didn't want to go, he told us he didn't much like the idea either, but we were all going and 'that was that'.

It was awful standing on the porches of people we didn't know, ringing doorbells, watching their horrified faces when they opened the door to see what was waiting to greet them: two scrawny kids and a woman standing beside a guy in a wheelchair, singing 'O Come, All Ye Faithful'. I felt like I was part of a travelling freak show.

Becky grew up singing in the church choir and sang loudly and confidently. My brother and I tried to hide behind our father and mumbled the words, wanting to sink into the ground and longing for the ordeal to be over. But house to house we went, until our obvious misery got us sent home and my father and Becky continued around the neighbourhood, shocking the neighbours all by themselves.

My father had very dry, irritated skin. I think it was a symptom of his condition, probably something to do with his poor circulation. Sometimes he'd instruct me to scratch an itch. I thought it was funny. He'd direct my hand, saying, 'Higher. Higher. A little to the left.' And then when I'd hit the spot, 'Stop! Right there!' and he'd let out a sigh of relief. It reminded me of scratching a dog when it had an itch it couldn't reach with its hind legs.

But my services were rarely called upon after they somehow discovered that apple cider vinegar was a remedy. Every morning Becky soaked a number of cotton balls in the liquid and rubbed it vigorously on his face and into his scalp.

Sometimes he asked me to get out the vinegar and repeat the procedure if there was a flare-up and Becky wasn't around. I didn't much like doing these things for him but I hid my distaste as best I could by joking that he smelled like salad dressing, which was exactly how he did smell. The scent of apple cider vinegar still reminds me of my father.

There were definitely upsides to his life in the wheelchair. Something that suited the cheap part of my father's character was that he never wore out his shoes. He had no more than two pairs at a time – usually a very long time. He would have had one pair his entire adult life but for Becky insisting he upgrade every couple of years.

Travelling anywhere was always a big challenge. The Begleys, befriended after my brother escaped his cot and Greta Begley scooped him up, didn't take sides when our parents separated, so they knew Becky too. They kept horses and sometimes came around to take Becky and my father to parties with their horse trailer hitched to their car. Compared with hoisting him in and out of the front seat and collapsing his wheelchair, it was easier and a lot more fun to wheel him up the ramp of the float, put the brakes on his chair and close the barn-like doors with him and Martin Begley in the back – particularly after they'd all had a few drinks.

When we started travelling in airplanes with Becky, in the mid-seventies, my father was handled like cargo. To disembark, a heavy-set flight attendant would stand in front of my father in his seat at the bulkhead, bend down to drape my father's limp arms around his shoulders, clasp his hands around my father's lower back and heave him up. If the flight attendant was taller than my father, his legs dangled in the air like limp ropes as the attendant stepped around to the wheelchair and folded my father into it.

Then he was wheeled to the emergency exit, where he waited while the long prongs of a large forklift raised up to the height of the door, came forward and hooked under the seat of my father's chair. Even my brother and I could admit it was pretty funny, once we got over our embarrassment. If our father didn't like the adventure of it himself, he never let on.

Sometimes, when he was in bed resting, our father's chair was a toy for me and my brother. The chair's leather seat was lined with matted sheepskin that was soft and warm to sit on. One of my brother's favourite games was for me to sit in the chair, let him wheel me to the top of Dad and Becky's steep driveway and then push me down the hill as hard as he could.

With the wind flying through my hair, I held on tight to the brake handles even though I was too little to push the levers on each side and tilt the rubber stoppers onto the tyres. Besides, my brother would have yelled at me if I had tried to slow down. Instead, I closed my eyes as I sped out into the middle of the street, where cars veered and screeched. This sport amused my brother enormously.

Eventually my father would hear the shouts and screeching brakes from his bedroom, guess what we were up to, and whistle as loud as he could. My ears were as trained to my father's whistle as a mother's to her child's cry. The whistle meant he needed something. Either that or we were in big trouble.

'What the hell are you bloody kids doing? Come inside! Three!' If he skipped counting to one and two and went straight to three it meant we were really in trouble.

When he was truly mad, he smacked me. 'Get the wooden spoon,' he'd say, red-faced, sending me to the kitchen drawer to get the foot-long wooden spoon Becky used for stirring pancake batter. When I returned, chin to my chest, with the spoon hanging limply from my fist, he'd say, 'Come here. Hold out your hand.' It always took him a few moments to manoeuvre the spoon's handle so he could properly clasp it in his feeble grip, during which time I patiently held my palm open on his tray, waiting for him to administer the hardest belting he was capable of – three feather-light taps. I cried as hard as if he'd given me welts.

Since he couldn't pick us up in his arms in time to thwart any one of a hundred daily perils facing a small and curious child, he had to rely on stopping us with his voice, making us believe that 'no' or 'stop' was meant as firmly as if he'd grabbed us by the arm and shaken us. I've never stopped believing that people mean what they say. If I say, 'Please don't do that,' I'm not kidding around. I'm constantly astounded that people don't take my words as the literal truth.

I grew up understanding the importance of words. My father didn't have anything *but* words. I learned from him to speak them carefully, and listen to them even more conscientiously. Perhaps that's why I've always been so drawn to writers – what other profession is as serious about the words it uses?

Seventeen

I wasn't an A student, but I loved school. I loved the routine of roll call, where it seemed like someone cared if I raised my arm and said 'here' or not. I loved running along the corridors between classes, the private space of my locker and, most importantly, I loved being with my friends. I relished it all.

Even though school wasn't always easy for me, I worked hard. I revelled in the days before the beginning of each term, when I rode my bike to the local newsagent to buy all new folders and exercise books. I covered these with sticky sheets of kitsch contact printed with horses galloping in speckled sunlight. I spent hours snipping the edges of the contact so it made perfectly diagonal corners and smoothing out the paper with my forearm – just like my father had done with the green felt of his tablemats – so there were no air bubbles under the surface. Then I made special labels for each subject, with my name, class and my teacher's name, written as neatly as I could, in large childish letters.

When my grade five teacher set us an assignment to write an account of our home life, I refused. I was a conscientious student, but how could I write about all the things that happened in our house? I was pretty sure that none of my schoolfriends' homes were called 'the flop house', which is what our place had been coined by the numerous guests and waifs we had stay with us.

When I told my teacher I wouldn't write the composition, he screamed at me and told me to sit in front of the class. He was a former army man who used to make us march in formation around the playground, no matter the temperature, including once when it was so hot I fainted on the concrete netball courts and had to be carried to sick bay.

When he wasn't marching us around the quadrangle like his own private army of miniature soldiers, he used to put my friend George in the rubbish bin and tell him he was garbage. George looked bad because he had a poorly made glass eye, but I knew him to be one of the kindest kids in my class. He had a pet sheep that he used to bring to the playground on occasion.

He never teased me about my dad, like other kids did, and I never teased him about his eye even though it looked like one of the marbles I used to flick across the playground. George was bullied mercilessly by the other kids when they decided to set upon him.

One day George had enough of the jeers. He pulled the painted ball out of its socket and, holding it in his outstretched hand, chased whoever it was who had teased him.

George's glass eye looked terrible, but it was worse when he took it out. The skin of his eyelid fell loosely across the gaping hole and his eye rolled around wet in the palm of his hand. If he didn't put it back in properly he had a completely white eyeball, which was even scarier to look at.

After our teacher sat me in front of the class as punishment, I went home and told my mother everything that had happened. I told her about George in the garbage, about my assignment. I described the marching, and the beltings he gave to the boys.

The next day my mother and I were sitting outside the principal's office at 8.45 a.m. My heart was thumping in my chest. I watched the hands of the big clock on the wall tick around to 9 a.m., heard the school bell ring and the sound of children's feet running along the corridors to roll call.

Eventually the secretary showed me and my mother into the principal's office, where I'd been only a few times before to get admonished for some wrongdoing or other. The principal asked a few questions before sending me back to class to fetch my teacher.

He must have known something was up, because the look he gave me when I told him the principal wanted to see him was withering. He told the class to be quiet and continue with the work he'd set, but the moment he closed the door, everyone erupted in cheers.

When he came back into the room it was almost the end of the period. His face was purple with rage and his usually slicked-back hair was falling down into his eyes. The next day we had a new teacher.

I was often put on after-school detention, where I had to sit in a classroom with the naughty kids after everyone else had been dismissed. The light streamed through the large open windows while we sat with our heads bent over our little wooden desks, writing lines. *I will not speak back to Miss Hornblower. I will not speak back to*

Miss Hornblower. I will not speak back to Miss Hornblower. I will not forget my homework. I will not forget my homework. I will not forget my homework . . . We had to write the lines one hundred times, as if that would set us straight.

It wasn't very often that I hadn't actually done my homework. Mostly it was that when things got tough at home and I packed my bags to stay with family friends, I forgot to include it with my clothes. I couldn't always keep track of what I'd need at school three days later. Invariably something I did need got left behind.

I often arrived at the beginning of class with a signed note from whomever I was staying with, explaining why I wasn't handing in the assignment we'd been set. After a while my teachers stopped believing me. If I wasn't put on detention I was sent to the school counsellor, who instructed me to sit in the wood and metal chair across the table while he or she, usually a Miss, asked earnestly whether everything was alright at home. 'Yes, of course it is,' I'd reply, rolling my eyes after I exited the room.

Eighteen

A year or so after my father left with Becky, my mother closed the gallery and enrolled to finish her last year of high school. It was the seventies and she had found feminism.

My mother was smart. She deserved a proper education and, in the beginning, I liked the fact that she was going to school just like we were. But the moment she found feminism, things got even more out of hand at our place.

My friends at school had normal families: mothers who weren't attending high school in their thirties, who wore bras and didn't have countless boyfriends. Mothers whose boyfriends didn't regularly beat them up or steal from them. Normal mothers stayed home and made tidy after-school snacks for their kids, as seen on TV. I wanted one of those.

Other families had able-bodied fathers who drove cars and had sheds and could fix things. I wanted to go and live at my best friend's place. Her mother ironed sheets and underpants and liked the English comedian Pam Ayres. Her father drove a Triumph Stag and played cheesy songs on his Hammond organ. They had a rumpus room and took condensed milk in their instant coffee.

Nowhere was anything normal for us. Becky made after-school snacks and kept better house than my mother, but there was still my father in his chair.

Even my mother's star sign wasn't a certainty. After reading the internationally bestselling astrology book *Linda Goodman's Sun Signs*, she came out one morning and announced that she was changing her astrological sign. My mother didn't like Goodman's assessment of Capricorns so she deemed herself an Aquarian. To her reasoning there was only a clutch of days between that sign and her birthday, so what real difference did it make? My father's sign happened to be Capricorn, so I'm sure that was part of her thinking too.

Dad and Becky had bought a new art gallery, next door to the new home they had moved to in North Adelaide. It was at this house that I really hurt my father, towards the end of the long and hot school holidays before my first year of high school.

My new school – a government school – had been an all-boys campus just two years before I was due to start. The school was largely made up of what were then the newest wave of immigrants – Greeks and Italians – and was considered pretty rough. Only a couple of my primary school classmates would be coming with me. The rest were off to private schools. I was eager for the change and the chance to make new friends, so I was even more excited for this new school year than usual.

A few days before the first day of term, my father called me into his room to tell me he and Becky were taking me to buy my new school uniform. I should have been elated; I'd done nothing but talk about my new school and all its trappings. But instead my heart sank.

'Okay,' I said. 'Thanks, Dad.'

I wandered out to find Becky. She could tell something had upset me.

'What's wrong?' she asked. 'Didn't your father tell you we were taking you shopping today? I thought you'd be happy.'

'Yeah, but I just want us to go. Just you and me, can't we leave him behind?'

Becky turned back to the sink to hide her disappointment at my meanness. 'I think he really wants to come with us,' she said, looking down at her gloved hands in the soapy water.

I told her I wanted to leave my father at home so we could be quicker.

Myer was the only department store in town that stocked my new school's uniform, so I knew I'd see other kids there getting themselves decked out. If they saw me with my father, I'd be branded as the freak before I even got started. For once I wanted to be normal like everyone else.

'We won't take long,' I said. 'Pleeease can *we* just go?'

'Alright,' she said. 'I'll talk to your father, but I know he'll be disappointed. He was looking forward to this.'

I didn't care, but the shopping wasn't much fun. I felt too guilty. Worse still, I knew I'd disappointed Becky.

When we got home, trying to make up for my cruelty, I ran straight into their bedroom to show off my new school gear for my father, the price tags still hanging from the collar. When I opened the door, I started screaming.

He was covered in ants. They had been attracted by a wound he had on his big toe, which Becky had left undressed to air while we were out. Thousands of the black critters were crawling over him. They were on his face, streaming up his legs in a long train, travelling fast across his body. When she heard me scream, Becky came running and I was shooed out of the room. She hoisted him up with the lifting machine and, dangling in the air, he was pushed to the bathroom, where she turned on the shower and the ants were swept down the drain.

Occasionally he recounted the story of the ants to shock people, and in his telling he was almost eaten alive, but he never mentioned to anyone why he had been left lying there on his own in the first place.

I rarely forgot my father was different, but sometimes he did. Once, he and Becky went to an All Hallows' Eve fancy dress party. They worked all day preparing the costume he'd been planning for weeks. Becky cut out a large O-shape from a thick sheet of cardboard and wrapped it in aluminium foil. Then she put the cardboard around my father's neck so it looked like his head was on a platter and added the final touch of oozes of red jelly to look like blood.

Becky wrapped him and his chair in a grey sheet and pushed him off to the party. She had painted her own face with white make-up and wore a pair of pink ballet tights. She strapped a number of my father's sheepskins from their bed around her torso. They arrived at the party as a sacrificial lamb and the head of John the Baptist. Depending on how you looked at it, they were either the funniest or most macabre people there.

When the host opened the door and immediately greeted my

father by name, he was absolutely crushed. 'How did you know it was me?' he kept asking. Even though they won champagne for being the best-dressed couple, his mood was dark for days afterwards.

Around this time my father enrolled to study Fine Arts at Flinders University. Along with these studies and the work of the art gallery, he held a weekly protest vigil outside the office of the university's architect to protest the campus's terrible accessibility. He had already been rejected by Adelaide University's law school because none of their buildings were accessible. But even at Flinders – a much newer campus than Adelaide's – Becky had to drive him up onto the pedestrian plaza in their little VW Beetle so he could get into the building where his lectures took place.

He never graduated. After finishing the first year, they informed him none of the second-year lecture theatres were accessible. He left university, but made sure they got the message; these days the campus has much-improved access.

While my father had Becky to help him, my mother was alone. After she got her adult matriculation from high school, she went to Adelaide University. Study and campus life now definitely got in the way of her other duties – housekeeping, and my brother and me. Even at the best of times, domestic duty had not been my mother's greatest strength. But once she was at school, things got looser still. She had other things on her mind.

She loved her crockpot. In the morning she threw in some loosely chopped vegetables, a chunk of off-cut meat, a couple cups of water, salt and pepper, put the lid on and let it simmer all day. Of course, it was practical, and she had better things to do than slave over a stove, but the idea of a crockpot still puts a pit in my stomach.

To the amusement of anyone who witnessed it, she made cake batter in a saucepan. There was no creaming the butter and sugar, or adding the eggs one at a time. She had no time for any of that. She dumped and slurped all the ingredients in at the same time before mixing them together so they were more or less blended and tipping the dough into a cake tray. Sometimes the cakes worked, mostly they did not. Although I'm sure my mother didn't see the ratio that way.

Years later, when he'd moved out of home and was living interstate, she sent my brother a cake with a five-inch nail in it. Other times she mistook salt for sugar. Sometimes the ingredients all worked, only to be forgotten about in the oven, so an hour later the kitchen was filled with plumes of smoke. With those cakes, my brother and I cut off the burnt bits and ate whatever was left with ice cream, to take away some of the burnt taste.

It was a wonder the house never burned down. Sometimes our backyard looked like an experimental art installation. When my mother burned something on the stove, which happened more often than seemed reasonably possible, she put the blackened pots out in the sun and doused the burnt bottom and sides in water, then tipped bicarbonate of soda onto the affected areas. There they sat until the black softened and we could scour or chisel out the inch-thick chunks of charcoal.

We had a large lift-top freezer the size of a small cupboard. It didn't fit in our kitchen, so it sat on the porch near the back door. Our mother filled the freezer with cartons of unfinished milk, squares of leftover cheese, meat, casseroles, fish heads and chicken bones she boiled to make soup.

The fish soup could have been delicious, except that the scales were never scraped off properly so you had to sieve them out between your teeth as you slurped. Lifting a spoonful of broth with a large fish eye looking at you took away a lot of the enjoyment too.

The problem with the deep freezer was that the food just kept stacking up. You could never find things or know what was underneath the last layer. There were no compartments, drawers or lift-out baskets. It all just built up and eventually froze into one solid mass. Nothing was labelled or put into containers. Leftover stews were tipped into a used plastic bag and dropped in for later. But later never really came and, if it did, I never wanted to eat it.

I thought of the freezer as a graveyard. I dreaded opening it or watching my mother take something out and throw it in the sink to be defrosted for the evening's meal. But one day the deep freeze was finally filled to the brim. I knew it would be down to me to make it right. I waited until my mother left, took the chair from the kitchen table and positioned it next to the freezer so I could stand on it and reach in.

'You can't throw that out,' my mother would have said of the two-year-old slab of meat scalded with ice burns. 'That's top-quality steak.'

The top layers were easily reached and I worked fast, throwing most of it into a large garbage bin. But the further down I went, my upper body folding deeper into the freezer, the harder it got. Everything was stuck together.

I knew I had to get the job done before my mother came back – otherwise the whole exercise would be pointless – so I boiled the kettle and poured it in. Jug after jug. Slowly the packages separated. I was making good progress – I was at least halfway to the bottom when I was overwhelmed by the smell of all the different meats, which had begun to cook, and the sour stench of milk from the unsealed cartons and unwrapped cheeses.

I had to hold back the bile rising in my throat. The chicken meat felt like still-warm dead babies, but I knew I had to keep going. Eventually my mother did come home and, after the shock had passed, she helped me with the rest. I felt sick and couldn't eat any dinner, but the freezer – that frozen graveyard – was cleaned out. After the mess I'd made with the boiling water, not even she could argue for a single item to be salvaged.

I wrote a poem about that experience and gave it to my mother, who thought it showed promise and stuck it on the fridge. She often said of her own writing that once it was written down, it didn't have anything to do with real life or real people. If only it were really like that. Still, I was grateful she didn't take offence and was proud of me for writing it.

Nineteen

We didn't have much money. We lived on our mother's student allowance from the government and rent from a boarder who had moved into the now shuttered gallery. I'm not sure if my mother knew he owned a pet eagle when she took him in. Shortly after he unpacked all his belongings he put a large chopping block outside the back entrance to the gallery, near my old swing. He swung an axe down into the surface so it sat there suspended in the wood like a threat or a violent sculpture.

My brother and I wondered what on earth it could be for. Maybe he was going to help us chop up the mallee roots we had delivered at the start of winter for firewood. Not so. Every morning he grabbed a few of the mice he kept in a cage and carried them to the block by their tails, screaming and whipping around trying to break free. There he laid them down and cut off their heads with the axe, then fed them to his eagle, which lived in the gallery with him. I don't remember a cage.

My brother and I had pet mice that we kept in an empty fish tank in the outdoor toilet. My brother named his mouse Continental Small Goods as a joke. I kept my cat, Mao Zedong, locked out on the other side of the door. We stayed out of the backyard near the eagle's feeding hour.

My mother was studying Classics at Adelaide University. She taught me to distinguish a Doric column from a Corinthian and how to count to ten in Greek. Best of all, she told me Greek myths. I loved Zeus the most and still think of him when it thunders. Even as an adult, when the sky roars and sparks I often wonder if it's not really an angry god stomping and throwing things around, as if there's a fight to the death taking place above the clouds.

It was around this time that my mother entered the university poetry competition – the Bundey Prize – and won. Suddenly she was a promising poet. From then on, I accompanied her to lots of readings. I sat on large cushions on the floor listening to readings at the regular Poet's Union events.

My mother had written some poems about me as a baby. I could feel my face get red as soon as she began. But I was proud of her standing up there in the spotlight reading her life out to the crowd. I enjoyed the readings, and writers seemed like nice people to me.

But there was something unsettling, too. Often the poems she read out on stage painted a picture of life that didn't match my own version of it. The poems described me as a flame of life, that having me around was like having a dolphin in the house. That I brought her immense joy and wonder. I know I did bring her joy at times, but mostly I felt like an encumbrance – a noose more than a dolphin.

I once cleaned up a rat that had died in the cupboard among the saucepans underneath the stove and always checked for weevils and wriggling maggots before eating dry goods. There just wasn't time in my mother's new-found life for any kind of domesticity. I had become her Cinderella and quietly cleaned up the dead bodies and threw out the evidence of neglect.

If treasuring something meant caring for it – which is what it meant to me and how I cared for the things I loved – how could you neglect it day to day and then tell the world it was your most treasured thing?

Over time, her poetry became another fable and I was complicit. My father was gone, so the narrative changed, but there was still a story to uphold. Now, though, with her reputation growing after the Bundey Prize, it was even more public. It wasn't just family and friends for whom we maintained a charade, my mother's representation of our life was printed in anthologies and newspapers. Printed, it was fact.

Sometimes, when things were good – and they really were good sometimes – I would happily fall into believing that it was all as we pretended. It was a relief, no matter how fleeting, that I had imagined the darkness and trouble. But the only time things felt real was when I walked out the front door and went to school.

Every second year, when the city played host to Adelaide Writers' Week, my mother took me to sit under one of the sought-after spots of shade under a tree, where we listened to the readings and lectures, eating sandwiches she'd packed for us. I'm not sure I was always a willing participant. It was often so hot I'd have preferred to be swimming or riding my bike with my friends, but she'd shoosh me if I complained I was bored.

When we rode our bikes home together, sunburnt and tired, she'd explain what the writers had been talking about. Riding our bikes together was a good time. Sometimes we raced with heads forward over the handlebars, pedalling hard. She was as competitive as I was and for many years she'd leave me in the dust and, by the time I dropped my bike to the ground in the backyard, she already had the kettle on the stove to make tea.

This was when home was referred to as 'the flop house'. There was an endless stream of people staying. Sometimes that was fun and they were nice people, but other times they stole from us, leaving in the middle of the night with their loot. There were constant parties and my brother and I got to stay up late playing charades with the guests as Nana Mouskouri played on the stereo in the background.

My mother may have been good at charades in everyday life, but at the actual *game* she was hopeless. She always ended up laughing so much at her own inability to express the word she was looking for in actions, she often simply blurted it out in frustration and got disqualified from the rest of the game. It was funny and, even though she rarely won, no one could argue that she wasn't the real victor.

My mother got involved in the student newspaper and thereafter our formal dining room was regularly turned into a printing workshop with people taking turns at winding the handle of the old-fashioned Gestetner printer. The clunky machine spewed out pages in blue ink, which we folded and stapled in impromptu assembly lines. They were fun nights too. My brother and I went to bed with ink on our hands and faces while the adults drank on, until my mother suggested they all go to Hindley Street – the local strip where bikies and prostitutes hung out – to visit the Flash Café for excellent coffee and gelato. My brother and I always knew when they'd gone to the Flash because we'd each wake up in the morning to find a couple of

Baci chocolates on our pillow. Chocolate kisses for breakfast was a sweet surprise.

Meanwhile, as an antidote to the flop house, my father decided it was his duty to instil in my brother and me a strong sense of heritage and structure, so when we went to stay at their place, he and Becky often arranged trips to our ancestors' stomping grounds and other personally significant heritage sites. We went on daytrips to Moonta to see the school where our great-grandfather had taught. I never understood the point of travelling all that way to see a school that had been turned into a museum and emptied of life.

Once Becky parked the car in the former school grounds, my brother and I scuffed our shoes through the dry red dirt to clearly demonstrate our indifference. The dust clung to our clothes and got into my nostrils. The air was so dry it made my lungs hurt.

Our father couldn't get up the stairs to show us the bronze roll call of former headmasters, which hung high on the baby-blue wall of the corridor outside what used to be our great-grandfather's office. Instead he waited in the sun in the buckled-concrete quadrangle while we went inside with Becky and reported back that we'd seen our family name up there, close to the top of the list.

My father was still in a manual wheelchair, which meant one of us had to wheel him from one spot to the next. If we had left him out in the quadrangle, he'd have died of heat stroke or dehydration unless a stranger happened by.

After we'd seen the plaque on the wall, and he shared stories about our great-grandfather and the school's history, we wheeled him back to the passenger side of the little two-door white VW Beetle. There we began the elaborate process of getting him back into the car.

The car had a manual lifting machine attached to the roof, once again concocted by Bob Todd and my father. The machine was soldered onto the roof exactly in the centre of the two doors. It consisted of an extending and retracting pipe, like a trombone slide, with a heavy hand-turned spool at the end. Around the spool was a high-density metal cord, which had a large hook attached to the end.

On the days we were going out in the car Becky sat my father in a bucket-shaped seat made of heavy canvas that she'd sewn with triple stitching to make sure it didn't tear. The seat had four thick loops of the same material, but even thicker and more heavily stitched, into which she threaded the lifting machine's hooks.

Once the hooks were in place and my father was clasped bottom and back, she hoisted him up out of his chair by turning the handle on the spool. As he was in the air, he looked like an old-fashioned picture-book illustration of a swaddled child held in the beak of a large stork.

When he was dangling high enough in the air – above the level of the car's seat – my brother or I pulled the wheelchair out of the way. Becky pushed my father with her hip and shoulder so the pipes retracted back into their socket and our father slid inside the car, hovering above the passenger seat.

Then Becky turned the handle in the opposite direction and lowered him into the seat. I secured the seatbelt around him while my brother collapsed the wheelchair and hooked it to the modified bike holder at the rear of the car. Finally, my brother and I climbed in the back seat and Becky started the car.

After visiting the old school in Moonta, we would drive to a dingy café on the town's main street for lunch. The place was dimly lit, with dusty fake flowers on plastic tablecloths, but they sold the best pasties and my brother and I couldn't wait to get there. This was by far the best part of the whole trip. Pasties were a hundred-year-old specialty of Moonta, having been brought there by the Cornish immigrants working in the mines. These delicacies were completely different from the dry, fatty version that we sometimes bought at our school canteen when we got money to buy lunch for a special occasion. It didn't matter that the pasties at school had been defrosted and then slowly warmed up in their individual cellophane bags in a heated glass cabinet, they made me feel like I was one of the cool kids. Cool kids bought lunch at the canteen.

Even my brother and I knew these pasties in Moonta were a whole different thing. These were made fresh daily. The pastry was light and flaky, and I slathered it in tomato sauce and spread it thickly across the top with my index finger. Usually I ate so fast I had to fan the large mouthfuls on my tongue with my mouth wide open so as not to burn myself. So many flakes of pastry landed down my front, when I finished I had to dust myself off like I'd been hit in the chest by a snowball.

Although he never said it directly, I strongly suspect my father's motivation in taking us to these old family sites was to show me and my brother that we came from a long line of adventurers. It's the same reason he took us to see my grandfather's long-dead monkey at the museum and constantly retold his family's history.

My father didn't want us thinking that we were frail, timid people who stayed in one spot all their lives, just because that's how his life had turned out after polio.

He was saying, 'This is your history. This restlessness and sense of adventure is in your blood.' I took up the mantel of my ancestors as soon as I possibly could, determined to do all the wild living, have all the adventures my father couldn't.

Twenty

Once my father finished with university, he volunteered in the state government's Department of Aged Care. He knew they'd never employ him without proving himself, so he offered to work for free and was determined to make such an impact they'd have no choice but to hire him.

My father was a 'systems man'. He was always telling me not to cut corners. There was a right way and order to do things, and he never let up instructing me which was which. Clearly he told the government people too, because not long after he joined their ranks as a volunteer, a whole new administrative system was in place.

A few months later, they offered him the job, but he wasn't allowed any of the standard-practice benefits and entitlements that would have come with the position for an able-bodied person. Those were the days before anti-discrimination legislation, when even the government tried to get away with whatever they could to save some money. My father was denied both a pension and any superannuation benefits. Their justification was that he was likely to not be able to work for long and would end up being a heavy liability on taxpayers.

Once again, they didn't know my father.

He also wasn't given any tax breaks for the often expensive equipment that made it possible for him *to* work. It was law back then – as it is now – that able-bodied people can claim items on their tax return that help them in their work, or make it possible for them to turn up and be able to reasonably conduct their business. Not for him. Becky drove him the forty-five-minute drive to and from his work each day and no allowance was made for her or the car. If he needed an electric wheelchair so he could get around the office independently, then he had to pay for it entirely out of his own pocket.

But even so, by 1977 he had earned enough money to buy a large stone house on the waterfront at Henley Beach. The local square, about a mile from their new home, was filled with hundreds of Harley-Davidsons belonging to the local chapter of the Hells Angels. Henley Square was the gang's regular hangout, so people tended to avoid the area when they were in residence.

The square fronted onto a long wooden pier, a suburban road with a large pub, a billiards hall, a small fun-parlour with dodgem cars and a little shop that sold cigarettes and sundry items. Not much in that store was family friendly, but occasionally my brother and I were sent to buy bread or milk with instructions to carefully check the expiration date. On most Sunday mornings, the square was empty of Harleys and on our way to the pier with our fishing rods and crab nets my brother and I picked our way through shards of glass from smashed beer bottles.

My brother loved fishing. He often woke me up early to go out to the end of the pier, where we'd sit for hours with the old regulars – weathered Greek and Italian men who always helped us out if we didn't have enough bait or lost a hook in a getaway fish.

The old men, with their big rods, caught large whiting and mullet and sometimes a shark. That never felt right to me, even though I didn't particularly like sharks after seeing *Jaws*. I forever regretted watching that movie because from then on, every time I went in the water, the theme music played in my head, sending me into the shallows.

But it was thrilling when someone caught a big fish. Suddenly we'd hear a shout or excitement in the old men's voices, which signalled a big catch. Hugh left his rod leaning up against the railing and I abandoned my little wheel of line on the ground and we ran to watch as the fish was reeled in.

My brother had a proper rod – nothing like the old guys', but a real rod nonetheless. He could cast out far off the end of the pier, into the deep water. My handheld reel of fishing line on a spool was nothing in comparison. On the way to the pier we'd dig up worms which he attached to my hook, still wriggling, because he knew I couldn't stomach it.

I wanted a proper rod like my brother's. Instead I cast out by pulling out the line until it sank under the surface of the water between the pylons. There we sat with our legs dangling over the edge for hours. We had an esky with juice boxes and sandwiches so we could stay out all day if we wanted. After consuming its contents, we used the esky to carry back whatever we'd caught.

The sea was full of fish then, and we always came home with loot we then prepared on sheets of newspaper in the backyard. My brother taught me how to gut and scale. It turned my stomach the first few times, but I took pride in being able to prepare a fish properly so it didn't have scales or any of the black blood attached to its inside cavity that made the flesh bitter.

If the weather was no good for fishing my brother sometimes took me into the dark billiards room and we pinged balls across the green felt of the smaller tables with long cues, trying to look like we knew what we were doing. The bikers looked on, amused. Some gave us pointers. Eventually we got quite good, even though I had to stand on tippy-toes to get far enough across the table to hit the balls.

Other days we took our pocket money and rammed each other as hard as we could in the dodgem cars. I loved the dirty, semi-industrial smell of the cars and the way they sparked electricity in the roof as we flew around the little rink.

I also enjoyed flooring the accelerator and driving into the back of my brother's vehicle at full throttle. I loved the sight of him jolting up hard against the steering wheel. I laughed so much I could hardly get my car turned around fast enough to get a lead on him, chasing me round the track to hit me every bit as hard. It didn't matter that I was three years his junior, when it came to the dodgem cars I got as good as I gave.

Every few months I went to stay with Muttee at her home in the country town of Gawler, about an hour from the city.

At Muttee's I felt like I could exhale. When I was little she made me smocked dresses and matching underpants so that when I swung around like a monkey on the jungle gym the boys wouldn't be able to tell what was pants and what was dress. She said I should be more ladylike and not swing around with the boys but knew I would never stop my antics. So rather than nag or ban me from boyish activities, she made me matching underpants. I now consider those underpants a wonderfully kind, thoughtful and accepting compromise.

I helped her thread sewing needles once her eyes began to fail and sat beside her as she whooshed the Singer treadle sewing machine across floral fabrics that she transformed into beautiful dresses. The outfits she made me always seemed to fit perfectly, although I have no recollection of her ever taking my measurements. Sometimes we talked as she sewed, but mostly I sat quietly beside her, watching as she pedalled her shoe on the metal plate that powered each stitch.

I was a tomboy who didn't like wearing dresses and had to be forced to put them on when I went to her house. But I was never truly reluctant, because she'd made them especially for me and I liked that feeling more than I objected to being in a dress.

Muttee was always there waiting to greet me on the platform of the little country station. When I stepped off the train I ran into her arms, engulfed by her ample body. We walked to the car and she opened the big heavy door and waited for me to squirm into the front seat before setting my suitcase at my feet and slamming the door shut with a swift nudge of her hip.

Muttee only learned to drive out of absolute necessity, after my grandfather died. She had a wonderful car – an eight-cylinder black Chrysler Royal assembled locally in South Australia. The car had fins like the Batmobile, a column shift along with push-button PowerFlite gears, and two-toned black and white leather upholstery.

When she got in behind the wheel, she'd say, 'Come and sit close to me now. Stay in the middle away from that damn door.' She drove with one hand on the big white steering wheel and put her arm around me every time she turned a corner, because the passenger door had lost its catch and was in the habit of swinging open in the curves.

At Muttee's I didn't have to hold everything in or together. I could just be a little girl. I loved it when she wrapped my hair in rags at night to make Shirley Temple–like curls out of my limp mop. Then one day she saw some workmen staring at me and one even whistled. After that, she let my hair stay flat, and the rags were used for dusting.

Muttee smelled like Ponds Night Cream. She had a pink powder puff on her dresser and there was often pink dust on the surface around the pot, which I used to trace lines into with my index finger. She let me sleep in her big bed with her, under the heavy cotton covers and thick woollen blankets.

I was not tall enough to get straight into her bed so I perfected a similar method to the one I'd used to get in beside my father. There were no walls to push off from, since the bedhead was between the two entrances to her large room. Instead I grabbed clumps of blankets in my fists and swung a leg up and over onto the thick white damask bedspread and hoisted the rest of my body up from there.

When I had settled on the down pillows, Muttee often reminded me I was the only other person who could ever be in that big bed with her since her beloved Brink's death. She said it was his spirit she felt when I was beside her, kissed me good night, and popped her perfect false teeth in the glass of water on the bedside table. She held me in her fat arms and listened to me breathe just as she had listened to her husband when he was alive, collapsed in exhausted sleep beside her after a long day on the farm.

Muttee made food I dreamed of. Her custard was as smooth as butter, rich with cream and thick with the egg yolks she whisked in from her garden chickens. She flavoured it with vanilla and sprinkled it with cinnamon before serving it to me in a little bowl with a sparkled gold rim. I could eat bowl after bowl of it, and usually did. After I finished I often went back to the serving dish in the fridge until I was so full I had to lie down.

She cooked chicken soup in beat-up triangular saucepans that came in threes so you could boil different vegetables on the same stove element. Later, I discovered that the soup was made with chicken's feet, but she thankfully kept that from me at the time.

Muttee loved to watch the tennis and the soap opera *Days of Our Lives*. One weekend we were watching the tennis with the air conditioner blasting. It was a long, extended finals match that had us both transfixed. During a commercial break she got up to quickly serve lunch. She brought out a large roasted duck's leg, with roasted rosemary potatoes and mushy green beans and peas, on a big silver tray that she placed on a wooden folding table in front of my chair. She went to the kitchen to get her own tray, set it on a matching table in front of her big chair, and we sat eating our lunch with the back and forth of the tennis ball.

The ball girls ran around the courts, chasing balls with their heads down, trying to be as inconspicuous as possible – how I carried myself most of the time.

As we were waiting for Martina Navratilova to serve for the second set, my grandmother said, 'Oh, this is so delicious. Daisy was a good bird.'

'What do you mean?'

'The roast. Daisy.' She took a bite, not quite understanding me.

'*This* is Daisy?' I asked with a sick feeling.

'Yes,' she said matter-of-factly. 'It's Daisy.'

My grandmother didn't think twice about telling me that we were eating the beautiful white duck, my favourite of all the gaggle in her coop. I vomited all over the silver tray and cried the rest of the day. Neither of us got to see who won that match until the six o'clock news.

I felt special at my Muttee's house. I often cried on the train trip home, at my feet a big box of vegetables from her garden, a supply of chicken soup, custard and jars of homemade apricot jam. Muttee wasn't blind to things and I'm sure she worried about what was happening at home with my father gone and wanted to make sure we at least had proper food.

There was tension between Muttee and my mother. I think Muttee disapproved of my mother going back to school and some of the other choices she was making. They spoke every Sunday morning when trunk calls, as they were called then, were cheaper. I loved running to the phone to speak to Muttee, but I remember my mother's reluctance and eye rolling when she took the receiver from me and they began to speak. Sometimes my mother raised her voice and hung up the phone before I got a chance to say goodbye.

I didn't understand it. I loved Muttee, but I'm pretty sure Muttee thought my mother was behaving irresponsibly. She once scoffed that my mother thought she was better than everyone else. 'Always a princess,' she said.

Twenty-one

In those years, my mother had a lot of lovers. Why not? It was the seventies. She was a student, a burgeoning poet who wrote about women and children, her lovers and her heartbreak, and the perils of domesticity. She was being published regularly and to acclaim.

Since she wasn't working in a regular nine-to-five job, she was often home when I came back from school. Mostly that was good. We'd drink tea and talk before I'd go do my homework. But often, particularly after she took a married man for a lover and daytime was their time together, I came home from school and the house was dark and moaning.

After a while I preferred going to my friends' places and I stopped inviting them to mine. On the rare occasion I did bring a friend home from school, I made a point of stopping in the street outside my mother's bedroom to talk very loudly to whomever I had invited over. I hoped she'd at least keep the screaming down. Later, she and a man would emerge, and my mother would smell like sex. Sometimes the whole house smelled like it.

Child rearing didn't really fit into her new version of herself and my brother and I were left to ourselves. My brother worked out how to shuttle between the houses, but I somehow got caught in my mother's web. In the same way she couldn't give my father to Becky despite no longer wanting him, she wouldn't give me over either.

Not that my father was making much of an effort. Maybe he thought I was happy, since complaining wasn't my nature, or perhaps he thought a little girl should be with her mother. They were in court over the details of their divorce settlement, but not over custody of us, as far as I know. He'd given up that battle and I stayed put.

I was moving house in my thirties when I came across a poster cylinder at the bottom of a box filled with junk. I almost threw the tube out along with the rest of the box's contents but curiosity got the better of me and I opened it and pulled out a large black-and-white photograph of me at about eight years old.

The image hit me like a blow to the chest. I clipped it with the pegs of a plastic coathanger and looked at it long and hard. It was a photograph obviously taken by a professional photographer. In it, I am holding a flame-shaped petal up to my chin. The 'fuck you' look in my eyes is chilling.

My mother was shocked when I showed her the photograph a few months later.

'But that was such a happy day,' she said in disbelief. 'We were on a picnic.'

It was a picture of deep unhappiness and my mother could see it as clearly as I did.

Once I said to her that I didn't think I had a very happy childhood.

'But darling,' she said, 'you had French wallpaper in your bedroom.'

I often thought my mother behaved like she had just stepped away from a car crash and wasn't quite in control of her actions. Taking responsibility for the wreckage was not something she would do easily. She could have put her foot down and driven headlong into a brick wall, got out to assess the damage and asked, 'How on earth did the front end get beat up like this?' And she would have meant it. There was a part of my mother that couldn't connect her actions with their consequences.

At an early age, I gave up trying to understand my parents' abandoning me. I went inside myself – silent, steely and resolute that nothing would hurt me. That no one would ever get close enough to injure me like they both had. Some people mistake this trait in me for coldness.

Many of my friends went through a vintage clothing phase – a rite of passage in most girls' lives – but to me it wasn't chic, it was poverty. Second-hand stores still fill me with dread, remembering the horrid little hand-me-downs I wore as a child. All those stores smell the same, no matter where in the world they are or how retro and hip they present themselves as.

When I was eleven I got my first job, washing dishes in the local retirement home. The big aluminium pots were so heavy I could hardly lift them or turn them in the sink to wash them, but I didn't care. I wanted my own money to buy myself new clothes.

I was eventually let go by the matron when she saw how upset I was after one of my favourite old ladies died. If not my parents, at least the matron knew an old people's home was no place for a child.

In 1988, I became fascinated by the groundbreaking television series *The Human Body*. In one episode, the presenter, Robert Winston, stands on the deck of a boat surrounded by many buckets of water. After he picks one up and tips it into the sea, he says with a sweep of his arm behind him that the buckets on the deck represent the average number of tears wept by a person in a lifetime. That was a lot of tears. I wondered how they calculate such a thing.

How many had I cried? When I was growing up there were people around who stepped in when they saw things were not going well at home. My mother didn't like me going to Dad and Becky's, but other people's homes weren't a threat, so I made it my business to escape to those places as often as I could.

My Uncle George (I called him that although we weren't related) was Chinese, and his real name was Patrick. He and his wife, Barbara, whom I called Aunty Babs, regularly took me into their home. Aunty Babs was a nursing buddy of my mother. She and Uncle George taught me to do the things they shared with their own children, including me in their family as if I were a member of it.

Uncle George called me his fourth daughter. He often joked that I was his only real daughter because I was the only one who ate the dark chicken meat. No one in their family of six made me feel like an interloper once, although I never excelled at anything like they did. They always thrashed me at tennis and ping-pong and were academically much brighter than me. In the beginning the kids must have wondered why I was always there. I'm not sure how Aunty Babs and Uncle George explained it to them, but whatever they said, I was accepted as a member of their family without any question that I ever heard or felt.

They lived in the hills out of town with a pool and a tennis court. Their three girls and I played elastics and jump rope endlessly in the large kitchen or out on the porch. The girls' older brother, Andrew, volunteered in the local fire-fighting brigade.

Life was ordered. Uncle George drove me to school every morning, even though it made for a third school drop-off on the way to his busy office. When we came home at the end of long hot school days, Aunty Babs made us snacks. Then we'd swim or play ping-pong, do our homework, eat dinner at the round kitchen table together, go to bed in tidy rooms and be woken up in the morning for breakfast, which was already laid out when we dragged our sleepy bodies in. More than four decades on, I can still remember their phone number as if I've been calling it every week since.

Their youngest daughter, Fiona, was closest to me in age. She and I used to tell other kids in the playground we were sisters, then be teased about the obvious nonsense – me blue-eyed and blonde, her with thick jet-black hair and Asian features. Aunty Babs taught me how to make rice the Asian way – the perfect absorption method.

Every Sunday Uncle George took us five kids to church. Aunty Babs stayed home and I mumbled through the hymns whose words I didn't know. I took my cues from Fiona about when to sit, stand and kneel, but when they all went for communion I stayed on the pew, feeling a little left out.

Uncle George taught me things my father could not. From him I learned to ski and to shoot a rabbit. The first time he took me skiing, we drove through the night to the ski fields. I stayed awake in the back seat, watching his eyes reflected in the rear-vision mirror, sure they were closing shut and he was falling asleep. I chatted with him and fought my own drowsiness to be sure he stayed awake at the wheel, as the other kids lay slumped on each other and Aunty Babs dozed in the passenger seat next to him.

The first morning on the fields he took me to the top of the black run, because I'd lied about how good a skier I'd been on a recent school trip. It took three hours for him to coax me down, slowly snow-ploughing the steep descent, rigid with fear and on the seat of my blue bib-and-brace ski pants. Other members of the family came searching for us, worried we'd been gone so long, but Uncle George sent them off. He stayed beside me, cheerfully encouraging me as we edged our way down the hill to the rest of the family, who were by then almost through lunch at the resort.

Later on that trip, when my skiing had much improved, I ran into Uncle George and knocked him down so hard I dislocated my jaw. He lay very still on the blinding white ice for so long I was sure I had killed him, although in the end it turned out I'd just seriously winded him. Nonetheless paramedics were called and they carried him down the slope on a stretcher. They asked if I was okay. I knew I'd hurt my jaw, but I said I was fine. Uncle George was the one who was hurt. I kept my own pain to myself, as I had learned to do with my father. As a reminder, when I talk my jaw still clicks and moves sideways a little.

Another lifeline was Amanda, a friend of a friend of my mother, who came to stay with us while she found accommodation after moving to Adelaide from Queensland. Amanda was ten years older than me – I looked up to her. She was always so kind, happy to see me, and interested in what I did and thought. She helped me with homework, put my hair in French braids and drove me around in her little Austin car, which she called Hetty. Amanda was well ordered and she took care with everything – particularly with me.

One night when she was visiting I wrote her a note in my best handwriting, explaining that I wanted her to be my big sister. I folded the paper over until it was a tiny square and then wrapped sticky tape around and around it to seal it tight. When Amanda left that night, I waited for her at the door and handed her the note and whispered that she shouldn't open it until she was in the car or at home.

To my delight Amanda agreed, and was true to her word from that day on. She took me to buy my first bras and in my teenage years, and far beyond, let me stay with her whenever I needed.

She dressed me for my primary school social like a character from a Bob Fosse dance show: a pair of fishnet stockings, a black leotard and my grandfather's beautiful top hat. She taught me how to cook with care, how to handwash delicate clothing and underwear. Most importantly, she taught me to care for myself in a way I had never known before.

What I understand about all this now is that I had my father's survival instinct. Children are incredibly adaptable and those lucky enough to have some smarts about them can invent all kinds of mechanisms and opportunities to cope where there are none. Where children in trouble are thwarted, though, is if there aren't good enough backups. Without a reprieve, without someone telling you, 'It's going to be okay,' it's hard to keep from going under.

Experts say you just need one person. One person to give you a break, to give you perspective, to tell and show you that what you are living through is not normal, nor something you brought upon yourself or are responsible for.

I was lucky to have more than one. My backups were Uncle George and Aunty Babs, Amanda, Marisa and Phil Wilkins,

Annie McCutcheon, others – who took me in. Their houses were calm and easy. I could regain my footing.

My father saw his lifeline out of the iron lung when my mother showed up in her starched white uniform and sass. He decided charming his way into her heart was his best route to escape. I saw my own route just as clearly – when these opportunities presented themselves in the guise of kind family friends, I grabbed them just as ruthlessly as my father had.

Of course it wasn't as thought-out as that – I was still a kid acting more on intuition than reason – but somehow I must have considered my options and acted. It was already my nature, but I made myself into the best-behaved little girl, because then I knew people would want me and I could get out of the chaos at home. Even if only temporarily.

At home I crawled into the darkness, hid myself and maintained a quiet heartbeat until I could escape. Most of all, I tried to forget.

Decades later, walking through the Guggenheim Museum one afternoon with a friend, I was struck by a piece by the artist Louise Bourgeois. It was a small bedroom with walls made of mirrored doors. On the neatly made little bed was an embroidered pillow. In tiny red stitches Bourgeois had written:

I need
my memories:
they are
my documents.

Standing there on the curve of the gently ascending walkway in the Guggenheim, I realised I had spent my life running from my memories of childhood. If I was ever to stop running, I had to remember.

Twenty-two

In 1975 Becky and my father took me and my brother to America to stay with Becky's family. We were ten and thirteen. My brother noticed that Mr Donothorn, his art teacher from school, was on the flight and spent the entire trip with his head under a blanket so he wouldn't be seen with the man in the wheelchair.

We never spoke about how these things made our father feel, but Becky vowed that when she and my father had children of their own, she would never let them carry the shame we had. It was seven years before they started a family, but Becky was true to her word. I was jealous when, a decade or so later, I heard that my father was coaching my little brother Morgan's school cricket team.

The humiliations to my father came from many quarters. I recently discovered a letter written by Becky's father addressed to the US embassy in Adelaide regarding our trip to visit her family. The letter reads:

> *Dear Sir:*
> *Richard Llewellyn is planning to come to the United States on December 9, 1974 and will stay until January 29, 1975. This is a pleasure trip during which he expects to visit friends. He has adequate resources to handle his own expenses. If there would be any problem we would be happy to assume responsibility for him.*
> *Sincerely,*
> *William L. Roberts*

Assuming that my father, a grown man, wouldn't be able to take care of his family on their vacation was patronising and must have come as a blow, although he never shared how it made him feel with me. I'm sure Becky would have known the extent of it, though.

Becky's parents had a pool. Becky encouraged my father to go in. She made him some shorts on her mother's sewing machine. Shorts were not something he'd worn since he was struck by polio, on account of his self-consciousness about his strange-looking, stick-like legs. But Becky was convincing and her three brothers agreed to help. They lifted him out of his chair, carried him down the steps of the shallow end and lowered him into the water. In my mind, I'd outgrown my father by the time I was ten, but in truth he was six-foot-two and it took all three of Becky's brothers to carry him.

It was an act of love, like a baptism or saving a beached whale. It was beautiful for him to float, to feel weightless after the constriction of the chair. And I got to go swimming with my father. I never knew how it was that he could float as perfectly as a blow-up mattress, but his body always stayed flat on the water's surface. My brother and I dive-bombed around him, trying to flip him over or make him sink. He never sank, but occasionally one of us bombed hard enough and close enough to make the waves roll him over facedown.

Being underwater didn't scare him after his training as a naval diver and he always came up laughing when we turned him onto his back. I pedalled my legs hard underneath the blue surface to get high enough out of the water to wipe the puddles out of his blinking eyes. Then I'd swim off to do more handstands in the shallow end while he floated on the surface.

One particularly hot day, they carried my father into the pool and I swam down to sit on the bottom to look up at his funny weightless body floating above me against the blue sky. He looked like Humpty Dumpty in a blue floatation tank: not quite as round as Humpty Dumpty, but his legs just as long and thin.

When I came up for air, Becky's mum announced a fresh batch of homemade ice cream. I clambered out of the pool and ran inside. It was the best ice cream I'd ever tasted. My swimsuit was dripping puddles on the kitchen floor so I was sent back outside, sucking the last of the strawberry cream from the bottom of the frosted cone, ready to dive-bomb my father again and tell him how delicious the homemade stuff was.

I pushed open the back door, dropped the remains of the cone on the hot concrete and started running. My father was facedown in the water. My uncles were sitting at a picnic table with their backs to the pool and in my enthusiasm for the ice cream I had failed to tell them to turn around and watch him.

When they heaved him out of the water he was very shaken, gasping for breath. He kept telling me that he was okay and tried to ease my guilt by saying his diving training helped him stay calm. He never blamed me, but I blamed myself.

The punishment for my stupidity was that I never got to go swimming with him again.

Later we drove to Puerto Peñasco in northern Mexico, about 100 kilometres south-west of the US border. We drove there in a large white Plymouth that one of Becky's brothers had bought for us in San Francisco. Using drawings Dad and Becky had sent him ahead of time, he'd jimmied together a lifting machine and welded it to the roof of the car. Dad and Becky wanted to be able to travel independently. Becky's brother sold that car back to the same dealer (minus the lifting machine, of course) after we left.

We arrived in Mexico like a carload of visiting aliens. I remember being scared by the local kids begging for money, squashing their faces to the windows and leaving behind dirty finger, snot and sweat smudges. Each time we stopped at a traffic light they tried to prise open the doors. I was sure we were going to be mobbed. I wanted Becky to turn the car around and drive us back to Tucson, to the pool and the homemade ice cream.

One night we went to a restaurant where a very beautiful waitress paid us extremely good attention. My father flirted with her, which made me cringe. Then, at the end of the meal, he made an exhibition of how much he was tipping her. She laughed and played the flirting game back, but when my father handed over the money her face fell and the mood of the evening changed. She said nothing more. It was only after we were back at the hotel that my father realised he'd miscalculated the exchange rate and only offered her a paltry amount. It was an honest mistake, but the show he'd put on trying to impress her, and knowing in the end we'd simply insulted her, was embarrassing.

My brother found a store that sold gigantic firecrackers – six of which, he told me, equalled a stick of dynamite. He convinced me to help him smuggle some back over the border to the US. He bought as many as he had money for and hid them in his luggage.

The morning we were leaving to drive back to Tucson, we did something we hadn't done the whole trip: we offered to help pack the car. My brother instructed me to shove some of the firecrackers into the cavities of the portable lifting machine they used when they travelled. This collapsible one folded down to fit inside a large denim bag that Becky had made.

As we approached the border we feigned sleep in the back seat. Our father knew something was up and quietly tipped off the border police to search the car. They found some of our stash, but not the ones I'd put into the lifting machine. Had Becky crashed on that drive back, we would have gone up like a mine blast.

Back in Tucson, when we let the firecrackers off, my brother and I were suddenly cool – not the freak children of the cripple. Our crackers lit up the sky in huge cascades of billowing glitter high up above the rooftops. The air smelled like gun smoke. The locals only had tiny little bangers that went off with a fizz; ours were magnificent. I went to bed that night with the smell of gunpowder in my hair and nostrils, dreaming of exploding stars.

Suddenly we were accepted. And, because we'd told them how we stuffed the crackers in our father's lifting machine to smuggle them across the border, he was seen as an accomplice. Suddenly he was cool too.

My brother was on a roll. A week or so later, he convinced Dad and Becky to let us go to the Grand Canyon. He argued that he and I should go alone and they could come pick us up after we'd made the trek. I have no idea why they agreed, but they seemed happy enough to put us on a Greyhound bus with enough money for food, one night's accommodation and the donkey ride down the canyon. We stayed in a small hotel on the South Rim so we'd be near the early morning muster of mules that we'd ride down into the mile-deep chasm.

I thought it sounded like fun, but when I met my beast and saw the narrow rocky track – not much more than a few feet wide – leading down into the abyss, I felt sick. I'd once before embarrassed my brother with my fear of heights and danger, when the Mad Mouse rollercoaster at the local fair had to be stopped to let me off because I was hysterical. He was so mad at me after that incident, he didn't speak to me for a week. So I knew I had to ride this mule no matter how sick I felt.

Hugh's mule and mine seemed to be the only ones to walk to the very edge of the steep track, reaching out over the cliff face to eat shrubs along the way. I looked down over my mule's withers to see its front hoofs right on the edge. There were hundreds of hairpin corners on our treacherous descent. The mules took each of them not safely hugging the rock face but right out at the unsealed path's edge. Peering down hundreds of feet of vertical cliff face to the canyon floor, atop a stubborn mule, I felt sure I was about to plunge to my death.

I'm not exactly sure what Dad and Becky were thinking, letting us go off like that. It was long before mobile phones or the internet. I suspect it was my father's conviction not to quell our thirst for adventure, or step in the way of our dreams.

Since contracting polio, he had listened to so many people tell him, 'No, you can't do that.' Damned if he'd ever say anything like that to us.

When my brother and I got home to Adelaide, my mother was furious. She called my father. 'You've made her fat!' she yelled down the phone.

Twenty-three

Dad and Becky built a wooden deck at the front of their house at Henley Beach, so my father could look at the ocean, smell the salt, feel the wind whip up from the south and remind himself of his beloved days in the navy.

Sometimes, if he lifted his head to a certain angle, all he could see was ocean and the dome of the sky; he could fool himself that he was far out at sea.

My father's mind could take him anywhere. Just like he'd read *Moby-Dick* and imagined himself out at sea, he could do the same simply looking out at the wide expanse of flat water that stretched as far as you could see left and right, straight to the edge of the world.

His great lesson was to teach me that we're as free as we allow our minds to make us. Imagination can save your life if you need it to. It saved my father. I was not sure if mine would be able to save me when my life depended on it most.

My father loved watermelon, but never so much as when we were in the backyard during our summer holidays, engaged in watermelon seed–spitting competitions. The rules were to propel our seeds at the same time. I took pains to line up my shoulders even to his, to have him believe our game was a genuine duel. Then I'd raise my arm in the air like a starting gate and shout, 'One, two, three, spit!'

I'd wait just a second or two before spitting mine, though, so I could aim my pips a little short of his. When he began to suspect what I was up to, I'd narrowly defeat him in a round or two to get him off the scent.

Out in the yard playing on my own, I could spit my pips three times as far as him. The little black seed would shoot all the way past the line of spindly beans staked up on bamboo sticks in his beloved vegetable patch. It wasn't much of a garden. As strong as his willpower and efforts were, they were no match for the harsh sun or the salt and sand that blew in from the beach. But he would not be defeated. He brought in pea straw to trap what moisture there was in the ground and hung shade cloths to dull the sun's rays.

He planted an olive tree, which thrived. But when I said he should just plant a grove of those and be done with it, he scoffed. He wasn't in the slightest bit interested in that. What he liked was beating the odds. There was no challenge in an olive tree. A tomato, though – in that soil – well, that was another thing altogether.

'Come and see my tomatoes. I just built the pergola last week to protect them,' he'd say, pointing with his chin to the four large pine posts stuck in the ground with dark mesh stretched tight between them.

He was always 'planting', 'mowing', 'chopping', 'building' and 'cleaning', when in reality he could only just brush his own teeth. But we all went along with it without question. It was our father's garden, and we all pretended he put up the pergola, and planted the tomatoes all by himself.

Taking ownership of tasks when all he actually did was tell other people to do them on his behalf was part of his fight for independence and dignity. He didn't physically do very much at all, but he did make arrangements and hustle to make things happen, so why shouldn't he lay claim to having actually done them?

He was always instructing me on the best way to make a bed, clean shoes, polish brass, wash windows, pull weeds, plant trees. When I was fed up, sweating over some task or other, and he reminded me of the benefits of his technique, I'd think, 'It's easy to have an opinion when all you do is sit all day and watch from the sidelines.' I like to think that I never said such a thing out loud, but I suspect I probably did.

In truth, the only thing he actually could do in the garden was hold the hose and aim it at the plants. Even then, someone had to put the hose in his hand and turn on the tap. But when we picked plump ripe tomatoes, bursting with flavour, the credit was all his. None of us objected.

Twenty-four

Four years after the trip to America, it was my mother's turn to take me overseas. The terms of my parents' separation and custody agreement stipulated that if one parent wanted to take us out of the country, the other had to grant permission. My father accused my mother of skipping that part. We hadn't been in London long when we received a stern letter from my father's lawyers. We had been summoned back to Australia.

My mother had rented out our house in Adelaide, planning for us to spend a few weeks in London, visiting art galleries and museums, before heading to the south of France for six months. I was looking forward to practising my French, and Amanda was coming with us, so I was especially happy.

We did visit the galleries despite the despair that fell over my mother when we got the letter from the lawyers. She believed in art as a sanctuary and I was glad to be out in public in a quiet, calm place where she had to keep it together.

I still remember being perplexed by the performance artists Gilbert & George, whom we watched one day at the National Gallery in a room of nineteenth-century oil paintings. I can't remember exactly what they did, but it seemed to me remarkably like what everyone else was doing, except they were cordoned off from the rest of us by a thick rope that made a large square in the centre of the room. Gilbert & George wore smart suits. They looked like they were on their way out to tea, but as far as I could tell they were just standing around, talking to each other.

I couldn't understand what all the fuss was about. After we sidled off from their performance, I kept asking my mother how what we'd just seen could be art.

'Anyone can put on a fancy suit,' I said.

My mother explained that sometimes art is just how you look at it. From then on I walked around the gallery looking at people sitting on the elegant wooden benches admiring the works, trying to decide whether they were more of the Gilbert & George trick or if they were real people looking at the art like we were.

It seems to me that much of life is like that. It all depends how you look at it, and from whose perspective. What you know or don't know, what you see or don't see, changes everything.

In a heroic gesture, given her grief and the turmoil we were in, before we went back to Australia my mother made sure we celebrated my fourteenth birthday as we'd planned. We caught the train to Dover, where we boarded the ferry that chugged slowly across the channel to Calais. I loved looking back at the steep bright cliffs knowing that we'd left one country and would shortly be in another. The proximity of two such different places was exotic to me. Once we disembarked in France we were met by a second train, which made its way to Gare du Nord in Paris.

On the day of my birthday we had a celebratory lunch in a tiny fish restaurant near the Centre Pompidou. The floor of the restaurant was covered in sawdust. A mangy dog with frail hind legs greeted us shakily before lying down on the ground as if the excitement of us entering had been completely exhausting.

An elaborate display of fish and seafood was laid out on crushed ice. I'd never seen anything like that before and the abundance seemed at odds with the place – the sawdust, the dog, and the owners, too, who seemed almost as battered by life as the dog. We selected the fish we wanted and it was taken to the kitchen and returned on large plates, steaming. It was a happy way to spend my birthday, but our little gathering had the forced cheerfulness of occasions that occur in the midst of a storm.

After we'd eaten, Amanda took a photo of me standing outside the restaurant. The handsome waiter who'd served us lunch and wished me *bon anniversaire* came out and stood beside me. Just as the photo was being taken, he said to me in beautifully accented English, 'And now you must look at me as though you are in love with me.' And I did. What that photograph doesn't show is that my mouth was full of ulcers, my gums bleeding and raw from stress.

Not surprisingly, relations between my parents worsened when we returned home. Since our house had been let for our planned trip we couldn't go there, so my mother rented a flat a block and a half from Dad and Becky's house, where my brother was now also living. The flats were called Allenby Court and we lived in one of the ugly blond-brick boxes for about six months. It would have been convenient had I been allowed to visit Dad and Becky, but that was now forbidden to me. I was not asked to testify in court for their divorce as my brother was, but we got pulled into their battle in differing but equally destructive ways.

I took up rowing and ran long distances. I needed to be busy, focused, successful and exhausted. I cycled to the rowing sheds on the banks of the Torrens River and was out on the river with my crew at 6 a.m. four or five days a week. After practice, I pulled a threaded needle through the large watery blisters on my palms. Then I cut the thread and got my crewmate Trudy to knot the ends so it stayed in place under the skin. This was a trick our coach taught us that allowed the air to quickly dry out the skin and form calluses. When I opened my palms up, they looked like a child's first crude sewing attempt.

It was beautiful to be on the river on cold mornings as the mist rose from the water. Skimming across the flat surface reminded me of ice skating with Becky. She'd first coaxed me out onto the icy surface with wobbly legs when I was about ten. It didn't take me long before I was able to skate backwards and do fancy turns like she did.

Out on the river, the focus it took to feather and dip a heavy oar in perfect unison with three other girls, and the strength it took to pull it through the water, required the kind of concentration I needed to get my mind off everything else going on. This was ordered and clear. You dipped, you pulled, the boat moved forward. We worked together as one. It was calm, controlled and it had a rhythmic predictability. Rowing was how life should have been.

We were the champion under-15 team but also upset the university crews by winning the ladies' Division One – the first time it had ever been won by a school crew. We were often in the newspapers with headlines such as 'Thrilling' and 'Hot Pace'.

Training for rowing didn't consist only of time in the water, but also circuits, weights and running. I took it further and joined the long-distance running team, training and competing with them too. I loved the solitude of running, setting my eyes on the horizon and steadily moving towards it. I loved being so tired at the end of the day that I fell straight asleep and didn't lie awake thinking about what was going on.

By the time I was fifteen I had two part-time jobs. I worked two nights a week at a pancake restaurant, where the manager pinched my bottom and liked to stand right up behind me when I was pouring sodas from the machine in the kitchen. He stood so close I could feel his breath on my neck and his hard-on against my arse.

I finished work after midnight and rode my bicycle home through the dark streets, because a taxi would have used up much of the evening's pay.

Friday nights and Saturdays I worked at the fresh food markets, where I had another job selling beautiful organic fruit and vegetables. My father's friends sometimes came by to tell me how much he missed me and try to convince me to see him. But he never came to the stall himself. I guessed he had a new family to look after now that Becky had given birth to a son, Morgan.

I started walking along the beach past Dad and Becky's house, hoping he'd be out on the deck, see me, and whistle to call me in. I tried not to stare too long, but listened for the sound of his warble on the wind. I figured if it happened that way I could tell my mother it had been an accident and she wouldn't be able to be cross with me. It never did.

Eventually I just went up to the house and knocked on the door. When Becky came out to see who was there, she said, 'It's good to see you,' hugged me and introduced me to my baby brother. Then she took me in to see my father, who was out in the backyard. By now we hadn't seen each other for about four years. Hugh sometimes relayed messages and there were the visits to the market stalls by his friends, but apart from those second-hand greetings, and a present for Christmas and my birthday, we were estranged. I was terribly nervous when I saw him. I wanted him to like me.

Throughout his life, no matter the bitterness of their separation and divorce, my father always acknowledged my mother's pioneering and bold spirit to have taken him on. Despite everything that happened subsequently, he was grateful. She'd done something truly remarkable and he knew it. She was his saviour. Had she not polished the brass or shown up to his hospital bed that day with the roses, he'd have lived a very different life.

My mother grew up going to dances in beautiful dresses. She read English *Vogue* – loved glamour and elegance. Yet she was willing, at least at one point – the best point, in fact – to hitch herself to the very unglamorous, inelegant daily routine of caring for my father. No matter what happened after that, or how any of us fared when it went sour, her actions at that time were heroic.

My visits to Dad and Becky remained a secret. Then my mother decided she needed to escape an affair with a married man that had turned bad and informed me we would be moving to Sydney within a few weeks.

I was about to enter my last year of high school in Adelaide, but the education systems were not unified across the country and in Sydney, where they did one more year of high school, I would be going into my second-last year. I liked school, but not an extra year of it. Let alone being pulled away from all my friends as I entered the most important year of school. There was little I could do to change that, but I did insist on being able to skip a year in the New South Wales system and jump straight into my final year. I was a year younger than my new schoolmates and far behind in every subject, but I worked hard and passed with an entry into the University of New South Wales.

At sixteen, straight after graduating high school, I left home to move in with my new best Sydney friend, Brigid. On the morning I told my mother my plan, she was irate. When I reminded her of that later, she said, 'But don't you remember, I waved you off from the balcony.' It was true, the day I loaded mybelongings into the back of a car, she did wave me goodbye from the verandah.

Brigid and I lived in a small terrace house in the inner-city neighbourhood of Redfern, which was filled with burnt-out buildings and abandoned cars. The streets were lined with trash and broken bottles. I slept on a foam mattress on the floor, made bookshelves from planks of wood and bricks, erected a portable clothes rack and pinned a Matisse print above my bed with thumbtacks. I only had the money I'd earned at Scoffs Bistro in Potts Point, where I worked all through my last year at school. I didn't care, I had French doors that looked out onto the street. I was happy.

The interstate move had put an end to seeing Dad and Becky for a year, but after moving out I invited them to dinner at my new place when they next visited. By now my father was disability adviser to the premier of South Australia, John Bannon. He worked for the premier for seven years. The posting gave him a platform to fight for change on the national level throughout the late seventies and early eighties, work that was later acknowledged with an Order of Australia.

I was terribly nervous about having them there. Brigid helped me clean the house and I measured the width of the front doorway to make sure my father would be able to get in. We prepared a meal I still remember in detail. We had talked about it for days, consulting recipe books – something I had never done before – and together we settled on veal.

It must have been expensive, but I bought premium cuts from a fancy butcher and asked him to pound them into thin steaks. I lightly steamed spinach, which I laid on top of the meat, then covered them with fine slices of provolone cheese. I rolled each steak and tied it with string like a package from a hardware store.

It was fiddly and I wasn't accustomed to cooking like this, but I wanted them to know I had taken care. Brigid, a master baker, took charge of dessert. Together, almost to our surprise, we created a proper, grown-up, three-course meal. We set the table with linen napkins and even lit candles. From that night on, my father and I began to slowly come back together.

But it took time. We lived in different parts of the country, although we talked regularly on the phone – after 6 p.m., when the rate was cheaper, of course. But it's hard to rebuild something so broken simply with phone calls. And I was broken. Even though I knew what had gone on, I felt like I'd been abandoned. My father was a fighter, but I felt like he had let my mother win, and she went home with a trophy she didn't even really want.

At my new high school in Sydney, we read TS Eliot and Patrick White's *The Tree of Man*. One day, our teacher, Miss Murphy, set us Sylvia Plath's 'Daddy'. I remember not being able to catch my breath as I read down the stanzas.

[. . .] I tried to die
And get back, back, back to you.
I thought even the bones would do.

But they pulled me out of the sack,
And they stuck me together with glue.

A few years later, I read Plath's *The Bell Jar* and fell into a deep depression. I stayed in bed in my pretty pink sheets for about ten days. I read books, smoked cigarettes, got up to eat and then returned to my hibernation.

The parallels between Plath and my mother rattled me then and still do. Both women walked around with dark secrets, showed a happy facade to the world but had another face for their families. *The Bell Jar* seemed to say it all and describe the person I had grown up with, but most importantly it let me see my childhood from the outside. I had lived this life, but I couldn't *see* or *feel* it until I read Plath's account.

But it resonated in other ways, too. The book reflected my own hopes and fears back at me. I wanted a different life to the one I was headed for. I wasn't being forced into stenography like Plath or a sewing factory like my mother, but my life was different to those of my friends and peers. I was still searching for a meaningful connection to the rest of the world.

Recently I opened a literary journal and thought I was looking at a photo of my mother in her late twenties. It was Plath. And despite his disability, my father and Hughes were similar men. Both had big personalities. Even in his wheelchair, my father was commanding in the way Hughes was. Then there were their two small children. And me and my brother.

After reading Plath's book, I felt as though I had all the stuffing punched out of me.

Twenty-five

At university I enrolled in an English and Political Science degree, but didn't last at it. My stronger urge was to reinvent myself away from my parents, so after six months I dropped out and flew to London with a one-way ticket and four hundred dollars in cash. I moved into a small apartment in the leafy suburb of Hampstead on a narrow street that led to the Heath.

In London I felt I could be anyone I wanted to be. I had no context apart from my foreignness. There were no reference points. I wasn't anyone's anything.

I dyed my hair black and went wild with a boy I called Tin Tin, because he had a blond quiff and pointy nose. He was from Birmingham, an industrial town in the midlands, which was worlds apart from the cosmopolitan life of London. He had moved from there a year before we met to get away from his past and try to make good, just like I was.

The first time we slept together, we made love in the dark. When I woke up in the morning I rolled over and put my head in the curve of his side. I saw he had a jagged, violent rip of a scar from high on his chest to just above his belly button.

'What happened?' I asked when he blinked awake. I ran my finger down the length of the thick ribbon of whitened skin.

'I got stabbed.'

He'd been in a coma for six months and now he lived hard and fast like it could all happen again tomorrow and I loved it. We were wild together, thrashing out our pain in flames of booze, drugs and urgency.

I had a full-time job working in a bar, but the salary was paltry. I needed more money so I answered a handwritten advertisement on an index card pinned to the noticeboard in my local laundrette. 'Cheerful cleaner wanted.' I called up, made a time to go see the ad's writer and soon enough began working for Adrian and Celia Mitchell.

They had a large house of four storeys, three girls, a dog called Daisy and a small backyard. Adrian, it turned out, was a famous poet and playwright, and Celia a Shakespearean actress. They could just have easily been accountants or lawyers, but by some strange twist of fate they were literary people. My long journey to a life in literature began in earnest.

In retelling them, many of my actions seem reckless and haphazard, but even then – as a teenager – I had a better sense of self-preservation and knowledge than it might have appeared on the surface. I couldn't articulate it then, or even think of it as a conscious choice, but I knew I had to break free.

I jumped when my life depended on it. My instinct for flight was correct.

Who could have known a little card in a Hampstead laundrette could set me on the right path? But something told me to answer that ad – over all the others on the board calling out for casual work – and with it began a new chapter of my life.

After a few months cleaning for them, Celia and Adrian became like parents to me. Celia organised for me to meet actors Jonathan Pryce and his wife Kate Fahy. I became a nanny to their little boy, Patrick, when Jonathan was starring in the movie *Brazil* and Kate was performing with the Royal Shakespeare Company. They had a simple, stylish apartment with a vase of fresh tulips always on the table.

One day when Jonathan came home, I told him I'd found the video of *The Ploughman's Lunch* and watched it.

'Did you like it?' he asked.

'Yes, it was wonderful. But I don't understand how they did the scene with you driving the Jaguar.'

'What do you mean?'

'When you were driving through that field!'

'What do you mean?' he asked again.

'Driving,' I said. 'How did they make it look like you were driving the car?'

'I just drove it,' he said like I was a bit daft.

'But you can't drive,' I said back, like he was the fool. 'You get picked up every morning by the driver to go to the studio.'

'Caro,' he said, holding back his mirth, 'I get picked up by the studio not because I can't drive but so I can rehearse my lines and arrive ready to work. It's Hollywood.'

I had no idea he was as famous as he was, or even that those kinds of arrangements could be made.

I seldom talked to my father while I was overseas. He was stingy about long-distance calls. So it wasn't too much of a surprise that I learned about my little sister, Anna, in a blue aerogram. My father had elegant handwriting despite the effects polio had on his ability to hold the pen. I was also surprised at how he managed to write in particularly straight lines.

My mother's writing, on the other hand, was hard to read. The words curved downwards at the end of each line. Her letters, when you held them in your hand, looked like a sinking ship. I remember receiving postcards from her when I was little that I read by turning them as I went along the lines. It was like reading with a steering wheel. By the end of the message the picture on the front – some exotic locale or a work of art – would be upside down.

With Becky's help, my father was now addressing international conferences and writing papers for government that shaped local and national disability policies. He delivered impassioned speeches about the need for major shifts of thinking in the care and treatment of people with disabilities. He changed the language. People were no longer 'cripples' or 'the handicapped', they were people living with a disability.

By this time, he'd taken a few more trips to the US with Becky and seen that Australia was far behind in disability rights and allowing people with disabilities to participate in society fully and equally. He took it upon himself to right the wrong.

Future generations of Australians have my father, and Becky in the wings making his work possible, to thank for helping to legislate for accessible public buildings, taxis that can transport people in wheelchairs, footpaths with ramps, accessible toilets. His tireless campaigning helped make it impossible not to hire someone with a disability if they were the best candidate for the job.

I was in England in 1984, just when the country was being reimagined by its new prime minister, Margaret Thatcher. The Falklands War was on and the conflict over Northern Ireland had erupted into the streets of London. I was sometimes scared to catch the underground. The miners' strike played out on television and in the papers every day.

The nuclear situation was also escalating. I joined Bertrand Russell's Committee of 100, which promoted 'the practice of civil disobedience in this time of utmost peril', as Russell explained at the time of the Committee's formation in 1961. I read Russell and then Steven Berkoff and Bertolt Brecht plays. I signed up for the Campaign for Nuclear Disarmament.

In the spring of 1984 I was staying at Celia and Adrian's cottage in Wales to discover some of my father's Welsh heritage, but I hitchhiked back to London in early June to attend a demonstration around the G7 summit.

The meeting was being held at Lancaster House on Pall Mall. Behind waist-high metal barricades stood a shoulder-to-shoulder line of bobbies blocking off the mall. The police faced us with blank faces. We watched one black limousine after another cruise down the red-paved boulevard with the leaders of the free world waving to us through the bulletproof windows.

I looked up the road to see that further along the mall, the line of police thinned out. I walked casually up to where there was a gap between guards, jumped the barricade and made a run for it down the centre of Pall Mall. I made it a good distance before being stopped by the dappled chest of a police horse rearing up in front of me. A moment later officers had wrestled me to the ground, then handcuffed and escorted me into the back of a police van.

My body was pulsing with adrenalin. When I looked out the little window through the metal bars I could see that my breakout run had drawn officers from their posts and a number of my friends had jumped the barricades. All of a sudden the police had 'a situation' on their hands. It wasn't long before the back of the van was filled with other protesters.

I don't know why I wasn't charged with an offence, but we were all let go with a warning. Later that night we went straight from the police lock-up to the nearest pub, where I was celebrated as something of a rebel hero.

When Celia decided to open a second-hand bookstore on Archway Road, I helped her set it up and then worked in the store. It was called Ripping Yarns, specialising in old illustrated *Boys' Own* and *Girls' Own* titles, as well as literary works and other classic editions. The shop was always filled to overflowing and we had to put tables of cheap titles out on the footpath to make room. Celia and Adrian's house became a warehouse of old books waiting for more shelf space in the store.

Walk-in customers were fairly irregular, so after I had fulfilled my basic responsibilities – rearranging misshelved titles, sweeping the leaves and soot that came through under the front door and covered everything in a fine black mist – I read books.

Some friends arrived from Australia around this time and we bought a blue Citroën 2CV for four hundred pounds in preparation for a road trip. Our destination was Northern Ireland. We never registered the car and got used to parking it wherever we wanted, shoving the parking infringements in the glove box, knowing there was no tracing them back to us.

We headed out of London and drove our little car into the belly of a large ferry that took us across to the southern tip of Ireland. We stayed in Cork and other places en route to the north and whenever the question of where we were headed came up, people pleaded with us to reconsider our plans. We were determined.

At one bed and breakfast, nestled right by the roaring winter sea, I decided to go for a swim. It was so cold I could hardly breathe in the water but I wanted to be invigorated by everything, including the trouble we were rushing into.

We reached the border late in the night and as we sidled up to the bright lights of the checkpoint, I wondered where the guards were. It seemed to be a very brightly lit but otherwise innocuous, unmanned border crossing. Until I looked closer and realised just how menacing it actually was. There was a large brick building to our left. Thick steel prongs stuck out of the road in front of us. A booming voice came across loudspeakers hung from flagpoles on either side of the road, telling us to hold our passports against the windows of the car. As I held my Australian passport open against the cold glass, I noticed a line of soldiers in camouflage lying in a gutter, machine guns pointed at our heads.

We hadn't made a hotel booking in Belfast and it was well past curfew by the time we pulled into the city. A car had followed closely behind us from the border and we were spooked. We knocked on the doors of a few bed and breakfasts, but no one would let us in. After many attempts, we were finally welcomed at an inn by a spooky man who looked as if he'd stepped off the set of *The Munsters*. He wore a matted black toupee that sat too far forward on his head, making it hard for me to look him in the eye. When morning came, I didn't want to stay for the complimentary breakfast.

We drove through more checkpoints into the city to get food. We left the car like we often did in London – on the median strip. When we came back an hour later, the street was cordoned off by dozens of police vans, and helicopters hovered above with snipers hanging out over the side. Two large police dogs were inside the car. I felt sick.

We agreed that Andrew, who was studying to be a lawyer and was by far the most respectable of us, should go talk to the police. Stepping out of the crowd and approaching the car, Andrew cut a Hugh Grant–like figure of cute sheepishness, as if to say, 'Terribly sorry for this cock-up, officers.' After a few minutes, arms began to wave and the dogs were called off. I have no idea what Andrew said, but we certainly toasted him at the pub later that evening.

A few days later I was out wandering the streets on my own when a bomb alert sounded and everyone had to take cover indoors. I went into the closest shop, which happened to be a camera store, and spent almost all the money I had left buying a beautiful Pentax. At the end of the alert, I went out into the streets and started clicking off rolls of black-and-white Kodak film. I saw a burnt-out facade in the distance and made my way towards it, heading down a narrow alleyway that opened out onto the front of the blackened building. I held the camera up to my eye and started shooting.

After about three clicks of the shutter, I was grabbed from behind.

'Who the fook are you?' said a male voice, the crook of his arm around my throat.

'I'm Australian,' was all I could think to say. I don't remember what else I said but eventually he relaxed his grip to forcefully turn me around by my shoulders to face him.

'Are you fookin' insane?' he yelled, splattering saliva into my face. 'You'll get yourself fookin' killed carrying on like that.'

After that trip, my politicisation was complete. I had found my cause.

My mother's had been her personal mission to save my father. For his part, my father took on discrimination where it impacted him and others like him. In London and Northern Ireland, I'd found a mission of my own.

As improbable as it was – my father in a wheelchair, my mother caring for all three of us – my parents opened a gallery in order to make a living. Despite many other challenges, it meant my brother Hugh and I grew up surrounded by art and artists.

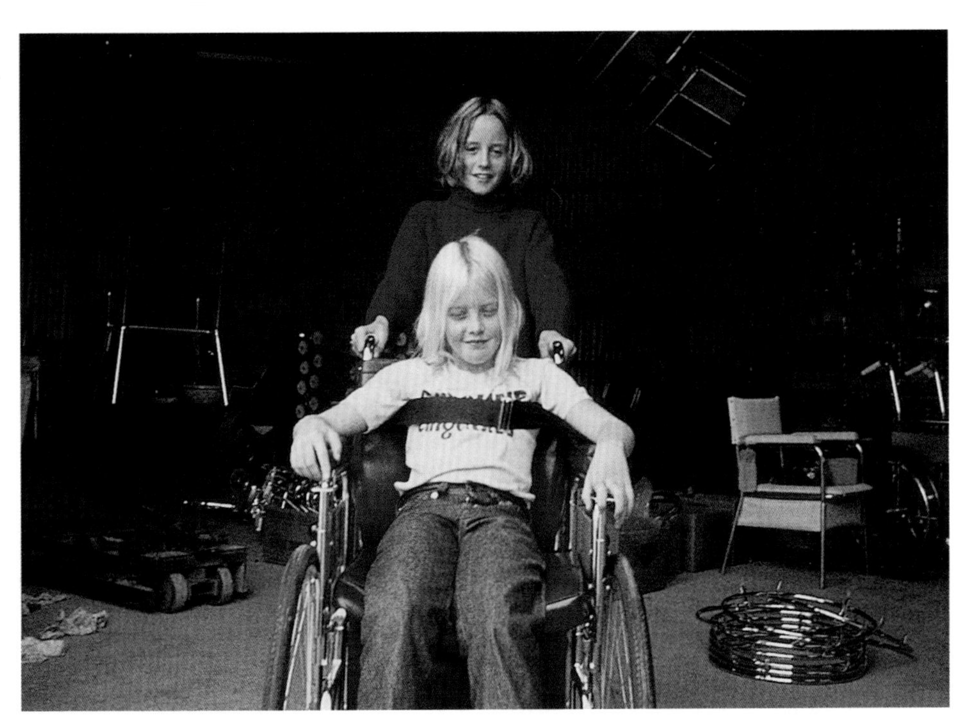

Kids can make mischief out of any circumstance. Here I am strapped into my father's wheelchair, ready for Hugh to push me down our steep driveway and send me flying into suburban traffic, one of his favourite games.

ABOVE LEFT: Life at home wasn't easy, so I loved my bike; it gave me some sense of control.
ABOVE RIGHT: The dark rings under my eyes and the look on my face say it all.

INSET: My father as a young sailor, before he was struck down by polio. BELOW: My father was determined to live a full life, but that was only possible with a lot of behind-the-scenes contraptions. He had this photo taken to show his employer what it took for him to get to work each day.

After my parents' divorce, my father built a new life with Becky, including opening a gallery of their own, in North Adelaide. Here they are at her family home in Tucson.

My father in the pool in Tucson, with Becky and two of her brothers. Bringing him into the pool was an act of love and faith.

This photo was taken after a long estrangement from my father. I was nervous and wanted him to like me.

My father loved being on his deck. At times it was almost like he was back in his favourite place: out at sea.

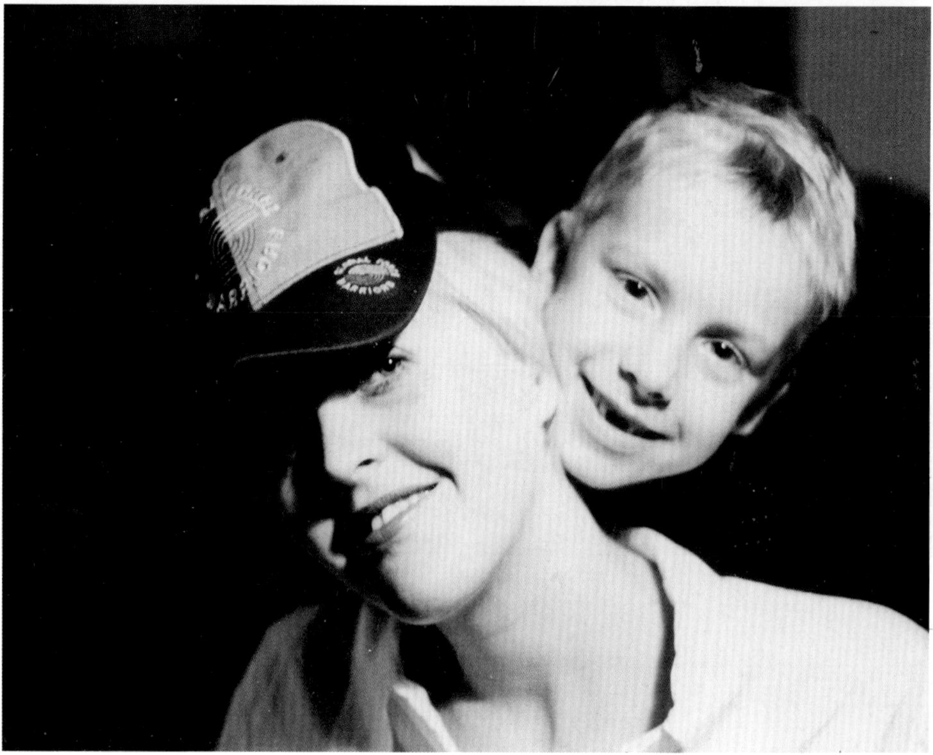

My son, Jack, the driving force in my life and my constant joy. Moving to New York without him, when he was a teenager, was the hardest thing I've ever done.

My boss, Salman Rushdie, at my last PEN World Voices Festival in New York in 2010. I had been diagnosed with MS the year before.
(Photo courtesy Beowulf Sheehan)

Accompanying my close friend Philip Roth on the 'Philip Roth's Newark' bus tour. His support and guidance during my treatment were invaluable.
(Photo courtesy Robert Sciarrino/ The Star-Ledger*)*

Delivering the opening remarks at an event at the 92Y, as part of the PEN World Voices Festival.
(Photo courtesy Beowulf Sheehan)

After running a literary festival in Paris, I came to Marina del Cantone in Italy. Climbing these steps seemed impossible, but it felt vital, and I made it to the top. I may not have found peace with MS as quickly or gracefully as my father did with polio, but his enduring influence has given me the strength to put the pieces of a beautiful life back together.

Twenty-six

I returned to Sydney from London in 1985, fully intending to collect my belongings and turn straight back around. Adrian and Celia had offered for me to live with them and to help me get into a university in London.

But when I arrived home, I realised I had missed my friends, and then I met a man I thought I was in love with, so I stalled.

After England, the Campaign for Nuclear Disarmament and the miners' strike, I got involved with the organised left in Sydney. We called each other 'comrade' and were encouraged to become a family, although they wouldn't have condoned that word. Family was nothing more than a bourgeois construct. Of course, I could relate to that idea. Like any kind of sect, the Socialist Workers Party discouraged fraternising with the outside world. We shared houses, became lovers ('companions'), worked and socialised together. Other relationships fell away, although my best friend from Sydney, Brigid, stuck by me throughout. The party demanded commitment and dedication, honoured hard work and intelligence, and, for the first time in my life, I realised I had both.

I became a 'leader', speaking at national conferences on topics like Recruitment and Radicalisation of Today's Student Population. I devised strategies and campaigns to attract young people to the party and then mentored the new recruits in the ways of party life. I organised film nights, with films such as *On the Waterfront* and *Apocalypse Now*, and ran the projector from atop a ladder in a small room at the back of the meeting hall. Today, my memory of all of those films still runs through a square hole above an office door in Chippendale.

We held dance nights with DJs who played eighties tunes that we could ascribe motivational meaning to. The Boomtown Rats were a favourite. Billy Bragg. Pretty much anything by British band UB40, who took their name from the unemployment form they had to fill out to get their benefits, stayed on repeat play. We danced and drank ourselves into political and sexual fervour.

I designed flyers with my companion – a former classical trumpet player who gave up a professional music career for the party. His trumpet, along with the sheets of classical music that were his repertoire, was stored under our bed on account of it being an instrument of the ruling class. Together we wrote what we thought were hipper and more attractive slogans than the ones we'd read when we joined. The youth wing grew with comrades who believed we could change the world.

After a while, I was invited to attend the party school in a suburb of Sydney, where I read Marx and Lenin along with about seven other students for about four months in a shared house owned by the party. It was a rigorous schooling of intensive reading. I read Lenin's speeches and critiques of capitalism, but I did a lot of it lying in the sunshine in the backyard in a bikini. We were taught by a number of tenured academics who had left their positions to become bus or train drivers and worked in blue-collar unions to recruit disillusioned members of the proletariat.

Once my Marxist education was complete, I was encouraged to put my learning into practice by going to work in a trade where I too could join a union and sway the minds of its blue-collar constituents. I tried out for the postal service but failed the exam miserably – and not on purpose. After that disappointment, I began working full-time for the party, which was good at accepting people's strengths and weaknesses and milking them ruthlessly all the same.

When I fell in with the socialists, I knew nothing about my father's experience on ships with those hard-line seamen who taught him about injustice. But I became a good young comrade who rolled her own cigarettes, just like him. My father hadn't joined a group or a party, but regarding social inequality he'd had his mind changed as forcefully and irrefutably as I had. We were around the same age when this radicalisation occurred, his on the deck of a ship out at sea, mine in an inner-city suburb wearing a Che Guevara T-shirt.

A big part of our work for the party was selling the weekly newspaper *Direct Action*. I wasn't a great fan of being on the streets, calling out slogans, but my sales were strong, so I was assigned a key spot outside a Woolworths in the centre of Sydney. There I could sell twenty to thirty papers in an hour.

One day I was in my usual spot when I was hit hard from behind so forcefully I fell to the ground. It felt like a baseball bat, but it was the crutch of a long-haired one-legged man. Once I was down, he stood over me yelling obscenities, threatening he'd do it again if he ever saw me selling this communist filth again.

I had often seen him around the city before he attacked me. A one-legged man is hard to miss. I had imagined him to be a Vietnam veteran. He was about the right age. As I lay on the ground with my papers scattering in the wind, he continued his tirade against me before lurching across the road on his crutches at high speed. A man in a business suit helped me up and then chased the guy down. I'm not sure what he said after he grabbed the one-legged man by the shoulders to stop him, but the man in the suit returned to make sure I was alright. He urged me to call the police, even though I was quite sure he felt pretty much the same way about my political views as the one-legged man who had attacked me.

The incident rattled me, just at a time when my commitment to the cause was wavering because I was starting to see that the party was as hierarchical and flawed as the systems it railed against. Something about the man in the suit's actions tilted my way of looking at things. In the party, everything was black or white. You were either with us or against us, yet a man with clearly opposing views could put them aside to help me. It made a mark.

While my formal ties with the hard-line left didn't last more than a few years, I never let go of the idea of justice and social equality. I don't think the party or reading Marx and Lenin instilled those ideals in me; I'd learned them long ago, standing beside my father in his wheelchair. Even a child knows what discrimination looks like.

My father didn't agree with the party's politics, or with how I dressed during these years, which was mainly in a pair of ripped and patched jeans and flimsy excuses for tops. Once I turned up to meet him and Becky at a conference he was speaking at and he told me I looked like one of the whores outside on the strip.

But he liked the broad strokes of my fervent political commitment – I was fighting for something I believed in, I was on the side of the underdog, and despite our estrangement he could see he'd still had an influence on me. Of course my mother influenced me in this regard too, her fight to save the parklands and her commitment to the feminist cause, the rallies where we shook our fists in support of women's rights.

After becoming disillusioned with the party, I got a real job, started missing meetings, broke up with my comrade boyfriend and eventually, after a few interventions by high-level members, resigned.

I'd fallen in love with a bald, hard-drinking, hard-partying, six-foot-four Polish musician named Leszek, fifteen years my senior. He hated communists. And I'd had enough of selling newspapers on the streets and being beat up for it, fighting battles I knew we'd never win with slogans and mantras from 1917 Russia.

Leszek was the frontman of a blues cover band called The Hippos. He played lead guitar and sang songs like 'Mustang Sally' and 'Shop Around'. He had a sonorous voice and played his black and white Fender guitar through a beautiful old Marshall valve amplifier. He was also a record producer, with gold records for his work with bands such as Midnight Oil and Spy vs Spy.

I didn't care that he had a number of teeth missing – he was the most handsome man I had ever met. Early in our relationship, my brother came along to one of his gigs and kept shouting into my ear over the music, 'He's one hell of an ugly guy, Caro!' But even he came around.

Leszek and I drank hard, played hard and argued hard. But I loved that he stood up to me. He wasn't a yes-man, yet he *was* a gentleman. He opened doors and sang to me when he was on stage and at home.

A few years later we were living together in Surry Hills and I became pregnant with our beloved son, Jack. I was happy pregnant, and stayed that way for ten months. Jack was a full month overdue when he was born on 6 May 1989, after a long and difficult labour. I always joked that it was Jack's stubborn nature that had him stay put all that time. Why change the incredibly comfortable and easy arrangement he had going on? Now I wonder if it was that I didn't want to let him go. Even before he was born I felt like this little human being was my life's purpose and meaning. I wasn't wrong.

During Jack's first night in the world the nurses came in to insist I wake him up for feeding. I refused, sure that if he was hungry he'd wake of his own accord. His birth had been so intense, I figured he was about as exhausted as I was. My mother taught me the highly underrated restorative powers of sleep, so I didn't care if they judged me an irresponsible, young and stupid mother; if my new baby needed to sleep, I would let him sleep. I may have been young, but I knew what was best for him. Of course when he woke up, I fed him. He thrived.

A week or so later, my father, Becky, Morgan and Anna were on their way to the US to visit Becky's parents with a stopover in Sydney. So Leszek and I took Jack to meet them at the airport. Jack was dressed in a red jumpsuit, wrapped in a blue cotton blanket. I gave him over to my father first. I placed my baby on my father's tray and lifted his arm, as my mother had so often done for him to hold me, and watched as he cradled his first grandson. Morgan and Anna each nursed him on their laps – an uncle and aunt at ten and seven years old.

I never questioned why they didn't arrange a stopover that allowed them to leave the airport and spend proper time with their new grandson. Perhaps they could have stayed a day or two to see how we were getting along, but my father had his eyes set on something else, so we sat in the Qantas lounge together before their flight was called and we waved them off to America.

Twenty-seven

My relationship with Leszek changed after Jack was born. We were lucky that he was in a band that played five nights a week and earned very good money. He was a good provider and we lived in a lovely house with a backyard and two dogs. At first he made an effort to come straight home after shows. Often I'd still be awake, so we could have time alone together, and in the morning he'd get up to tend to Jack and make me tea. It was exactly the romantic idyll I'd dreamed of, but after a while it all changed.

It wasn't too long before Leszek was staying back after the shows, drinking late into the night with the band and its groupies. I tired of bourbon and cigarettes crawling into our bed at 3 a.m. and resented tiptoeing around the house with Jack while his father slept off another late night.

By Jack's first birthday, I was a single mum. I was twenty-four.

We managed as well as we did in large part because Jack was such a great, easygoing baby. I never bothered with all the paraphernalia of babyhood – change tables, portable playpens – that I see so many modern-day parents hauling around with them. Much of it seems a nonsense designed to exhaust everyone. Jack had a simple collapsible stroller, but mostly I carried him in my arms. He slept in a beautiful old wooden cot, which a friend bought in a second-hand shop and painted pink and blue. When we visited my friends, he slept in their beds, cushioned by pillows to prevent him from rolling off. It was simple. We travelled light.

I was parenting how I had been raised. My brother and I – at least until we became rebellious in our very different ways – were quiet when we were told to be. We sat down, stood up or fetched this or that whenever we were asked to. Our parents didn't have the luxury of only half committing to what they wanted us to do. So when I told Jack to be quiet or behave, that's what he did. He knew what I said was what I meant, just as my brother and I had known it when we were toddlers. We didn't have the option to be defiant. Jack didn't either.

After separating from Leszek, I knew I had to make something of my life – for Jack's sake, if not my own. I was a 24-year-old single mum with a high-school education and no particular skills to make me employable.

I got a full-time job working as a secretary for a progressive company that sent me to typing school, where ironically I got a certificate with my name printed on it in large looping cursive.

I wasn't going to argue with Leszek about the morals of providing for his son, so I also began working in a bar two nights a week to supplement my secretary's salary, while Jack stayed home with my flatmate. I'd get home at 2 a.m., then wake Jack early so he could attend pre-school childcare and I could be at my desk at 9 a.m. Of course I was tired, but didn't feel I had much choice.

Jack was a little over two when I quit my job as a secretary to begin working with my good friend Frankie. We ran a small music booking, publicity and management company. Most of our clients were jazz musicians. We eventually got established enough to rent a sunlit office on Druitt Street, with an enormous balcony looking over the Sydney Town Hall. Many friends told me it was irresponsible to have quit the security of my stable job, but I contended I was no good to Jack if I was unhappy.

Once again, what seemed like a foolish and reckless move worked out. Working with Frankie was fun and a whole lot more interesting than answering phones all day.

In 1992, on a trip to Adelaide to visit Dad and Becky, Jack gave my father his favourite nickname. It was a hot afternoon and there were guests over at their beachside house to celebrate Becky's birthday. By now my father had an electric wheelchair that he could control himself and as always he was in his element as host.

Jack wandered into the sunroom, looking for a lost carriage from his train set.

'Chair,' he said, looking up at my father, trying to make himself heard over the babble of guests. 'Chair,' he said more loudly, since nobody was acknowledging him. Still there was no response, so he pulled on my father's trouser leg and yelled in his baby voice,

'Chaaa-iirr!' My father answered, 'Yes, Jack?' and the tiny human at his feet asked if he knew the whereabouts of his lost caboose.

My father pointed to the *Thomas the Tank Engine* carriage lying on its side under the window in the corner and Jack said sweetly, 'Thank you, Chair.' Political correctness had arrived with a vengeance and a strained silence came across the room. The guests either turned their heads out towards the horizon or peered into their drinks. Jack waddled off, his drooping nappy making him swagger like a cowboy, completely ignorant of the bomb he'd just dropped.

People who met my father generally fell into two categories. There were those – the majority – who did their best not to stare at the ugly chrome wheelchair, though you could often see the effort in their faces. There were also those who assumed his mind was as sedentary as his body and spoke very slowly and loudly at him.

Yet here, in the pink and orange glow of the sunset, a toddler had named the obvious truth. It didn't take long for my father to begin laughing. Slowly everyone joined in, watching him and me to make sure they really did have permission.

It was a name my father loved, in no small part because he enjoyed the horrified look that came over people's faces when one of us called the guy in the wheelchair, 'Chair'. It was a name I loved because it was honest. My father *was* his wheelchair. The name stuck and Jack called my father Chair from then on.

During the same visit home, I visited Muttee in hospital to introduce her to Jack. She was eighty-nine and had never approved of me having boyfriends; she wanted her little girl to have a wedding ring. After Jack's birth, a distance had opened between us. But I was hoping that with death in sight she might soften to the living.

She didn't. She was steely in her demeanour and disapproval hung in the air as I sat on the edge of her hospital bed. I rubbed hand cream into the frail, arthritic hands that I had known so well when they were thick-fingered and strong. I tried not to let my anger come through in my touch. Jack played on the floor with his toys; my grandmother ignored him.

'You know,' she said, 'I still feel exactly the same. It feels no different today as when I was sixteen. Nothing has changed except this body. Inside I still feel like a teenager.'

I wasn't sure if that was the best or the worst thing I'd ever heard about old age. At that moment, sitting next to my grandmother, I decided to take the positive interpretation.

Even though she couldn't shake her disapproval, I felt short of breath when Jack and I walked out of her room, knowing I'd probably never see her again. We walked hand in hand down the corridors. Trolleys and wheelchairs squeaked along the linoleum floors. Children skipped with 'get well soon' helium balloons, oblivious of their environment, parents trailing behind holding sad flower arrangements wrapped in bright pink tissue paper.

I don't like hospitals at the best of times. I often faint in them even if I'm not the patient – particularly if I'm not the patient. Watching other people's agony drains all the light out of me. I'm sure it's some residual trauma from having spent half my childhood in a bed with a chart hanging at my feet.

And so, as we approached the enormous glass doors leading out into the street, I felt myself exhaling. I blinked in the bright light and, as we stepped out onto the path, a raucous noise broke out above our heads. I looked up to see two large black birds fighting in the blue sky above the exit. There was a loud guttural sound before one of the enormous crows plummeted through the air, landing with a thud at our feet. Jack screamed and I picked him up, held him as tightly as I could so he couldn't see the tears streaming down my face. I walked quickly away across the trimmed lawn of the hospital grounds.

Shortly after, my Muttee was in a black box.

A year or so later, I booked myself in to see a medical doctor who also acted as a counsellor. Dr David Isaacs saved my life. There is no way to get it all right in rearing a child, and I knew I would make mistakes all of my own with Jack, but I would not use my parents' example of parenting as my guide. I would not be the neglected who neglects, or the abandoned who abandons. I would do better.

Not surprisingly, I had internalised some of the tricks I'd witnessed, and in the early days of my relationship with Lezsek, I could flip into a jealous fit that had me chasing him across town in my little orange Datsun 120Y.

Dr Isaacs worked with me to help me see that I had not made up or imagined my difficult childhood. Talking to him in his snug office overlooking a park in North Sydney, I began to understand that I had lived in a house of distorted truths. I began to see the great divide between the stories I'd been told and my memories. Slowly, slowly, I learned to trust my own version. I also began to see the damage I carried with me and grew determined to cleave it off.

For many sessions we simply talked, but after a while, Dr Isaacs suggested hypnosis. He believed I had been so conflicted about the version of childhood events I'd been told and my own memory of them, that the only way to make me see and truly believe my memories was to have me relive them. I was sceptical of his methods – hypnosis sounded to me like something from an old movie, performed by a charlatan swinging a fob watch – but, as he counted back from seven and told me my arm would rise off the pillow he'd placed under it, I felt my arm lifting.

On the first day, I went back to a memory of playing at the foot of my father's chair in the gallery. I had one of my brother's rubber toy snakes, which I trailed around like old rope. The ghoulish reptile had long red fangs and blood on its bottom jaw.

I looked up when I heard my mother enter and saw her clasp her long red nails to her face and tear into her flesh. She opened her face in the same way I dug into wet sand on the beach to make a road around a sandcastle for a toy car to travel along. Her skin flayed in ribbons and blood streamed down her face onto her blouse. I pressed myself up against the spokes of my father's wheel.

My father called his parents on the phone in the gallery, which he always had within reach, on his tray.

I wanted to climb inside Grandfather when he arrived. He scooped me up in his long arms and took me straight outside and put me in the back of his old station wagon. I waited in the car while he went back inside and called the doctor and a friend of my mother. When the doctor arrived, Grandfather came back to the car and we drove away.

Gran was waiting for us when he carried me into the house. She had set one place on the table and right away brought me soup in a green scalloped-edge bowl. She gave me that same set of bowls years later, after Grandfather died and she moved to a nursing home.

I woke from that 'spell' in Dr Isaacs' office with near cuts in my palms from clenching my fists so tight. My mother had always played that incident down when I asked her about it. She told me I exaggerated it. But the grooves in my palms and uncontrollable shaking rippling through my entire body made me see just how bad it had been.

I was so disoriented, Dr Isaacs worried for my safety. So did I. When I got home, I went to bed and stayed there, sobbing for most of the following week. When I was finally able to leave the house, I remember standing on a train station platform, hoping I'd be able to stay where I was.

Twenty-eight

When Jack was seven, I became involved with a well-respected, kind and clever music journalist. I was no longer working in the booking and promotion business with Frankie, but that job had taken me to a role overseeing the ABC's jazz label.

I met my husband to be when I was in Wangaratta for the annual International Jazz Festival. He was having dinner with a large group of other critics and presenters when I walked into the bar. One of his colleagues waved me over and introduced us. He had dark eyes, olive skin and thick black hair and when I sat down next to him, I was the only woman at the table.

'Usually I only meet men with beards at these weekends,' he said, promisingly.

Later that night we were wrapped around each other. When I drove off a few days later, I felt as if I had been skinned. I knew I wanted to be with him.

All this came on the heels of my first book, *Jobs for the Girls: Women talk about running a business of their own*. After that I wrote *Fresh! Market people and their food*, a tribute to the cuisines of first-generation Italians and Greeks who'd come to Australia after the war.

With the confidence I'd gained from the books, I'd tried my hand at fiction. My first short story was published in an anthology edited by Susan Johnson called *Women/Love/Sex*. I couldn't believe it when I saw my name in the list of contributors alongside *real* writers. I felt I was beginning my real life's journey. I was becoming a writer.

When the man I'd met at the jazz festival returned to Sydney, he asked me out for coffee and told me he'd bought *Women/Love/Sex* and had read my story. He was the first person who spoke to me about it. He took me seriously. It was intoxicating.

I tried not to put Jack in the company of men I was seeing unless it was serious, but this was the most serious I had felt about anyone since Jack's father and I wanted them to meet and get to know each other slowly. I dreamed of the three of us being together as a family. We arranged to 'accidentally' meet after school at a favourite café, the Tropicana in Kings Cross. I had ordered Jack a hot chocolate and I was halfway through a latte when he walked in. I feigned surprise.

Jack was always a polite child, he shook people's hands and looked them in the eye when he was introduced, but on that day he was rude. He gave yes and no answers to inquiries, didn't look up from his mug until, embarrassed, I excused us and left.

'What got into you back there?' I asked him in the car.

'Nothing,' he snapped.

'Come on, darling,' I pleaded. 'I've never seen you like that. Didn't you like him?'

'You love him,' he said from the back seat. I was stunned into silence. How could he have possibly picked that up in the ten seconds between being introduced and acting rude?

This man was wonderful with Jack and eventually – after a few false starts – we moved into his apartment on a tree-lined street in Kings Cross, which had a large balcony overlooking the city. We had lots of friends, held magical dinner parties and he enrolled Jack in the Conservatorium's music program for kids. There Jack took up the violin, and his love of music and natural talent for it flourished. It was a magnificent gesture and I loved this man for it all the more. Jack had lessons twice a week, practised every day and learned not only to play but also to perform. Under his influence, my son was blossoming.

We'd been living together for about two years when we went to a friend's wedding. There was an oyster bar set on a huge ice slab, champagne and a band, and we were dressed to the nines. On the way home, stumbling slightly in my high heels after too many champagnes, I was upset.

'What's wrong?' he asked, holding my elbow.

'You'll never marry me,' I bawled.

He was silent. I was desperate to be wanted and to be owned. I wanted security and forever and for someone to publicly declare to the world, *I want you* over all others.

'If you won't marry me, I will leave you. I want to be married,' I said through tears. 'If you won't, I'll find someone who will.'

And there was my ultimatum. I should have wanted him to propose to me of his own free will. But there it was. A few months later, for my birthday, he gave me a card asking me to marry him. He never spoke the words, he wrote them.

We were married in front of 120 friends and family in a little boatshed on the lip of the harbour. The long dark room where all the boats were stored we lined with baby olive trees I'd bought for each of the guests to take home and plant.

The day before, my mother and I had been up at 4 a.m. to go to the early morning markets. We walked around among speeding forklifts and piled the car with armfuls of tulips. I carried a sack of potatoes over my shoulder and we bought all the ingredients for the menu I was preparing with my friends. When we got home my mother filled the top-loader washing machine with water and put all the flowers in it. The house was full of friends and, together, we cooked for the wedding the next day.

At the ceremony Jack and Becky performed a violin duet. During the proceedings the celebrant kept referring to my husband by another man's name. I wondered if it was a bad start to things. We didn't take a honeymoon and, when he lost his wedding ring in a rainstorm in the week following the ceremony, I thought it probably had been.

For years we sat on an old sofa of my mother's – once smart and elegant, twenty years into its life it had lost all of its Italian chic and was sagging and threadbare. Every time I looked at it or straightened up the white sheet I used to cover the shabby upholstery, it depressed me. I felt I should have discarded the past, not carried it around with me like a bowerbird.

Many of our weekends began with newspapers on the bed, our cat, Rocket, curled in among the rummage, while we looked in the lifestyle section for nice write-ups or special sales and markdowns.

After breakfast we set out with newspaper clippings and a plan for the stores we'd visit.

It didn't matter how many times we did this – hours and hours of fruitless shopping – I still managed to convince myself at the outset of each expedition that today would be the day I could put that old sofa out on the street for someone in need to lug home.

The shop owners always sized us up as customers to attend to well. We looked like we were shopping with new love in our hearts. We'd be on first name basis with them in minutes. Every swatch of fabric came out and the assistants would patiently answer my husband's many questions about durability and cleaning.

We'd wander off from the counter every now and then to talk about the fabrics and whether they would match our paintings and the colour of our walls. We bounced heavily to test the springs. We lay down to make sure we could stretch out fully and asked strangers to come sit with us to test if the couch would comfortably accommodate a visitor or two.

The assistants would write down the details. They discussed possible delivery dates with us and, inevitably, promised they could rush the order through.

We danced this step again and again. Shop after shop for three years.

'Perfect,' I'd say enthusiastically. 'Yes?' I'd look to my husband, pleadingly.

'Okay. Thank you so much,' he'd say, extending his arm to shake the salesperson's hand, clasping the colour brochures and fabric samples under his other arm. 'We'll go away and think about it and call you back.'

And with those words, another small death came over me – a shadow that darkened with time. It dulled me so subtly that I didn't feel the glow disappearing, wearing our marriage away.

By now my professional prospects had significantly improved. I'd worked in publishing and in cultural marketing and was now director of the Sydney Writers' Festival. I loved the job: it was challenging and rewarding, and I had the privilege of working with writers I admired. But each day I would come home to sit on my mother's couch. As the springs gave away, we were pulled ever more deeply into it. 'Hard to get out of,' people commented cheerfully when they came over for dinner parties. To sit on this couch was to be embraced, clasped. It grabbed you.

One day a sofa is a sofa and the next it represents something much grander and you're left wondering how you could not have seen it this way the day before. What clears at those moments? A fog? I couldn't sit in the sofa without feeling the grip of our marriage pulling me down. 'It's just a sofa,' I told myself firmly as we ate dinner on our laps, watching television. But by the time the weatherman came on with the forecast, it was, again, everything that was wrong with our union.

It wasn't that my life with my husband was awful. He was a good man, loving, gentle and kind. He was conservative – not politically, but in a way that made him sensible and deeply cautious, which is what I had wanted when we first met.

We did share values and believed in the same ideals, something I always thought was important. Yet we were different in the most fundamental of ways. I didn't see it at first, but his default position on almost everything was 'no'. Mine was 'yes'.

How could I be with a man like that after growing up with my father, who believed 'yes' was his only option?

It didn't take all that long until I began to think 'no' for myself, to save my breath. His starting point was always 'that's not possible' or 'that's not sensible' or 'don't wear that'. Perhaps worst of all for a person like me, 'don't do that'. In essence, don't be who you are and don't do the things you want to do.

I felt old when I wasn't yet forty. I longed to dance again. I ached for some of the risk and edge of my life before marriage. I'd lost the truth of myself in our safe married life. Without realising, I'd turned out the lights and shut the door on a room I loved.

I often went to other literary festivals for inspiration and to meet new writers to feature at the Sydney Writers' Festival. It was at one of these that I met an author who woke me from the slumber of my marriage.

I'd long admired his writing but it was during his on-stage interview that I saw the full extent of him. He had a beautiful liquorice voice. Afterwards, there was a long line of people for his book signing. I watched as he graciously accepted compliments from his readers, was attentive and genuine to every person in the long line. He didn't flag in his attention to his readers.

After he signed the final copy of his book, his publishers and a group of other industry people introduced me to him and invited me to join them for dinner.

'I'm sorry,' he said, excusing himself from the invitation. 'I'm exhausted and really need to go to sleep.' I felt a slump of disappointment. I had wanted to be seated next to him at dinner.

But it turned out we were walking in the same direction and the others peeled off and we waved them farewell.

'Good,' he said.

'Sorry?' I asked.

'I don't really need to go to sleep. I want to have dinner just with you.'

We walked along the edge of the dark harbour, the lights of boats and ferries flickering in the distance.

The restaurant we came upon was expensive, with views across the water. He ordered duck that came in thick slices. I had scallops that arrived swimming in delicate foam that I thought looked like bubble bath. I told him I didn't think food and foam really went together no matter how fancy the restaurant, but he tasted one and said it was superb. Then he told me he didn't like to share food. He asked questions and he listened.

It was late by the time we made our way outside onto the footpath. The street was hushed. We walked in silence in search of a taxi until I stopped him. 'I want to kiss you,' I said. He turned towards me.

I wrapped my leg around him and he pulled me into him. He had a firm and confident grip. I felt any reticence rush out of me. I wanted to devour him. I closed my eyes and didn't think about anything other than this.

He held me tight and I pressed into him. I felt like I could just keep falling into his frame, that he could envelop me. I caught glimpses of his beautiful face in the midnight darkness only as beams of light from passing cars swept by. I raised both my hands, palms flat towards him. A stop, or surrender – I wasn't sure which. He placed his palms to mine and we pushed against each other, wanting more. His hands were on my hips, wandering. He put his leg between mine and raised his knee up to me and I ground down into him, wanting.

We were all in a rush now. I pulled his shirt out from his pants and slid my palms up on his chest. I was so excited by his strength. He bit my neck gently and I felt weak and bent to him, putting my lips to his stomach. His skin was soft like a child's. I put my tongue in his bellybutton, licking him along the rim of his brown leather belt and reached down and felt him hard in his pants.

'Come back to my room with me,' he whispered in my ear when I stood up, his tongue wet on my earlobe. He took my hand and I followed him.

We moved apart from each other in the hotel lobby as the bellboys and receptionists smiled to greet us. I felt sure the world could see the charge between us. The lobby was grand and silent, just a hush and the sound of my heels clicking on the marble floor. The heavy pulse of my heart made me slightly seasick, as though I was being knocked off kilter with every beat. The doors to the elevator slid open and shut silently behind us. I fell back into his arms as we were whisked up tens of storeys to his room looking out over the curve of the world.

Our time together was brief; only snatches between his heavy festival, media and publishing commitments. I felt alive with him near me. He only had to put his elbow next to mine on an armrest for a charge to run through me.

His kiss ignited me. I'd forgotten the taste of that kind of intoxicating desire. I'd let the thought of it slip from my mind. He brought it flying back, with a force that left me winded.

'I'll call you when I get home,' he whispered on the last day of his stay. I was lying with my ear to his chest, listening to his heart. I didn't believe him.

'Tears,' he said, 'are for kissing.' He kissed mine, whispering, 'Don't be sad, honey.'

He walked me down to the lobby and out into the hotel driveway, where the concierge hailed me a taxi. The writer was wearing black and white Nikes with no socks. I noticed he had beautiful thin ankles. I could also make out the faint outline of his cock as he waved me goodbye. He blew me a kiss as the taxi pulled into the busy street.

There was no turning back. I felt dead towards my husband. Our marriage was over. He was being retrenched from his job and I should have waited for him to be in a better place before delivering the news, but I couldn't wait. I arranged to meet him in a park near the Art Gallery of New South Wales. We sat on a bench in the dusk light, overlooking the harbour, and I told him I was leaving. It was brutal, but I couldn't pretend.

I didn't tell him about the writer because that hardly felt like the point. As far as I was concerned our marriage had been over for a while; I just hadn't seen it that way until I experienced an alternative way of feeling. My husband and I had propped ourselves up with friends and buying an apartment, but the joy of it had gone. We were a dull version of our former selves. I'm not sure if he saw it that way. He was blindsided and I hit him when he was already down. I was cruel.

I slept on couches until I was invited by my friends Vyvian and Pete to spend some time in their beautiful cottage by the sea, near Wollongong. Long coal trains wailed along the bottom of a steep escarpment, so close by that it felt I could stick my hand out the kitchen window and touch them as they whooshed past.

As the trains ran along beside the house, rattling their way across the mountain, I thought about what it would feel like to walk onto the track and lie down. I imagined the waiting, the feel of the hum of the train's approach through my spine, wishing for the bright blue of the sky to turn to black. Where would I rest my head? On the track, or with my neck against the metal?

To feel the steel and screeching bearing down on you as you determine to simply lie still and be delivered. An end to the interminable black line you've been on for God knows how long. I wasn't suicidal, I felt liberated and free, but listening to those trains, for the first time in my life, I could *understand* the darkness my mother had felt.

My marriage was over and the man I loved was living happily with his wife on the other side of the world.

The writer and I had done some high-octane fooling around, but what really hooked me was his mind and his voice. I couldn't shake him. As I was folding my clothes and putting them in boxes, he was unpacking his suitcase and putting his clothes into the cupboard beside his wife's dresses and blouses. I'd hitched myself to an unavailable man.

One day my mother loved my father, the next day she did not. Here I was, in the same position.

My husband didn't ask if there was another man. Had he, I would have told him. But he let me go as easily as he'd accepted every other disappointment in his life.

I went around our echoing apartment, wrapping my things in newspaper, taking books out of bookshelves and placing them in two separate piles.

A real estate agent came and gazed around our apartment contemplatively. His black BMW was parked illegally out front so he could make sure it wasn't getting keyed or broken into.

'You must,' he said, 'give people an idea of the lifestyle they aspire to. You have to show them that they can live a certain way in this apartment.'

He paused for effect. 'You need a stylist.' He looked at each of us, unsure who was the decision-maker. 'You see, it's about lifestyle.'

He was a brochure of himself. 'It's got good bones – great bones – but it needs, well, something, a lift . . . All new furniture. That will do it.' He looked at the old couch and declared confidently, 'A sure sale if you can make it look right. I have a friend I can recommend. She works magic.'

I bit my bottom lip, trying to hold in my fury. 'My arse', I thought. 'We'll do it.'

More than anything I wanted to punish us both. Push the tragedy so far up into our faces that it screamed loud and clear, 'What a fucking waste!'

A week later I went back to pick up my husband and we drove in silence to the shops we'd been to over the years. In one afternoon, we bought all the furniture we'd passed over during our marriage. A dining table, matching chairs, a coffee table, rugs, a beautiful red throw, an occasional chair and, of course, a new sofa.

'Does this strike you in any way as ironic?' I said, as we drove away from the last shop with a pile of receipts on the dashboard. I wanted to punch the windscreen. Smash it all.

'What do you mean?' he asked. 'I don't understand why you are so angry at me.' He was staring at the road ahead.

'We've bought all this beautiful furniture for an empty nest to be sold. In one afternoon, we've furnished our home as we were incapable of doing in the three years of our marriage. Can't you see that we've just made a showroom of how *not* to live?' My throat was tight.

He continued to look at the road ahead. 'You are upset,' he said. 'I don't want to discuss it.'

He was right: I was upset and there was, indeed, nothing to say.

I realised all these years that I'd been looking for matches, trying to strike something in my husband to ignite him. I might as well have been trying to light water, or trying to bring movement back to my father's limbs.

None of it mattered but my leaving. I would sleep on a single mattress on the floor, just as my mother had done in the gallery. I'm not sure if she had felt like this, but I was excited to reshuffle my cards and see what happened next.

Twenty-nine

What happened next was that my father got very sick. Becky called early one morning and told me they were in the emergency room. From the sound of her voice, I knew it was serious. I packed a small suitcase and Jack and I were on a plane to Adelaide a few hours later.

We went straight from the airport to the hospital to find them still in the emergency room, my father sitting in his wheelchair, almost eighteen hours after Becky had brought him in. His eyes were rolling back in his head and he was speaking nonsense. I'd never seen him like that before and I was frightened. The doctors and nurses, I realised, had assumed he was physically *and* mentally disabled and had been ignoring him for all those hours based on that assumption.

I kept thinking about the matron who had refused to come in for my father's emergency when he was admitted with polio. It felt like I was in some kind of altered reality. My father's behaviour and his wheelchair were all the proof these doctors and nurses needed to confirm their assumptions. Nothing I said – that he was accomplished, sane, had an Order of Australia and wasn't behaving like himself – could convince them that he needed to be seen and treated immediately. I felt like I was screaming underwater.

The medical system was failing him again. No wonder he never wanted to go to the doctor when he was sick. The first time the system failed him, over such a simple thing as a key to a room, the consequences were catastrophic. This moment was looking to be every bit as dangerous.

When the doctors finally attended to him he was diagnosed with sepsis. By this time, after such a long delay, the toxins were all through his bloodstream and he was delusional.

Once they administered the drip of antibiotics and sedated him, he quietened down a bit. I told Becky and my brother Morgan to go home and take a break. They took Jack with them and I was left alone with my still delusional father, who had now at least been put in a bed, but we were still in the emergency room. As I watched the rest of my family walk out through the automatic swinging doors and into the bright daylight, fear gripped me. I had been alone with my father thousands of times, but I had never been the one to care for him. I had fetched him things or scratched an itch, but I'd never given him his pee pot. I used to lift his arm and drape it around my shoulder so I could lie with my head on his chest, but I had never touched his legs.

They had always been ugly and scary, so thin and straight they looked like they'd snap if you didn't handle them carefully. The skin was tight and shiny, as though it'd been greased. I'd watched my mother and then Becky move his limbs around unceremoniously, but his legs had always creeped me out.

So, when he turned his head towards me and told me he was uncomfortable and needed to move, I panicked. He'd settled down by now and was quite lucid. I stood up and walked to the bottom of the bed, where his legs were resting on a folded hospital pillow. 'I don't know how to,' I said. 'Becky always does it.'

For a long time, I didn't know he had feeling in his legs. Somehow the idea didn't make sense when nothing could move. He used to get mad at me for that. 'How many times do I have to tell you?' he'd say, like I was a fool.

'Just pick them up,' he said. 'They won't break.' I tried to look calm, taking his thin ankle in my hand and very tentatively lifting it from its resting place and laying it down a few inches to the left. Then I did the other leg. 'That's better,' he said. 'Thank you.'

I sat down on the plastic hospital chair beside him wanting to cry, wishing Becky would come back.

After a few days of heavy antibiotic treatment my father was physically much improved, but the episode had changed him. He stopped speaking. I knew being back in this environment was hell for him. When he got out of hospital after contracting polio, he vowed that he would never return to another ward or gurney bed. Not only had he been unable to keep the vow, this new experience seemed to be bringing back all the feelings of powerlessness that he'd tried his best to forget. The smells, the sounds, the dulled chatter in the corridors, doctors talking about you like you weren't actually in the room.

I felt he'd given up. The man who had refused to be beaten, to be silenced or hidden away, was quietly but resolutely in retreat. One day I came in and his lunch tray was untouched. No one had noted on my father's chart that he couldn't feed himself so the orderlies had unquestioningly removed his untouched tray after each meal. He hadn't told anyone he hadn't eaten since arriving. He refused his medication with clenched teeth. My father was killing himself.

Hugh yelled at him through tears and then tried to prise open his mouth. My father locked his jaw tight until, defeated, my brother gave up. I argued with him that Dad had had enough and we should be able to let him go. He had demonstrated time and again that he was no quitter and I felt he had earned the right to tell us he was done with this battle. We had no idea of the pain and the struggle he'd gone through every day sitting in that chair. If he wanted to end it, we should allow it.

Two days later, he came back to us. I arrived at his bedside and he spoke to me like as though nothing had happened. He said he was hungry. I went home and made him soup, which I drove back and fed him for dinner. From then on, I visited twice a day with his favourite meals, prepared with as much love as I knew how. I sat at his bedside and fed him with a silver spoon I brought from the house.

My father was admitted to hospital with a curable problem but, unbeknown to me, had been subsequently diagnosed with terminal cancer. He didn't mince his words when he told me he didn't have long to live. I hoped he had softened the blow when he told Morgan and Anna.

Thirty

Even though it seemed like he'd wanted to just days before, my father couldn't give up on life. He couldn't stop fighting and we said goodbye to him three or four times before his body finally succumbed after the ravages of forty-seven years of living with polio. When he was first discharged from the infectious diseases hospital all those decades before, weighing eighty-five pounds, the doctors told my grandparents their son wouldn't see out the year. He called every year he survived beyond that gloomy prognosis 'cream'.

Watching him as he was really dying was like waiting for a huge pendulum to stop. Death had stalked him ever since he was twenty, but he hid that fact from me and everyone else. Now there was no hiding it. In the end, it wasn't polio that got him. It was cancer. He was leaving us.

He had been discharged from the hospital and come back home. Every day, while he slept, I sat for long stretches, looking at the sea outside the big sliding windows. When things got really tough, I went down to the beach and threw rocks into the water and skimmed pebbles across the flat glass surface. On the other side of the world, the American writer I'd kept in touch with through daily emails threw pebbles back to me from his beachside home. I imagined the rocks colliding on the water's surface and settling gently on the seabed, where they'd roll together, buffeted by the tide.

My father's impending death unsettled everything. I'd felt abandoned by him before, but then he returned. Now I would have to let him go him once and for all, when we had so much to make up for, so much still to talk about. And here was this whole new me, liberating myself from a stifling marriage and slowly becoming the person I wanted to be. I wanted him to see who I would become.

We were lucky. Our father was not instantly and unexpectedly snatched from life as Uncle George had been. Uncle George was fit and healthy. He had a skipping rope, which hung on a hook on the back porch, and he skipped religiously for thirty minutes every morning before he went to work.

He took his family skiing to places like Vail, played tennis and squash regularly. He ate healthily. Uncle George was the strong, able-bodied father I never had, yet he died aged fifty-four, coming down the black run of an Italian ski field. Aunty Babs had to arrange to have his body flown back to Australia in the midst of her blinding grief.

The guilt I felt when he died was enormous, because I knew it should have been the other way around. It should have been Uncle

George's family that had time to make proper arrangements and tell him the things that needed to be said. He was too young. It was too sudden. They should have had more time. Surely they wondered why it had been their father instead of mine. I would have.

In the weeks before my father's death he took to watching a lot of television and it was that, more than anything, that scared me. In the past he only watched the news and foreign language films and those, I always thought, mainly for the sex scenes.

Now it didn't seem to matter what he was staring at. From the moment he woke until he fell asleep at night the television, turned up too loud, beamed and blared nonsense at him. I knew this meaningless distraction meant that he couldn't quite bear the thought of death.

One night, towards the end, to give Becky a break I slept beside their bed on a fold-out mattress on the floor, while Becky stayed in the spare room. My father woke all through the night in a fevered delirium. Every two hours I drew morphine into a syringe and shot it into his gasping mouth. It stilled him.

The following evening at dusk, haggard from the night before, I walked along the water's edge. The enormity of the simple fact that I had never been on the beach with my father hit me. Of course I had thought about it in passing, but as he lay dying, it struck me like the devastating blow it actually was. I suddenly saw that to live at the lip of the ocean yet never once build a sandcastle with your father was a cruelty that had hurt me more than I had ever admitted.

As the sun melted down into the curve of the horizon, it looked like the sea should bubble from the heat. I left my clothes in a pile on the sand and waded in until the water reached my belly.

The sea was so flat it mirrored the pink and orange sky. I faced the horizon and propelled myself off the seabed. I felt as though I was diving into glass. I swam out far and when I came back to shore

I was covered in goosebumps. I sat on the warm sand and patted myself dry with my T-shirt. The sky had softened while I was swimming. It looked like someone had come along with a giant brush, painting it and the water in a wash of colour. I went back to my father's sickbed, where he lay hooked up to air pumps and other contraptions, and placed my cool palm under his nose so he could smell the sea.

My father made all the funeral arrangements himself and enjoyed doing it. 'I'm dying, so let me see the box, let me think about my body being lit in flames. Let me now face this off.'

He made us promise there would be no roses or baby's breath. He wanted wattle, because it was South Australia's state flower and because 'Wattle' was the name of the street where he had lived with his aunt Molly and his parents after being released from hospital. Wattle meant home.

He also wanted his funeral to be an inexpensive affair and wattle, considered a weed by many, is as cheap as they come. He had chosen the cheapest casket, one with removable handles, and told the undertaker to make sure they took them off before they threw him in the furnace so they could be used to carry another dead person to their resting place.

'Put the dead in the ground, if you must, or throw them in a furnace,' he said. 'But don't, don't – I beg you – waste all that nonsense on me.'

In an ideal world, he would have been buried in a cardboard box – he even made inquiries, but there were health regulations against it. He decided someone should make a DIY coffin. The entrepreneur in him wished he'd had that particular business idea a few years before he was due to be in one.

He knew he'd found the right funeral home when he discovered one close to the two-dollar shop warehouse. The two-dollar shop was his favourite place to shop. He still liked nothing better than a bargain, so the warehouse seemed like a good omen, or a fitting symbol. I joked about it. 'Dad's getting buried at the two-dollar shop.'

The coffin could be cheap, I thought, but the flowers, my mother had taught me, should always be spectacular. Not too surprisingly, though, my father chose a mean little florist with spindly blooms and gauche oil paintings of sunsets by local artists in ugly frames.

It didn't matter that we were arranging his wreath, he flirted with the young woman behind the counter. I realised that as well as the price point of her flowers, her enormous breasts had also caught his attention.

The florist agreed to the wattle but my father knew she'd try to sneak some baby's breath in and he warned us when we left the shop. 'Watch her. She'll get carried away. I don't want any of that,' he said. 'Promise me.' I gave my word and kissed his forehead.

By now I was a few years into my tenure as director of the Sydney Writers' Festival. All this was going on during the final stages of preparation for this juggernaut of an event, but I was flying back and forth to see my father as often as possible, bringing Jack with me when I could.

Whenever I was there, I cooked. Food is love and cooking was the best thing I could do that made any difference to Dad and to Becky. Cooking was also a welcome distraction from the sadness. When Jack came with me, he spent most of the time sitting up in bed beside his Chair. He chatted away as though nothing were unusual, that this wasn't breaking his heart. But when I tucked him into his bed each night, the stress showed. Sometimes he cried, but I knew mostly he saved his tears until after I'd left the room. He was being stoic for my benefit too.

During the day, watching the two of them reminded me of all the times I'd sat up in my father's bed as a child. It was like watching a version of myself. Jack knew of jigs, too, and I watched as he got those whenever my father had the strength.

Chair was Jack's champion and a father figure in his life. Years earlier, he boastfully declared he would teach Jack how to defend himself in a knife fight. When we laughed at the absurdity of the idea of *him* giving that advice, he told us how he'd had to get out of numerous knife attacks when he was on the docks. He also managed to suggest that pretty girls were often at the root of the dispute.

We were standing around the kitchen while dinner was being prepared when my father said, 'Jack, get the carving knife.' Jack, thinking he was just passing the knife for its usual purpose, put it in my father's hand with the blade stood upright.

But once the knife was in his hand, my father told Jack to take his elbow and lunge the knife towards himself, as though my father was attacking him. Jack obliged, jabbing the knife towards his stomach with one hand and defending himself with the other. When my father told him he'd done everything wrong and would have been cut in a real fight, Jack didn't protest at the absurdity of the whole thing. He played along and took every instruction to memory. Jack still likes to recount the story of how he learned from his 95 per cent paralysed grandfather how to defend himself in a knife fight.

A few days later, I was back in Sydney scrambling to ready what was to be my second-last festival.

I remember calling my father near the end of the festival, while I was in the back of a cab, taking three overseas writers to the festival reception at the governor's house. 'I promise I won't die in the middle of it all,' he said. His voice was frail but cheerful; he said nothing of how close he knew he was. Becky told me they had been out for a coffee that morning with his breathing mask strapped to his face and the canister of air hooked up to the back of his chair. She laughed that he looked frightening, but he'd gone beyond caring. I was glad that all that mattered to him was that he was still punching.

The festival finished on the following night. He died very early the next morning, at home, with Becky and Anna sitting beside him.

'He waited for the festival to be over for you, darling,' Becky said. My father died with all the wilful determination he had possessed in life.

And sure enough, when I rang with the news that the time had come to prepare the wreath, the florist said she couldn't get wattle.

'What do you mean, you can't get it?' I asked. 'You said it was easy when he paid you.'

'Well, I can't,' she said. 'I just can't. No one has it. And anyway, it's ugly.'

'You may think it's ugly,' I said, my knuckles turning white around the receiver, 'but it's what he wanted and it's what we're going to have.' I hung up the phone.

In the end, determined to deliver on her husband's wish, Becky got in the car and drove through the suburban streets and filled their decked-out van – with all its now redundant hydraulics, straps and belts – with the bright yellow blooms. She stole them from parks and people's front yards.

'Okay,' I said, as we carried armfuls of yellow foliage into the florist's depressing little shop, 'Can you do something with this?'

'I guess I can. But don't you want anything decorative in it? It's so plain. Some baby's breath. A rose or two . . .' She trailed off as she saw my expression.

'My father only wanted natives.'

That was her cue. The colour came back to her face. 'Well, how about a little decoration with something red to offset it? It'll be lovely, I promise. But you can't just make me make do with *this*,' she said, pointing at the yellow branches on her countertop as if they were noxious weeds. That was part of my father's joke, I suddenly realised. 'Bury me in the weeds, where I belong.'

'It's hardly a job for a florist, is it?' she said.

'Okay,' I said. 'But only natives and do not, not, not use roses or baby's breath.'

I went home and sat in my father's wheelchair, which I'd always loved to do. I decided to be brave and say my final farewell before they turned him to dust.

I drove Becky and my father's van to the funeral parlour and laughed as I passed the two-dollar warehouse nearby. I parked in the disabled spot even though my father always reprimanded me for doing that if he wasn't with me. I sat for ten minutes with the engine off, steeling my courage.

I had never seen a dead person before and the first thing I noticed as I stood above his pale body was that he didn't smell like salad dressing anymore. I never imagined that death would take away your scent.

It is true what they say about dead people. He looked peaceful.

The undertaker had wrapped a cloth around my father's neck that looked like a starched doily. The rest of his body was covered in white satin and reminded me of his John the Baptist fancy-dress outfit.

I cried black mascara all over his shroud and then he looked a little less angelic. The funeral attendant tut-tutted before he shut the lid of the coffin, but I thought it was appropriate for my father to appear a little smudged.

Thirty-one

For close to fifty years, driven by the vow he took against the matron who'd 'cared for him' when he was first admitted to hospital, my father fought for the rights of disabled people. He was determined that others like him would not face the impediments to success and independence that he had faced. He believed everyone could and should contribute and he prised open closed doors so people with disabilities could play a role in society and have their voices heard.

So on the day of his funeral, the crematorium courtyard looked like a wheelchair convention or an accessibility protest without the placards. The fountain set in the middle of the rose garden was surrounded by every kind of wheelchair I had ever seen – electric, manual, fancy racing chairs cut down low. The people on wheels almost outnumbered the able-bodied mourners.

Our family stood behind the hearse as he was pulled out. The shiny black box swathed in yellow branches of wattle slid out onto a waist-high chrome trolley. It looked like a bright yellow firecracker had burst across the lid of his cheap coffin.

As the service was about to begin, all the chairs wheeled into the hall, running into each other like dodgem cars. They vied for room down the front and took up all the aisle space, so to make their way into the pews the able-bodied had to climb over their footplates or push them this way and that.

When I sat down in the front row next to Anna and properly set eyes on the floral arrangement on top of my father's coffin, I began to laugh. The florist had set a large, stiff red Banksia right in the middle of my father's coffin.

'Dad's got a hard-on,' I whispered to Anna, who smiled for the first time that day. Becky overheard what I said and winked, while my brothers shook their heads disapprovingly.

My opinion of the florist changed forever. This was a wonderful parting gift from the big-breasted florist in the mean little store. It was either an incredible piece of unplanned, hilarious luck or that girl was very funny.

It was a wonderful irony to see my father – the man whose body confounded people when they saw his children – memorialised by a big red phallic salute, exactly the joke he would have initiated himself had he thought of it. From then on I held on to my sister's shoulders, and we cried and laughed through the service.

My mother attended, although I am not sure where she sat – not with us in the front.

After the speeches, Jack stood next to the coffin with a large wicker basket filled with Italian Baci chocolates. Hugh's daughters, my nieces Sophia and Claudia, each held matching baskets of fresh coastal rosemary picked that morning from the path outside the house.

As people paid their last respects, they took either a sprig of rosemary from the girls or a chocolate kiss from Jack, then laid it on the coffin. Becky wanted to send him up in flames covered in sweet kisses, so he knew he was adored, and rosemary, so he would never be forgotten.

The night of my father's funeral, more than a dozen dolphins danced out of the water at sunset. We'd often seen small numbers of them together – three or four in a group, making their way along the coastline – but never so many. My father always had his eyes cast out to the sea when we sat on the deck or in the sunroom, so he was usually the first to spot their fins ducking and diving.

Once, in my thirties, he pointed to three fins swimming as close to the shore as I had ever seen. 'Go on, run,' he said, sensing my thoughts. I tore out the door, scrambled down the rocks and ran as fast as I could across the sand. I waded into the water with the dolphins swimming around my legs. Their strength and power shot through the small breaking waves as they hunted down a school of tiny silver fish.

My father was delighted when I came back up to the house charged with the thrill. It was exactly what he would have done, and watching me do it, and hearing me describe it, seemed to give him as much pleasure as if he'd done it himself.

I sat beside him one afternoon with my feet up on the spokes of his wheel, watching Morgan and Anna playing a game of cricket on the beach, and he said, 'I wish I could be down there with you kids.' That was as close to a complaint or regret that I ever heard.

I understand now that my father's time in the iron lung was like a monk's meditation. He lay there and for a long, dull, isolated and largely silent year, he thought. He thought his way out of his rage so the people around him would never feel it.

After the wake, the sadness I felt when I was finally alone seemed selfish, because he was finally free and I knew that's what he'd wanted. But I would miss his fighting spirit, his whistle, the smell of vinegar, his jigs and the sound of rubber tyres squeaking on wooden floorboards as he motored himself around.

I pictured him flying and swimming and doing all the things he hadn't done since he was twenty. He was released from his confinement. There was something about my father's death that felt freeing, not just for him, which it certainly was, but for me too.

As I lay in bed that night listening to the waves crashing outside, I remembered my childhood hunt for matches to set my father on fire. On the day his body was turned to ashes, I realised he didn't need flames to get him out of his chair. His mind got him out of it every single day.

I also knew once he was gone and Jack was old enough, which he would be in a few years, there would be nothing else holding me in Australia. I began to hatch my plans. A year later, I was gone.

Thirty-two

Shortly after the funeral, I travelled to New York to invite a delegation of *New Yorker* writers to visit Australia as guests of the writers' festival. It was on this trip – my father just dead, my marriage in tatters, and my heart tuned to a married man – that an inspirational greeting card changed my life.

The message called out to me from a spinning display rack at the overcrowded Universal News & Magazine shop on Eighth Avenue, near Columbus Circle. The store sold thousands of magazines, seemingly all on display except for the more hardcore pornography, which a little notice said was available on request. 'Who reads all these?' I wondered, straining my head to make out the titles near the ceiling. A ladder with wheels had been hooked to a railing that ran along the top shelf.

I wanted to look put together for my meeting the next day, so I wandered into the shop in search of a felt-tip pen and a Moleskine notebook. I was about to go to the counter to pay when I saw the greeting card.

Written on a black background, the words 'Leap and the net will appear' spoke a truth different to the other motivational mumbo jumbo on that rack. *Old ways won't open new doors, dance like no one is watching, love like you've never been hurt, sing like no one can hear you, live like heaven is on earth.*

We take notice of what we want to hear. *Leap and the net will appear.* I simply had to have it. I added the card to my purchases and when I returned home to Sydney I stuck it to my refrigerator with a yellow NYC taxi magnet. A few days later, motivated by a final quick reassuring look at the greeting card, I called a meeting with my boss to tell her I'd succeeded in securing the *New Yorker* writers for the next festival – and gave a year's notice on my wonderful job.

'I'm moving to New York,' I said once my boss had recovered from the shock and asked what I was doing next.

'Wonderful! What's your new position?'

'I don't have one.'

'What do you mean you don't have one?'

'I don't have a job yet.'

'Okay . . .' she said dubiously. 'What about a green card?'

'I don't have one of those either.' The plucky arrogance drained from my voice. Her questioning made me realise I had nothing in hand but a dream.

My friends advised me against it. There was Jack. I had big responsibilities. I also had a perfect-fit, high-profile job and wonderful friends. There was plenty to keep me right where I was, but I wanted to leap and never questioned that the net would appear.

I was born into restlessness; I learned from my father to keep my eyes set to the horizon, to plot a scheme for what was next. I didn't understand the idea of contentment. I had to strive for more, push myself harder. Goals weren't met simply for their own sake. I turned my back on my successes like they were cast-off lovers and went looking for the next, like a true addict.

Sometimes my actions did look like those of a reckless addict, even to me – quitting university, flying to London with a one-way ticket, having a baby at twenty-three! This was not the first time I'd given up security and comfort for some risky big idea or fairytale dream. But usually I was successful. Doubt from others fuelled my commitment. The harder, the better.

Three months after the festival finished, with Sydney Town Hall packed to hear the *New Yorker* writers talk about life at the magazine, the stars aligned. I was on a plane to New York for a job interview.

Every convincing lie comes with a core of truth. It was true that I was looking for the next step professionally and that I wasn't sure that was on offer in Australia. It was also true that, a decade earlier, when I went to New York with my best friend Sophie, I had declared, hugely hungover while waiting in line for bagels, 'One day I have to live here.'

And it was also true that I was very aware that the clock was ticking. There's a use-by date on a woman reinventing herself from scratch in another country, and mine was fast approaching. At forty, I guessed I had one or two more years before my dream of living in the city that never sleeps would be well and truly out of reach. It wasn't fair, and it wasn't the same for men, but much in life isn't.

With those three things clear and true, my ruse was unshakable. But the carefully omitted fact was that it would bring me closer to the American writer, and I believed I could make him love me enough to leave his wife.

Of course, that was not something I could share openly. Professionally, I couldn't afford a reputation as a festival director who ran off with married writers. Nor did I want the story of my divorce to be that I had left my husband for another man.

Whenever it came up, I said I had resigned and was planning to move to America because I was ready for the professional challenge of my life, to make a mark in the epicentre of the publishing world. Which was true, but not the whole truth.

Even more than I wanted others to believe it, I wanted to convince myself. How could I justify leaving my life behind – leaving Jack – for anything other than professional reasons?

I was ambitious. I had looked, but couldn't see a clear career progression in Australia. Perhaps I would have realised my dream to live in New York anyway, but the American writer certainly put gas to my flame. We often fool ourselves into thinking we're making a carefully considered choice by tallying the evidence that supports an already-made decision.

That first night at dinner with the writer, I was only halfway through my entrée when I thought, 'I'm in trouble.' By the end of the meal, I knew my marriage was over. A week later, I was sleeping on my friend's couch.

Through my work I'd met and dined with any number of wonderful writers, but this one was a prize-fighter on the page. Over the course of the coming few days, in our time together, he told me such carefully and kindly observed stories about human frailty, his own included, that I often found myself holding back tears.

He spoke in perfectly constructed sentences, usually with a coded message lying right under the surface. He was someone who warranted paying attention to.

I felt like I was being read to and once we stopped talking, when it was just our heat and sweat and his breath in my ear, he was the first man from whom I held nothing back.

Our initial time together was only a clutch of days, but it was what happened when he left that gripped me most. After he flew back to his home in America, all we had was our words and we held on tight through those, no matter the implausibility of our continued romance. I told him everything and he whispered back to me.

I imagined being wrapped around him, which sent a shiver up my spine and made the hairs on my neck stand on end, all the while telling anyone who asked I needed a new challenge.

Thirty-three

PEN stands for poets, playwrights, editors, essayists and novelists. It's the oldest human rights organisation in the world and defends freedom of expression. Its US membership included Norman Mailer, Susan Sontag and Toni Morrison, as well as almost every other US-based literary luminary. Under the presidency of Salman Rushdie, PEN America had established an international literary festival, called PEN World Voices.

In a post 9/11 environment, the US was closing itself off from the rest of the world, looking inward when it really needed to look outward. Americans were not reading the works of foreign writers – less than

3 per cent of books published in the US are translations. Salman resolved that PEN should bring those important voices to the US. His thinking was that if Americans weren't going to go out and read the world, then they would bring the world's writers to America. The job interview I had was to become the director of this festival, in 2007 still only in its third year.

Over the course of a week I had eleven hours of face-to-face interviews with staff and board members. We talked about books, writers, freedom of expression and how we could put the festival on the map. My final appointment was with Salman himself at his home. I arrived early and walked around the block to kill time despite the almost 40-degree scorching heat. I felt nauseated, not so much from the temperature, which *was* sick-making, but from nerves. Finally, a perfectly planned few minutes early, I walked up the stoop and knocked on the front door of his brownstone.

Salman greeted me warmly and showed me up the narrow staircase to the first floor, where we sat together on a large cushioned couch in his living room.

'My inbox is clogged with emails from writers all over the world telling me to hire you,' he said, laughing. 'Every time I log on there's someone else, somewhere in the world, singing your praises. I'm tempted to give you the job just to shut them all up so I can get on with my work.'

'I paid them all, you know,' I said, jokingly. But as the words came out of my mouth, I wished I could pull them back in. I knew I shouldn't be fooling around when so much was at stake. But it was too late, I had no option but to continue with my folly. 'Fifty bucks. That's all it took.'

'Ha, that'd be right!' he exclaimed. 'Writers! So easily bought.'

And that was it. I think he knew then that we'd get along, and we did.

The evening before I was due to fly out of Sydney to begin my new life, Jack broke his hand. I was kneeling on the floor, cramming a jar of Vegemite into a sock to add to my suitcase, when he walked into my bedroom with his right hand raised, blackened and twice its usual size. He'd got into a fight and, rather than hit the person tormenting him, he punched the reinforced glass of a bus shelter.

Jack was no fighter. He had never hit anything or anyone before. When he was three, being teased by a boy at day care, the teacher told me his solution was to gently but firmly lay the bully down and sit on him.

We were in the emergency room for six hours. It looked like he would have to have surgery.

Of course, I had considered Jack in my decision to get all this in motion. I'd tied myself in knots worrying about the right thing to do. I'd asked him over and over whether he was okay with me leaving and he'd say, 'Of course. It's your work, you've got to go.'

But what choice did he have? What choice did *I* have?

Despite my pleas to delay my arrival until after Jack's HSC exams, PEN told me I had to start work at the office by the beginning of October or not at all. I had left it as long as I could and booked a flight that arrived on the Friday evening, the weekend before I started work.

Carefully timed plans were put in place. My friend Tanya, who'd known Jack since he was born, agreed to look after him for the weeks before Becky was able to come and take over. Becky had been a teacher and had more patience than anyone I knew, so I thought she might actually be able to help Jack with his exams better than I could.

Jack and I had never had serious conflict, but the past year had been a battle to get him to focus at school. One day, arguing about his homework, I threw a heavy candle at him. Thankfully he ducked, but we were both shaken. It was a violent act. For the first time in his life we were at odds and the confident parenting that had come so easily to me – even at twenty-three – seemed to have deserted me. I was completely at a loss.

But the arrangements were put into place and it was agreed that he'd come join me after he'd completed his exams.

To meet PEN's deadline, everything had to happen fast. I had a month to secure a visa for an 'alien of extraordinary ability' – notoriously difficult to get – and begin work. I hadn't had time to stop and really *think*. But as Jack and I waited in the emergency room for the results of his X-ray, sitting in the cold plastic seats with a tiny television blaring above our heads, the enormity of what I was about to do hit me like a baseball bat in the stomach. I sat on my hands so Jack wouldn't see them shaking. I thought about how to call the whole thing off, cancel my flight and tell Salman and PEN they'd need to find someone else for the job.

Eventually the doctor determined surgery wasn't required. He wrapped Jack's hand and forearm in gauze, slopped wet plaster of Paris over it, and forty-five minutes later, the cast set, we drove home. It was after midnight when I tucked Jack into bed, his arm resting on his Simpsons duvet cover. I stroked his hair and kissed him goodnight for the last time in six months.

A few hours later Jack was standing on the footpath, dressed in his school uniform, waving me off with his good arm. My friend Peter was driving me to the airport, and as we pulled away from the kerb I watched Jack get smaller and smaller in the side mirror. Then we went around a bend in the road and he disappeared from view altogether. I put my head in my hands and could hardly believe what I was doing. I thought about telling Peter to turn the car around. But I didn't.

What I should have done was wonder what kind of job doesn't allow a mother to see her kid through his exams. I knew the work could be done from anywhere. I didn't need to be in the office in New York to start inviting writers to the festival. I knew what I was doing and how to do it. All I needed was a computer and the internet.

A friend who worked at Qantas organised an upgrade on my ticket, so I was in business class from Sydney to New York, which was a blessing for more than just the extra leg room. I was a mess. Even with the additional luggage allowance in business class, at the check-in counter I had to jettison things from my suitcase into the trash.

Suddenly I was one of those chaotic travellers I'd always derided, down on the floor to open their overstuffed cases with its privacies for all to see as they determined what they could discard. None of what I threw out mattered. I'd left my beautiful son behind; losing a few possessions was the least of it.

I arrived in New York with the ephemera of my life in two large suitcases. Some of the rest of it was making its way across the sea in the hull of a large container ship. I felt ripped in half by two equal hands. On the one side I had left Jack, the one person who had focused and driven my life. But on the other, against no small odds, I had set this dream alight.

When I was in town for the interviews, I met with a writer who mentioned that he and his wife were subletting a one-bedroom apartment in their building while renovations were being done on their own. They'd be leaving their temporary accommodation around the time I was due to arrive. Real estate is notoriously difficult to secure in New York, so the timing of this was seamless. When I got the job and they offered to help make the complicated arrangements to take over their lease, I jumped at it. It didn't matter that I would move into the apartment sight unseen, I'd have my own place right away.

From JFK airport I went straight to their freshly minted Upper West Side apartment on the thirteenth floor, where I was greeted with a bottle of French champagne. I could tell from their place that my new digs were going to be better than I could have dreamed. A few glasses of champagne later, I wheeled my suitcases into my beautiful new parquet-floor apartment, six flights down from theirs. The writer's wife, Lisa, had prepared a blow-up mattress in the bedroom, towels in the bathroom, a couple of pots and pans, and enough crockery to get me started.

I can't say I wasn't excited about all this. Since Jack would be following me once his exams were over, our separation seemed temporary and bearable. I stuck the 'jump and the net will appear' card to my new refrigerator in my new apartment in my new city and thought – all things considered – I'd made a magical leap.

The next day I caught the subway to the Whole Foods at Columbus Circle. I had heard that Whole Foods stores were laid out according to the principles of feng shui, which I thought sounded like a joke, but, in fact, I *was* oddly calm as I took my place at the back of the long line. I'd walked through the supermarket twice. The first time filling a large cart with all of Jack's favourite things, then, remembering it was only me, reversing back along the aisles, returning items to their shelves, swapping the big cart at the entrance for a small plastic basket instead.

After clearing the check-out I made my way past the glittering stores of the Time Warner Center, where everything promised luxury and prestige. I realised just how effective that feng shui had been when my arms started feeling like they were detaching from my shoulders from the weight of the brown paper shopping bags.

As I waited for the subway in the bowels of Columbus Circle, I watched a busker dancing as though he was inside a child's music box. He was a tall, elegant black man, with his face painted white with theatrical makeup. He wore a pair of loose black breeches with braces and a stiffly starched white shirt. He stood with his feet together on a block of smooth white formica just bigger on each side than his worn-down shoes.

He twirled a thin baton between his fingers in time to the twinkle of the children's nursery rhyme 'Hickory Dickory Dock', which played from a small boom box strapped to a portable trolley behind him. He spun and swayed with his eyes closed as people put dollar bills into the bowler hat on the ground in front of him.

I was transfixed by his grace. He was such a sad and beautiful sight there on the subway platform, I let three trains go past. He swivelled around so smoothly on the soles of his shoes atop the formica block, I wondered if there were little wheels in them. I bent over to see, but there was no trickery. He deftly glided around on his tiny stage, flopping down and dancing back up again – a perfect doll in a music box.

I had put down my shopping and watched him for about fifteen minutes, until I remembered my peas would be defrosting. I placed three singles in his hat and he swirled up, like a ballerina nailed to her spot inside the music box, and winked at me. I mouthed a soundless 'thank you' back, put my hands together in prayer, bowed in respect, and got on the wrong train.

When I finally got home I put my groceries away, opened a bottle of wine, put my headphones in my ears, turned my iPod up loud and practised swivelling around seamlessly in one spot. I imagined the busker looking at me through a distant window, seeing me dance and then slowly realising that I was the woman from the platform, now trying to imitate his act. I couldn't get the perfect glide of his feet and instead rotated with little shuffles, but I just about managed his fall from the waist. I lurched my torso up again with a mechanical jerk before making another slow spin on my heels.

It was fall when I arrived. The days were cold, bright and filled with colour. There was a growers' market around the corner from my apartment where I shopped every Friday morning before work. I'd come home with large bunches of basil and bags filled with sweet tomatoes, just-plucked mushrooms, salad mixes of bitter mustard, radicchio and fresh herbs.

My apartment may have had no furniture but it was filled with light. Sleeping on a blow-up mattress in New York only added to the sense of adventure. I cooked meals in a single pot and fry pan and ate them sitting on the floor of an empty room. I was happy.

My mother wasn't big on giving the usual parental advice – the kind of words that gently guide you away from mishaps and set you up for living in a sensible way. 'An apple a day . . .', that sort of thing. My mother considered fruit 'empty calories'. I swore off it.

Her guidance was more along the lines of 'Don't wear nice underwear on a date if you don't want to fuck the man.' I don't think I understood what that even meant when she first said it to me, but it was repeated often enough that I eventually got the gist.

She taught me through example, though, that if you have proper cutlery, a linen napkin, a nice china plate to eat off, and a teacup and saucer, the rest of your life circumstances can fade away. Once she took me to stay with one of her boyfriends in Sydney. There was no glass in the window frames, but when we sat down to dinner, we had napkins. Every day, when he was at work, my mother took me to the art gallery. I've always known that if a napkin can't save you, art certainly can.

So along with the jar of Vegemite I'd shoved in the sock, in my luggage I had tucked away four Liberty plates and four sets of silver cutlery, my favourite teacup and saucer, and some linen napkins. You never know when you might have guests, even in an empty apartment in a city where you know virtually no one. With those things, apart from Jack's gnawing absence and my guilt about leaving, which sometimes I could set aside, I was happy.

However, the writer I had dreamed of being closer to had become a shadowy figure. I had imagined I'd see more of him when we lived in the same country, but I had less to do with him now than when I was in Australia. I had my hands more than full with the festival and trying to get acclimatised to a new city so, thankfully, he wasn't the focus of my attention. He reneged on carefully made plans and made excuses. I worked.

The writer's absence was one thing, but what really shook me was that, in the weeks and months that passed after Jack's exams finished, it became more and more evident that he had no intention of packing up and following me.

Thirty-four

In the PEN office, on Broadway in SoHo, I had a small workstation in a narrow internal corridor, wedged between an executive's secretary and a junior member of staff. It was a crummy workspace, particularly for a senior member of the team, which I had been led to believe I was going to be. But the box of beautiful business cards – a thick cream-textured stock, a simple design with my name and new address – made me forgive the slight and, for a while in disbelief. It was a miracle that I'd pulled this off and was here in my dream job in the city I'd fallen in love with – the city that made me feel prettier, smarter. I smiled more. I was starting anew.

But nothing was quite as it had been promised. After just a few days, I began to feel like I'd walked into an environment more akin to the places an organisation like PEN might be drawing international attention to rather than its own place of business. Everything was a distortion of the truth and of what I had been told I could expect. My agreed-upon salary had been mysteriously calculated down while I was on the plane to America. My title had changed.

Most of my colleagues were wonderful, but everyone cowered around a couple of individuals. The atmosphere was toxic and, for some reason, particularly acrid when it came to me.

The day I received my first pay cheque from PEN, I left my tiny desk in the corridor and walked up Broadway to the large Crate & Barrel homewares store on the corner of Houston. A thin, well-dressed man introduced himself as Nigel. He didn't look like a salesman; he looked like a well-dressed editor about to go out to a work lunch.

'Does that couch over there come in another colour?' I asked, pointing to the smart simple-lined showroom prop. 'I don't want it in white.'

'Mocha or charcoal.'

'I'll take it in mocha.'

'That was quick,' he said. 'Did you even sit on it?'

'Yes, when I first came in. It's perfect and I'll take it. I'll also need a bed, a table and chairs . . .'

A little under twenty minutes later, I was swiping my credit card.

'That's the quickest sale I have ever made,' said Nigel. 'I've never seen anything like it.'

'You have no idea,' I said, thinking about the last time I'd bought a full house's worth of furniture in a single outing.

After about six weeks in the job, a colleague asked me to join him for breakfast at Balthazar, a buzzing French-style bistro in the heart of SoHo.

'You're a lousy actor,' he said. He ordered a café au lait which came in a large French coffee bowl, like a cereal bowl. 'It's very plain that you're unhappy in your work.'

'Well, it's not quite what I imagined,' I said, holding my voice in check so it didn't waver. 'I'm not sure why you've brought me here. You overrule everything I suggest. Surely my experience has to count for something.'

'I don't know how it is where *you* come from,' he said venomously, 'but that's not how it works here. And this is too important.' He sipped his coffee, taking his time for effect. A narrow line of milk froth trimmed his lip. I took a small moment of pleasure from him sitting there like a seven-year-old who'd just drunk a glass of milk, but then he leaned forward across the narrow table and began jabbing his index finger in the air a few inches from my chest.

'Listen,' he spat. 'You are just going to have to get used to the fact that I am going to be all over you like a cheap suit.' He leaned back in his chair and took another swig from his bowl. He didn't seem like an innocent seven-year-old anymore; he seemed exactly like a thug.

A chill ran through me. 'I can do this job. You know I can.' In my four years at the helm of Sydney Writers' Festival, I had more than doubled audiences, tripled box-office takings, doubled book sales. For my final festival I had curated 300 events with 300 writers, the PEN World Voices Festival was a small undertaking by comparison. From what I could tell, audiences at the first festivals had been about a tenth of the size of Sydney's. It's not that this was a program I could do with my eyes closed, there was a ton for me to learn and to be challenged by, but none of it was out of my reach.

'Well, you haven't been doing it here, not in *this* city. And this is too important. Until I know you can do it, I'm going to ride you.'

My breakfast stayed untouched. I'd ordered a boiled egg and toast soldiers because it was the breakfast my grandmother used to make for me. I thought it would be comforting because I knew ahead of time this meeting would be stressful. I remembered staying over in the big house where my father lived after he got polio, feeding the chickens, and then dunking strips of buttery toast into the yellow yolks of their eggs. This serve went cold on the plate.

Two weeks later another member of staff summoned me to a café where they played loud commercial radio that was more ads than music. Advertising was everywhere in America, even on subway turnstiles. Billboards appeared in the sky, plumed out from the back of tiny skywriting planes. It seemed no public space was exempt.

'Well,' he said with an evil chuckle, which you might have mistaken for merriment if you didn't know better. 'I told everyone straightaway that no one was really qualified for the position.'

I stared into my polystyrene cup of coffee in silence as he explained in detail that these first two months had been my 'honeymoon period'.

'Jesus,' I thought. 'If this is the honeymoon, I hate to see what the divorce is going to look like.'

When I got back to my desk I was shaking. I opened the *New York Times* and the words 'adversity is the first path to truth' jumped out at me from the page. I cut out the newsprint and stuck it to the edge of my monitor. It became my daily mantra.

The next day, on the subway to work, I watched a tall man as he stepped into the carriage. My eye was drawn to his striking stature and his distinguished leather hat, which was the shape of a short top hat. When he sat down next to me I turned and smiled. He smiled back.

When I next looked up, a man with his wrist slung through the hand strap above us seemed to be dangling rather than standing. In New York you quickly learn who not to make eye contact with on the subway or on the footpath, so when I noticed the barcode tattooed on the side of his neck I averted my gaze to the ground.

But I looked up when he addressed the man sitting next to me, 'I like your hat. I'm not bold enough to wear something like that.'

'Bold enough to tattoo a barcode on your neck, but not bold enough to wear a beautiful hat?' I thought.

The man in the hat nodded. 'Thank you.'

I thought that was the end of the exchange, a compliment paid and an acknowledgement back, until the man in the hat said, 'You know, you don't think you're bold enough until you are called on to be.' And the man with the barcode, as if he was ready to be scanned and paid for at a check-out, nodded and got off at the next stop.

'You sure are right there,' I said to the man in the hat, thinking of my nightmare at PEN.

While this exchange had taken place, a man in an expensive suit sitting on the other side of the carriage stared into his phone playing some kind of game, earphones plugged in his ears, as New York City in all its infinite wonder passed him by.

When I got out of the subway I came upon a cavalcade of empty drink cans rolling along the footpath. The wind had whipped the cans along at quite a pace before they rolled off the lip of the footpath and stopped in the gutter.

I looked around to see a homeless man slumped up against the wall of a convenience store like a half-emptied pillow. He'd obviously collected the cans, planning to trade them for money, but in a moment of 'Why bother?' he'd unleashed them to roll away from him like tumbleweeds.

As I got closer, I realised the man was ripping up dollar bills in his hands, throwing the pieces into the wind and watching them dance like confetti in the air, until they fell, painting the footpath or settling in the gutter along with the cans.

It wasn't the first or the last time that an encounter like that produced a moment of recognition. The truth, the real raw stuff of life, happens in the street, not in fancy corridors – you just have to be paying attention. I knew all too well the futility of trying to make a castle from crumbs.

Thirty-five

Work went from bad to worse. I cried on the subway. I cried at my desk. I took up smoking after having quit for more than a decade. I cried at home every night with a bottle of wine and cigarettes.

I couldn't tell anyone the full extent of the cruelty. Who would believe me? I had no track record here and no one knew me. And most damning of all, this was PEN – one of the most respected human rights organisations in the world and the pinnacle of literary life in the United States. What chance did my reputation and word have against that? I was alone.

But there were moments of light, when the nightmare faded into the background and I remembered exactly why I'd sacrificed so much. I'm not sure these remarkable instances made up for the stress or the pain but when they appeared I grabbed them with both hands.

After the toughest six months of my life, it was opening night of my first festival. I was standing in the wings of New York Town Hall, peeping out from behind the heavy curtains at a packed auditorium.

'Why are you dancing, Caro?' asked Don DeLillo in a whisper, sucking on a lozenge, trying to soothe his sore throat before his reading.

'I'm in New York, it's opening night, there are 1500 people out there, and *you* are here,' I said.

Don had been a hero since I read *White Noise* at university during one of my failed attempts at getting a degree. Now he was standing beside me.

Don DeLillo was cool and steady, but he smiled. After that, whenever I called or saw him, he'd ask, 'How's it going, kiddo?'

The festival was a hit. The closing event featured a capacity crowd at the historic Cooper Union. During the sound check before the show started, I stood on the stage at the very same podium from which Abraham Lincoln delivered his speech against slavery on 27 February 1860.

Suddenly all the strife felt worth it. To be on *that* stage was everything. I savoured the moment standing in the spotlight, delivering something important.

The next morning, I woke to an email from Salman. *Congratulations*, he wrote, expressing how much he'd enjoyed our first festival together and inviting me over to celebrate.

When I arrived at Salman's place a few days later, a bottle of champagne was set chilling in an ice bucket on the coffee table. Seated on the same couch as for my interview, we recounted the highlights and laughed about the best and worst bits.

Salman's highlight was the cabaret, where Patti Smith performed and Sam Shepard read at the Bowery, along with Saul Williams, the slam-rap poet as cool and well-dressed as Prince. Huang Xiang, a performance poet who fled China after repeated imprisonment and torture, delivered his show in Chinese with wild arm-waving and yelling. *New Yorker* cartoonist Victoria Roberts, appearing as her alter ego, a Japanese geisha, was the MC. It was a riot of a night and only just hung together, but right on the edge of chaos, it was a magical show.

Finally I plucked up the courage to tell Salman some of what had been happening in the office. For the first time in my life I had to admit defeat.

'You should have come to me,' he said. I knew he meant it, but I also knew it would have been my word against theirs. Salman offered to speak to the people in question. A little reluctantly, but wanting to be tough and to fight my own battles, I said I'd like to try to handle it myself. The thought of facing them made me feel sick, but knowing I had Salman's support gave me courage.

The American writer warned me. 'Be careful. If they can't fuck with you straight, they'll screw you sideways.' He was right. I got a desk out of the corridor, but every obstacle was put in my way to make the job as difficult as possible.

Finally, Jack came to visit. The driving force of nearly my entire adult life was back. I tried to put on a good face, because that was the only way to survive the absence, but with Jack returned I realised having him gone was like missing a limb. Worse, I'd actually lost all sense of what was important to me.

I took him to all the places I thought he'd love. We went to Generation Records on Thompson Street in the West Village. The cigarette smoke a heavy fog as we pushed through the doors. I bought him CDs and limited-edition T-shirts of his favourite heavy metal bands. It was unabashed bribery.

We walked up Tenth Avenue, before it was the galleried hipster spot it is now, in search of an unmarked loft space on the western edge of Chelsea. Jack had heard about an exhibition of an underground artist who had done the cover art for his favourite band, Tool. As we walked up the steep creaking staircase, I wondered what we were getting ourselves into. The place looked more like a dive where you'd buy a hit of heroin than an art gallery. I clutched my handbag to my chest.

I did everything I could to get him to fall for the city, but no matter how shiny I tried to make it seem, or how enthusiastically I spoke about the opportunities New York could offer him, he always wanted to go home. In Sydney he had a girlfriend and a close-knit group of friends.

He visited a few times over the years, but it broke my heart each time he left. I had to accept that his life – at least for now – was in Australia. At the airport I couldn't bear to watch him walk away or wait to see if he turned to wave goodbye before disappearing into the security line. I left the moment I kissed his forehead and he let go of me, so he wouldn't see how distraught I was. But he knew. Eventually he wouldn't allow me to see him off at the airport. We bade our farewells at the apartment.

My choice to move to America seemed foolish. What was it all for? It was looking more and more as though I'd left Jack, the guiding force of my life, for a fantasy.

The American writer often said work saves us. Now I was working day and night simply to get around the roadblocks that were deliberately being put in my way.

I made good and strong friendships quickly, but I didn't talk about what was really happening at work, or my loneliness, or my doubts. With my work life as bad as it was, these friendships were even more important to me. And besides, I felt that I couldn't talk about my misery because it seemed to be entirely of my own making, having chosen to move from Sydney.

Many of the writers I worked with at PEN became friends, so meeting Philip Roth at John Updike's memorial in 2009 was exciting, but this kind of event had become common enough in my work life that I wasn't overly starstruck, even though it was a thrill to meet such a legendary figure.

I found it remarkably easy to make witty small talk with Philip on the way to the elevator that took us to a private reception on the second floor. He asked me a question to which I made a joke I no longer remember. But I remember the sound of his laughter, which was full and unbounded. When he laughed he threw his chin up and the sound echoed and bounced along the near empty marble corridor. He had the laugh of a young man.

A distinct hush came over the room as we entered. He seemed not to notice, but I did. He steered me to the makeshift bar on the edge of the room, the palm of his hand in the small of my back, and slowly the muted hubbub of the reception began again. 'Bold,' I thought of his touching me like that.

He ordered himself a water and a glass of white wine for me. Soon I became aware of people hovering, trying to break into our conversation to get time with the reclusive novelist. At one point I told him he didn't have to babysit me, that he should mingle and talk to his fans. 'I don't want to monopolise you,' I whispered to him, leaning in.

'I know where I want to be,' he said without pause.

Our game was on.

I told him that I'd read only one of his books, *American Pastoral*, and only because I was assigned as the publicist when I worked for Random House Australia in my twenties.

Since becoming the Sydney Writers' Festival's artistic director, my reading had been dictated by writers I knew I could invite to the festival, and Philip was known to be elusive. Roth, the reluctant stage presence, was dead to me.

To my surprise he laughed, as though I'd told him another hilarious joke, and seemed relieved I wasn't an adoring fan.

'Come to dinner,' he said.

'Thank you,' I said. 'I can't.'

'Why not?' he asked. 'Do you have plans?

'No, I don't,' I said, envisioning my grim evening home alone. 'I can't intrude on the *New Yorker*'s dinner,' I explained, fearing editor David Remnick's reaction to discovering *I* was going to be a tag-along to his literary powerhouse dinner.

Philip told me the dinner wasn't a formal part of the Updike tribute, just him and a few friends. After more rebukes, he finally said, 'You have to come. It's my birthday.' How could I refuse?

We hailed a cab on Forty-Second Street with Judith Thurman from the *New Yorker*. We all piled in the back seat and headed across town to the Russian Samovar. Three friends were waiting for Philip at the table at the rear of the restaurant, near the swinging door to the kitchen. We ate smoked salmon and caviar in the soft glow of pink and apricot coloured lampshades. The piano player's tip jar – a glass fishbowl stuffed full of singles – sat on top of the reflective lid of his baby grand. The menu listed more flavoured vodkas than I had imagined possible. It was a lovely evening and all the while I was thinking, 'How did *this* happen?'

Afterwards, Philip walked me to the Fiftieth Street subway. As we approached the stairs down to the entrance he joked that he hadn't ridden the subway since 1969, when his novel *Portnoy's Complaint* had made him a celebrity.

'I want to see you again,' he said as he took my hand and kissed my cheek. I rummaged through my bag in the glow of the streetlights and, with a shaky hand, scribbled my number on a piece of paper I tore from my notebook. He folded the paper and put it in the pocket of his jacket. 'I'll call you,' he said.

The poet Luke Davies was staying on my couch at the time. We sat up late that night as I recounted my extraordinary evening blow by blow. We laid bets on whether I'd get the call and, if I did, how long it would take.

Luke was still asleep on the couch when Philip called two mornings later, inviting me to see Cleopatra's Needle and the saucer magnolias, which he said were in full bloom in Central Park. Luke watched as I danced around the room and then he helped me decide what to wear on a date to Cleopatra's Needle with Philip Roth. After a few false starts – too formal, too conservative, too casual – we settled on jeans, a cotton shirt in baby blue that showed just the right amount of cleavage – a lot – and my favourite Arche brown suede wedges.

'You're tall,' Philip said when he kissed me on the cheek. 'Good,' I thought.

The trees were laden with flowers, their branches drooping from the weight of their bright white and pink blossoms. We sat under an enormous arbour of cherry blooms and talked for some time. Every now and then a fan approached. Philip handled these sweet intrusions graciously. He asked the person where they came from and engaged in small talk.

He was warm and easy company. He seemed interested in what I had to say, but most importantly he made me laugh – doubled-over laughter.

A few days after our afternoon in the park, he took me to dinner at Eli Zabar's on the Upper East Side. He asked a question about my childhood and I told him about my father's polio.

'That's interesting,' he said. 'I'm writing a book about polio.' I was intrigued by his wanting to write a book about a topic that, as far as I could tell, hadn't directly touched his life.

He asked what it was like to grow up with a father in a wheelchair. 'I don't know,' I said. 'I haven't thought a lot about it.' I realised that, as true as it was, it sounded strange.

As we looked over the dessert menu – he ordered clementines that came whole and unpeeled in a large glass bowl – he asked if I would read his manuscript and comment on his portrayal of the disease. He insisted on us stopping off at his place on my way home so he could give me a copy of the manuscript. Not long after, he called me a limo and I was on my way home – fare paid – clutching a large manila envelope containing the manuscript of Philip Roth's final published work of fiction, *Nemesis*.

Philip had the disease exactly right. In fact, I learned things about polio from *Nemesis* that I had not known. I saw in the book a deep and profound humanity, which warmed me even more to its author.

It also made me think about my parents and their choices. In the novel, Bucky's sweetheart promises to stay by his side after his paralysis, but Bucky shuns her, believing he should not inflict his suffering upon another human being. He sees himself as unlovable because of what's happened to his previously athletic body. That single decision, based on the shame and anger at what's befallen him, those few words he utters to a stunned, devastated, loving girl, dictate the rest of Bucky's life. He lives alone, isolated and bitter.

My father did the opposite. He reclaimed his life the moment my mother presented herself as a willing participant at the side of his iron lung. In return, she got to be the saviour.

In *Nemesis*, I recognised a cautionary tale my father had avoided. I saw cowardice where my father had been brave, bitterness where he had been hopeful. In the midst of my own great leap into the unknown, my parent's story still signified nothing to me but wisdom and fortitude. The despair in Philip's creation could never touch me.

Thirty-six

My initiation to New York had been its own special kind of hell on account of my troubles at PEN and Jack deciding to stay in Australia, and I was still recuperating from the festival when my landlord notified me that he was selling my apartment.

Even though I now knew the city, it was daunting to go househunting in New York. My first apartment was lovely but, best of all, it was in the same building as my now very good friends. It was like *Friends*, we were always dropping in on each other, sharing meals or having a drink. The thought of losing them and the sense of security in having them close by was scary. But

I had no choice. Time was up. I had to stand on my own two feet now.

I decided to find a two-bedroom apartment. I reasoned that perhaps if Jack had a room of his own when he came to stay, he would be more likely to consider a move. I worried that he felt I had left Australia as a way to escape the responsibilities of single parenthood. He never said or implied such a thing, but it played on my mind. He'd already grown up without his father and I was sensitive to the feelings that absence left in your life, having felt the same myself. I did all I could to make it not so, but you can't change reality. I had, in fact, left him.

Of course my desire for him to move to New York was selfish too. I felt whole when Jack was with me. Parenting and being with Jack was never anything but a joy, even when I was working two jobs and we were dead broke, staying with friends on a mattress on the floor. I had always felt he was my reason for being. In a way we had grown up together. I felt ripped apart having him gone.

In the first days of my apartment search, I was taken to one hole after another – dark, cramped and noisy. At one there was a dead bird on the back step. I walked straight out.

In a moment of bad timing Jack had come to visit just when I had to be out of my apartment. Thankfully new friends allowed us to stay in their homes while they were travelling. New Yorkers are like that. It's a big city but people are staggering in their kindness.

I got a call to inspect a townhouse in Harlem I'd inquired about. It had looked gorgeous in the photos on the web: a fireplace, big windows, but even so I was suspicious. I'd seen enough to know how much can be done with a wide-angle lens and some lights. I told my friends I was going to see a place in Harlem; they warned me, 'You can't live there.'

When I arrived at the street it was cordoned off by police tape and two police cars. I thought maybe my friends had a point. I clutched my handbag, thinking, 'I've come this far,' and walked past the flashing lights. A man called out hello from his front stoop. I smiled and waved back even though it seemed like an odd encounter in the midst of a crime scene.

No one answered when I rang the doorbell of the townhouse. I went downstairs to the basement flat, which had an old bicycle chained to the bars on the windows. The door was beat-up and rubbish had collected in the foyer. My heart sank.

I was about to leave, but thought I should call the landlord, to make sure I was in the right place. The phone rang out and I thought, 'lucky escape'.

I started back towards the subway when someone called my name. I turned around and the landlord was standing on the stoop, waving me back.

'Sorry!' he yelled. 'I was outside. Didn't hear the phone or the door.'

Reluctantly, I turned back and went inside.

'You haven't come on the best day,' he said.

'No,' I thought to myself. 'There's obviously just been a murder.'

'There's a block party about to happen. Once a year the whole street gathers for an all-day celebration, that's all. That's why all the cop cars.' He waved his hand at a pile of wood off-cuts and plaster in the hallway at the bottom of the stairs. 'All this is going as soon as we finish the renovations,' he said.

We walked up to the second floor, light shining in through a domed skylight in the stairwell. He opened the door and I knew this was it. The apartment was filled with light. It had pressed tin ceilings and a pretty parquet floor. There was a large fireplace in the living room and another in the master bedroom, which itself was the size of a studio apartment. There'd been no trickery in the ad. This was even better than it had looked in the pictures. I'd found the place where everything could start again.

Not long after, Jack and I were unpacking boxes. I opened and closed the dishwasher ten times just to look inside it. I hadn't lived in a place with a dishwasher for more than a decade. We hung up my paintings and I felt like this was an all-new kind of home. A permanent home.

'I'm never leaving. You'll have to take me out in a box,' I joked to my new landlord, who looked like a cross between Ryan Gosling and Bradley Cooper. I felt the tides had finally changed. It seemed Jack was happy too. He said he wanted to stay. My gambit paid off.

Thirty-seven

I'd been in New York for three years when I took that run in Central Park and felt my legs go numb underneath me.

When I called my doctor early the next morning to make an urgent appointment, he told me to come straight in. An hour and a half later I was sitting in his office, recounting what had happened.

First he ordered an X-ray, thinking I might have a pinched nerve. When the results came back indicating there was nothing to be seen there, he called a colleague and an hour later I was recounting the same story to a neurologist, who then stuck my feet with safety pins. 'I'm sending you down for an MRI,' he said when

I couldn't feel the pricks. 'Wait here, I need to make a few calls to get you in.'

My emergency MRI appointment was squeezed into an already overbooked schedule and the nurses seemed none too pleased when I arrived.

'You'll have to wait,' one of them said gruffly from behind the reception counter.

'That's fine. The doctor warned me it could be a while. I'm grateful to you for fitting me in,' I said, trying to soften her.

I sat in the waiting room with its apricot-coloured walls and filled out another of the endless forms. Name, age, symptoms, date of last period . . .

I returned the clipboard and sat down again as an episode of *ER* came on the little television set in the corner. I watched as the patient suffering some acute trauma was rushed in on a gurney, blood pouring out of her, and realised it was making me anxious. Finding entertainment in someone else's medical ordeal was great at home, but watching it in a hospital in the middle of your own disaster is a very bad idea. It seemed an odd choice and I couldn't believe no one had changed the channel.

Eventually I was ushered in to have the MRI. I'd seen coffins up close. The only difference between this MRI machine and a coffin was the MRI had a sound system. No such indulgence for the dead.

The nurse told me to close my eyes. She put a round cotton pad on each lid and kept them in place with surgical tape. The room went black. She stuck ear plugs in my ears and fastened a cage around my head. Then she told me to relax and slid me into the tube. Beside my right ear was a speaker for the technician to speak to me from the control desk. There was a microphone for me to speak back or call out if I needed to. In my hand I clenched an emergency buzzer.

The machine itself pelted out an unrelenting cacophony of very loud clanks and bangs.

'You have to stop crying,' the technician said through the speaker. 'You are moving around too much. You are going to ruin the imaging. Calm down and try to stop crying,' he pleaded from his booth.

An MRI produces sound between 85 and 110 decibels. An ambulance siren is 120 decibels, a jackhammer 130. A rock concert is about 110. I tried to pretend I was back in my twenties, at a rave, going with the flow of the clanking in my ears, trying to forget that my eyes were strapped closed and my face secured by a white plastic cage so I couldn't lift my head. This was the scariest day of my life.

Finally the technician told me the nurse was coming in. I knew it was like failing an exam at school. I was the difficult one, the troublemaker. Always the one who couldn't sit still, who fidgeted and made trouble for the rest of the class.

The nurse grabbed my foot and started stroking it. I felt calm again, but then she started massaging my foot with more pressure, moving it forcefully in large circles. I knew she was annoyed with me.

At one point, her massage became so forceful that she began rotating not only my ankle but my entire right leg. I struggled against her from the knee down, worried that *she* was moving me too much, that the imaging would be ruined and they'd have to start again on account of her. At least this silent fight with her stopped me from crying.

They pulled me out of the machine an hour and fifteen minutes after they had begun. 'I never want to see you back in here without sedation,' the nurse said sternly.

How can you relax when you feel like you've been buried alive while being blasted with terrifying noise?

On the other side of the world, almost fifty years after my father's, I was having a catastrophic moment of my own. Overnight, life as I had previously known it lay shattered around my feet as if I'd walked through a plate glass window.

I knew from my father that one day you could be a sailor, the next a rag doll in an iron lung. But nothing prepared me for when the phone rang at 8 a.m. the day after my MRI.

The neurologist and I exchanged the very minimum of pleasantries. 'It doesn't look good,' he said.

'What does that mean?' I asked.

'Pack a bag, I'm admitting you,' he said. 'You have MS. I want to see you here in an hour.' He hung up the phone.

I walked back into the bedroom like a ghost and burst into heaving sobs.

I packed my bag in a daze. I was bewildered. Fear gripped my throat. What could this mean? Why hospital? Sure, I'd had that terrifying incident in the park, but I was functioning. My legs were numb but I didn't *feel* sick.

Some things are never easy to say – there's no good way to break up with a lover, for example. No softening words that will make the abandoned feel any better. Even so, I wondered if that phone call hadn't been a fairly callous way to tell someone she has an auto-immune disease that, in a few years, could put her in a wheelchair.

I pulled my little suitcase up to the neurology ward on the eighth floor of New York–Presbyterian. The words 'STROKE VICTIMS' were above the nurses' station.

I spent the next five days in a cotton hospital gown having every kind of test the doctors could think of performed on me. I was terrified. My friends visited and Philip, who was new to my life at that point, came too. His father had schooled him from a young age on the importance of paying visits to the sick. Philip often went with his father to the homes of Newark's infirm, to check in or drop off a meal prepared by his mother.

Always the dutiful son, Philip came to the hospital and called me a brave soldier. He told me jokes and made me laugh despite myself. When the doctors came on their rounds after his first visit, I commanded a new respect. Doctors who had previously answered my questions with no more than a dismissive wave of their hand were suddenly happy to actually engage me in conversation. Before Philip turned up, it often felt like the doctors didn't have time for the living, thinking part of their patient. It felt as though what they wanted to say was, 'Listen lady, just take your medicine. Alright? Trust me, I'm a doctor.'

Of course, doctors are busy people. There are many more patients like me in all the rooms along the corridor, and then even more sitting in the waiting room once they finish their rounds. And every one of us is needy. Every one of us is terrified. It must be exhausting and exasperating. How many times do you have to explain this stuff, which they won't understand anyway? I can see it from their side of things, but this is my life and I *do* have questions. Lots of them.

Once all the medical staff and visitors had left my bedside and I was lying there alone staring at the ceiling, all I could think about was Jack. I kept thinking of my relationship with my father, wondering how I would ever be able to tell Jack that he was about to become what I had always been: the child of a parent with a disability.

Shortly after I was discharged from the hospital I started receiving large parcels in the mail, pharmaceutical brochures written in sixteen-point type packaged with pens and DVDs. They depicted people 'just like me' peeling vegetables or packing their bag for a family holiday. Living their lives so fully with MS. At the cost of $2500 a month for a prescription, no small effort went into advertising and marketing these drugs.

I was suddenly being guided through life by a pharmaceutical copywriter. But my life was not peeling vegetables or going on family holidays with a container to dispose of medical sharps and a letter from my doctor explaining all the syringes in my hand luggage. I was meant to have a big, skidding-around-corners-and-grabbing-it-in-fistfuls kind of life. I was devastated to be contained by this. I had watched my father in that chair and decided from an early age to do all the dancing and living that he could not. I didn't want to sit down; I wanted to keep on with an outrageous adventure big enough for the both of us.

The neurologist's small waiting room had couches at either end and a row of chairs under the window. Whenever I went back for check-ups I'd take one look around that room – the bodies slumped over, people dozing, the wheelchairs, the chatting – and a fury came over me like a bleak storm.

Rather than join them, even in waiting, I chose to stand outside in the corridor until my name was called. I didn't want to be associated with those people in any way, certainly not by the one thing we all had in common.

A petite social worker sat in with the MS specialist as he delivered the final, no-doubt-about-it diagnosis. She sipped coffee from a Starbucks cup about the height of her face while trying to look sincere.

'It's not so bad,' the specialist said, pushing the Kleenex box across the table.

I only had one question. 'Will it make me stupid?'

I'd seen the MRI scans of my head with small white masses indicating where the disease had lodged itself. I envisioned my brain becoming like a sea sponge, holes eating away at my memory, my capacity for language, my intelligence.

'Probably not,' he said. 'But there are no promises with MS.'

No holding back the truth.

At least with polio, my father never had to worry about becoming an idiot. He was often the smartest person in the room. His mind was perfectly nimble and that's what saved him. That and his lust for life.

What hope did I have? As far as anyone could tell me, I could have a deadened body and a deadened mind. Worse still, while my father's sexual function was spared, the same would not be true for me. Once MS got me fully in its grip, chances were I'd be numb all over.

I am my father's daughter, yet all I could think was 'Why me?' I wanted to scream, '*This is not fair!*' Not so much because it happened to me, my adult self, but because it happened to me, my father's child. It wasn't just that I got sick, it was that I got sick after he'd already suffered so much. *I'd* suffered so much.

The neurologist scrawled the name of a psychiatrist on a pad and said my feelings were normal – that lots of people had trouble adjusting to a diagnosis like this. I realised then that the doctor's desk was as big and as deep as it was in order to keep distance between himself and people like me. I wanted to reach across the table to grab him by his stupid pink shirt, or by his even more ridiculous bow tie, and scream in his face that this wasn't about adjusting.

I wanted to get up close to his detached coolness and say through clenched teeth that I didn't need a shrink, I needed a loaded gun.

Instead, I sat politely in silence like a good middle-class woman. Fury boiled inside me. He stood up to reach across the desk and shake my hand, saying, 'I'll see you in two months.' I was dismissed.

The social worker opened the door for us. As we walked out into the hallway, a young woman walking with forearm crutches came lurching towards us. 'Fucking great,' I said audibly at the sight of her propelling herself along by a series of massive jerks and lunges. The social worker corralled me into her office, where I sat in the far corner with my arms and legs folded like twined ropes.

'You might want to consider a support group,' she said. 'Most people find them very useful and a great way to share feelings and experiences. It's important not to isolate yourself. Studies show that people with support do better.'

As a child, I had known this to be true. I had sought out people like Amanda and Uncle George's family to support and look after me. Yet to her, I said, 'I would rather shoot myself in the face.'

I wasn't a joiner at the best of times, but joining in with a group of strangers, united by nothing more than our disease, was the *last* thing I wanted. I didn't believe in the power of sharing. None of them would want to hear what I thought about having MS, anyway. I wouldn't inflict myself upon them. Support groups were all about coming to acceptance, going through a process and arriving at some state of peace. I didn't want that; I wanted to throw a hand grenade at the world.

Had the social worker heard my internal commentary, she would have underlined the notes I knew she was making about me. 'Not dealing with it very well.' That was right. I wasn't at my best by a long shot.

How could my father have been so accepting, so at peace with his terrible fate? I remembered all the times I'd asked him, 'Weren't you mad? Didn't you get angry?' I never truly believed his denials. I know now he wasn't pretending or putting on a good face. Acceptance is not something you can fake. Anger can't be hidden.

It seeps out of your pores like a toxic fume. I did pretty well at hiding the truth from my friends and colleagues, but for the people treating me I maintained no such charade. They got the full extent of my black and stinking fury.

Thirty-eight

About a year after my diagnosis, in 2010, Philip invited me to join him for weekends at his country home. For nearly every weekend over two summers I arrived Friday evening on the train with my little rolling suitcase, and his wonderful driver Pete, or Pete's son Reid, picked me up from the station and took me to the house, where a glass of wine and dinner were waiting.

I didn't cook when I was there. Philip enabled me to rest, and encouraged me to swim laps in his heated pool to keep up my strength. While he spent most of each day working in his studio, I had the run of the house. I used his laundry to do my washing, which I then draped over the bushes outside his kitchen door and on a small drying rack I set in the sun at the side of the house to keep it from view. I didn't like using the dryer for environmental reasons, but it also reminded me of home to smell sheets and clothes that had dried in the sunshine. Philip joked that I was turning his home into a trailer park but never insisted I use the dryer.

Philip looked after me. I didn't have to do anything when we were together. He planned where we'd eat and made the reservations, and when we were in the city, if he noticed I was tired, he ordered me a car service to take me home. If we stayed in to watch a ball game, he ordered and paid for our take-out. When my insurance no longer covered my physical therapy sessions, he sent me a cheque in the mail unannounced with a handwritten note that read, 'MERRY PHYSICAL THERAPY!'

For once in my life I needed someone else to take charge and he did it graciously, without making me feel coddled, disempowered or that I owed him anything in return.

Most of all, Philip made me laugh. It didn't matter how many times he told me a joke, I laughed as though it was the first time I'd ever heard it. He said I was like a goldfish who, by the time it had swum a lap round its small bowl of water, had forgotten what it had just seen and believed it to be all new again.

One day we pulled into the car park of the Stop & Shop supermarket and he started pronouncing it as 'Stop 'n' Shop'. Then he went on a tirade of riffs on all the novels that could be abbreviated that way. *War 'n' Peace*, *Crime 'n' Punishment*, *Sense 'n' Sensibility*. On he went, howling anew with every title. Philip always laughed at his own jokes but this one particularly tickled him. He had his head back against the headrest, laughing in full flight. He could be dark, but he also knew how to laugh. It didn't matter how bleak or desperate I was feeling, he could always bring me around.

Philip's country home in Connecticut was outside a small town called Sharon, which struck me as a strange name for a town. Somehow Warren, also close by, didn't seem so odd.

Philip fought hard for his privacy and for silence. In the city, he'd bought the apartments above and beside his and leased them to quiet tenants. In the country, he'd bought the land around the house's large parcel so he'd never have to worry about intrusions or disturbances from neighbours.

The country property was edged on one side by a dirt road, which we often took as a shortcut to Philip's favourite restaurant in town. Along the road, about a mile and a half from the house, there was a bridge over a little stream. One day I told Philip I was going to try to walk there.

'Watch out for bears,' he called over his shoulder from the computer desk in his studio.

'I'll call you if I meet one,' I said.

The road was rarely used except by a handful of locals, so I was a little worried about the bears. Once I'd told Philip I was brought up watching Yogi Bear and consequently didn't really believe bears were dangerous. He took my hand and walked me out to the roadside trash can to show me the holes in the lid, which looked like someone had made them with a shotgun but were in fact from bear claws. 'Does that clear things up for you?' he asked.

It was a cool but sunny day and I was thrilled to be out, feeling good about being strong enough to attempt this walk. The walk was beautiful, the sounds of the stream running alongside the road and the chirping birds. The woods were dense, green and fecund, so different from Australia and still a novelty to me. When I reached the bottom of the hill I sat on the bridge's metal railing, watching the water fall over the edge of a pond and down into a smaller, light-speckled stream that ran over mossy rocks.

Almost as soon as I started back up the hill my right leg began to drag. I had to stop every fifty metres. Once the dragging began it couldn't right itself. The lower half of my right leg felt as if a heavy weight was strapped to it. I stumbled a few times.

Halfway up the hill, I lay down on the road, sobbing. I wished a car would come around the corner and end it all. I began crawling along the road on my hands and knees. Finally, when the road flattened out at the top of the hill, I managed to walk again. I made it back to the studio where Philip was working. When he turned from the computer to greet me, he saw I was a mess.

He sat me down on the leather couch under the window and I blubbered, 'I hate this fucking disease!' I punched my leg with my fist.

'I know, I know,' he said with his arm around my heaving shoulders. He said the hill was steep and that when he used to run it, he'd found it hard going. He was trying to comfort me, but I couldn't be consoled. I was undone.

'It's here and it's now,' he said. 'You have to focus on that. It's here and it's now. Nothing else.' And those words did help. *It's here and it's now.* They have become my silent mantra whenever my illness overwhelms me.

Philip taught me about baseball and we watched many games – him sitting in his Eames chair, me lying on the couch with my shoes off. He'd used Joe Girardi, the Yankees' manager and former catcher, as a model for Bucky's physique in *Nemesis*, and I came to love the game as he explained its nuances to me.

For three years we spoke on the phone two or three times a day and often saw each other three or four nights a week, when he was in the city or I joined him for weekends in the country. I had my own room at both his apartment and his house in the country, and I climbed into bed with him most mornings if he wasn't already up before me. I used to like resting my ear on the hard metal of the implanted defibrillator that sat just below the skin of his chest. We talked and sometimes he made up stories or told me jokes. Then we went to the kitchen and he poured himself a bowl of Great Grains while I made toast. I always thought cereal was for children, but he loved Great Grains – just like a little boy would.

Philip's first defibrillator had pride of place in the kitchen. When he first handed it to me I twirled the smooth metal disc in my palm. I almost dropped it when he told me what it was. He thought it was hilarious and, eventually, I came to appreciate it too and often picked it up and held it in my hand.

During the summer of 2011, after having publicly announced he was done with writing, Philip started behaving oddly. It wasn't that his behaviour was out of character, it was that it was exactly in character – when he was writing.

'What are you up to?' I said jokingly after about a week of him heading to the studio with the purpose of a man up to something.

'Nothing, nothing,' he said, waving his hand in the air as he went out the front door and disappeared until lunchtime.

Whenever I went into the studio he was at the computer, working. Over time I noticed a growing pile of typed pages stacked neatly on the desk where he sat to read and write correspondence and to pay bills. Still he insisted it was nothing. 'I quit writing!' he exclaimed. 'Didn't you see? It's all over the papers.'

Then, over a number of days and weeks, I saw him carry into the studio a succession of large black trash bags from one of the sheds he kept locked with a large padlock. Whenever I went in to see him he'd be seated on a chair surrounded by the contents of one of the bags, which seemed to be filled with a mixture of papers, medical records, old chequebooks and diaries.

Still he insisted he wasn't up to anything.

During that winter ice got in under the eaves and the whole house was flooded. While the extensive repairs were taking place Philip was sleeping in my room and I was out in the studio. During the months of this mystery – him clearly up to something, and no small thing as far as I could tell – his mood was darkening.

One day, as I walked from the bathroom to the bed in the studio's back room, I noticed on his desk that the ever-growing pile of pages now had a cover page and a title: *Notes for my Biographer*. I was terrified. I had already been worrying that none of this was going to end well. I'd read *Exit Ghost*; I knew what he was capable of. I was convinced he was planning to kill himself.

I could have flipped that title page and read what followed, but I never did. Instead I pleaded incessantly with him to tell me what he was planning. I watched him like a hawk, ready to intercept whatever his macabre plan for his exit might be.

Finally I asked him straight. 'Are you planning to kill yourself? Is that what all this is about?'

He laughed and laughed, but by now I didn't think it was funny. All I could think was that in his very meticulous Philip Roth way he was working towards suicide. It would be *Exit Ghost* for real. 'Okay, okay,' he said. 'I promise I'll show you soon.'

A few weeks later, he handed me the manuscript *Notes for My Biographer*. 'Take it,' he said, holding out the stack of pages held together by a large rubber band. 'I want you to read it.'

The book was a rebuttal to Claire Bloom's *Leaving a Doll's House*, Philip's ex-wife's account of their marriage, which was published in 1996. Many of the stories he'd already told me. He'd talked a lot to me about both Claire and his first wife, Margaret Martinson.

So some of it was not new, but all of it was upsetting. Philip's manuscript was the saddest thing I'd ever read. I read three or four different drafts and most of my feedback encouraged him to write the good with the bad. 'No one will believe you if you don't admit at one point you loved her. Be the gracious one.'

Philip wanted the book published. But no one would touch it for fear of the lawsuit Bloom might bring against them. At one point we discussed the idea of Philip offering to pay any damages arising from a legal case brought by Claire. More than anything Philip wanted to put the record straight. I wanted for him to be able to put the record straight. I knew how forcefully he'd been struck and blindsided by *Leaving a Doll's House*. After its publication, Philip told me *New York* magazine published a photo of him on its front cover with the word 'MISOGYNIST' written across it. Philip went into hiding.

I never bought or read another copy of that magazine after he told me that. How could it be that he could be attacked so viciously by Bloom and a magazine editor but had no right of reply? Surely whatever money it might cost him was worth it to have his side of the story told. To me, knowing him as I did and having seen the documentation – the bags and bags of it, the medical files, the chequebooks – I believed him.

But finally all options were exhausted and he had to let it go. He kept two copies of *Notes for My Biographer*. Every other copy – and there were many of them – I collected from under his desk in the studio and put into trash bags. Pete loaded them into the trunk of the Volvo and drove us and them back to the city, where I collected the remaining copies and then threw them all down the trash chute in the apartment building. The last I knew, one copy of *Notes for My Biographer* was with Philip's lawyer, locked in a safe in Connecticut, the other, as the title would suggest, was with his biographer.

Thirty-nine

Just as there is no definitive test for MS, there is also no sure-fire way to predict its course. No one even really knows what causes it. My doctors couldn't say for sure how helpful the preventative medication I was taking would be. Nonetheless, I had to self-administer daily injections that left dark bruises on my skin.

My father taught me to face hard facts straight. There was no sugar-coating it: my future was completely unknown.

From an early age, I understood that life is chaotic – one day you could wake up and find everything gone to hell. I had always lived with urgency and hunger. Now I knew why.

Open your eyes and you can always see someone worse off than you. I was in my forties when I was diagnosed. Many people contract MS in their twenties. I had left PEN for a good job running The New York Public Library's centennial celebrations. I had great friends, I was living in New York. My feelings for the American writer had lost their headiness over time but I had somehow struck up an intimate friendship with Philip Roth, and that's where my attentions were. Jack was with me. By any standard I still had much to be grateful for.

But I couldn't summon up any enthusiasm. Somewhere down the track I would be living a life I'd never chosen or wanted. It made the thought of going on unbearable.

Over the years my mother's attempted suicide had me thinking a lot about what drives someone to take their own life. The man who found Mark Rothko dead in his apartment mopped up the artist's blood with towels. Rothko took razor blades to the veins in his elbows and bled himself out of life, the blood oozing onto the floor like his big, pulsing, moaning paintings. Life in red and black and then just the still and stop.

I have made a living of being very good at details – I knew I wouldn't make a misstep – but I would never do that to Jack. I could never leave him so cruelly, but I have to admit that in the days and months following my diagnosis I stopped caring about daily life and thought about how easy it would be to accidentally slip onto the subway tracks.

When I was still living in Sydney I returned to London once, to revisit the haunts of my youth, and looked out on the Hampstead High Street to see a man in his late fifties crawling on his hands and knees in the middle of the road. It was clear from his fine suit that he was a Hampstead resident with a lot of money. Cars were honking and driving around him and he was swerving in his slow crawl to try to get in their way.

Everyone was watching, but no one was acting on the scene that was playing out in front of us. I walked over to him in the middle of the road, standing with my arms outstretched as cars swerved around me. I was trying to stop the traffic and yelled for the people standing aghast on the footpath to call the police.

'Let me die,' the man pleaded, looking up from the bitumen.

'No,' I said. 'I won't. Not here, not like this.'

'Please, leave me alone,' he said politely. 'I just want to die. My life is nothing. Just leave me.'

'You have to get up,' I said more softly. I bent over to get eye-level with him. 'Please.'

Still he refused. I continued talking to him but he wouldn't budge. I hitched up my dress, saying a silent farewell to my new fishnet stockings, and told him, 'Well then I am going to crawl along here with you.'

It turned out the man had lost his wife to divorce and his kids were gone too. He could see no end to the sadness. He begged me to let him be delivered.

'What you are doing,' I said, 'is not fair. Some poor person hits you in the middle of this goddamn street and their life is ruined as well. I'm just going to crawl along here with you until you stop.'

Finally the police made it through the traffic. I was relieved of my post by an officer, who eventually led the man into a police car while the other questioned me.

I often wonder whether that man finally saw his way to end it or if he was able to forget that dark day on the sunny High Street.

I thought of a line from the poet Philip Larkin about death:

Not to be here,
Not to be anywhere,
And soon; nothing more terrible, nothing more true.

Larkin had also said, 'Beneath it all, desire of oblivion runs.'

On the tube home to my hotel a few hours later, I began to shake from shock.

Often I think our children know more about us than we give them credit for. As parents, we think we know them the best, but I'm not sure the opposite isn't the case.

I tried to hide from Jack the desperate thoughts I was having about my situation and diagnosis. As best I could, I put on a cheerful face and tried to make everyone believe I was doing better than I was. I think I was pretty convincing, but there was no hiding anything from Jack. He saw right through it and I watched as he hovered and kept an eye on me. I knew he was doing everything in his power to make sure I didn't act.

Forty

When it comes to facing change and challenges, I'm cut from the same cloth as my father. I run from comfort. But I couldn't immediately find peace with my illness in the way he had. MS was never the adventure I pictured for myself. My father may have seen his diagnosis as something interesting but I already knew exactly what it meant, how much suffering was involved, not only for the person facing the disease but for those around them.

The nurse who came to my house to start me on the new medication told me, 'This medicine for you to inject three times a week is made from the uteruses of Chinese hamsters.' She couldn't understand why that made me laugh and I only stopped when she took hold of my wrist and said, 'Oh, don't worry, they're not really Chinese.' Like that was my problem with it – the nationality of the rodents whose uteruses I'd be injecting for the rest of my life.

Those hamster's uteruses made me sick for twenty-four hours each time I injected them into my muscles. They stopped my periods and made me fat. Addled by the medication, sick three days out of seven, I was so desperate I actually began to think about how I could kill myself. Putting the bigger question about Jack aside, I knew it wouldn't be difficult to get myself admitted to the hospital again, where I'd inject myself with enough heroin – which I could easily get hold of on the streets of New York – to put myself to sleep for good. God knows the injecting part of it wasn't a problem anymore. Killing myself in a hospital was a genius plan. I didn't want anyone to have to deal with my dead body. I wanted trained professionals to find me, just a short gurney-ride to the morgue.

For three twenty-four-hour periods a week I had debilitating, flu-like muscle aches and blinding headaches. I felt like I was looking at life through a blackened lens. If I had been convinced that the pain, the bleakness and discomfort of the medication was keeping my MS at bay, perhaps I could have stuck it out. But it wasn't. My symptoms were worsening.

When I called to talk to someone from the pharmaceutical provider about the side effects, it didn't improve my mood.

'Hello and welcome to 1800-Special-Pharmacy-Services. Your unique ID number is 399 997. Please memorise it or keep it in a safe place – you'll need it at all times.

'We would much prefer you to think of your ID number simply as a random computer-generated figure. However, you probably know it is not. That's right! There are 399 996 sick people just like you on our medication. Don't do the math for what that makes us worth because the numbers will blow your infirm mind.

'I'm sorry, patient 399 997, would you mind if I put you on hold for a moment?

'Hello? Are you still with me? I apologise for keeping you waiting for thirty-three minutes and fifteen seconds. I hope you enjoyed the music and hearing our special infomercial however many times we've inflicted it upon you during your wait. Did those inspiring testimonials from John, Judy and Harry make you feel like you too can still achieve great things despite your recent diagnosis? Isn't it amazing that Judy went on a cruise all by herself! See, you can do it! Chin up.

'Now, what were you saying? I'm sorry, the line seems to be breaking up. It sounded like you said you were having trouble with your medication. I think we must have a bad connection. Surely I must have misheard the bit about severe and debilitating depression. Did I hear thoughts of suicide? Oh, this really is a terrible line.

'I have to say you are sounding a little agitated now. Really, if I can offer a little advice, just entre nous – *that's* not good for you. You should really try to keep that in check.

'Okay, I understand you've done everything we told you to do, exactly as we told you to do it, and you're still having trouble. Have you talked to your doctor about all this?

'No? Not yet? Good! Yes, I understand, it takes three months to get an appointment with your specialist and you read in our brochure that we're open from 8 a.m. to 10 p.m. EST and there's always a nurse on call. I'm glad you took the initiative. That's a very good sign.

'Well, yes. All our health professionals are on the payroll and it's true it was a bit of a revolving door of nurses a while ago. Apparently some of them felt working for us compromised their Florence

Nightingale pledge. I can assure you, though, that since unemployment hit double digits, no one's made any mention of Florence!

'Now, what did you say your little side effects were? Hair loss, depression, thoughts of suicide, fatigue, nausea. And you haven't had a period in how long? Oh dear. I mean, well, that's in the range. Now, let's see . . .

'Sorry? And your symptoms don't seem to be improving either? You read what? Now really, 399 997, you shouldn't go worrying yourself with so-called "facts" and silly statistics. They'll just get you in a muddle. Leave all that to us.

'You can't go getting yourself all in a flap about scientific research that says our very expensive medication doesn't actually work. Like I said, getting stressed out is really not good for someone with your condition. At any rate, I'm told that scientist is quite shady – he's Italian, you know – and you know how easy it is to put things up on the World Wide Web. There's all sorts of harmful misinformation out there from people trying to take advantage of vulnerable people like yourself. I can't tell you how simple it is to pull the wool over people's eyes.'

I stopped calling and went cold turkey. I didn't care if being off my medication meant that my symptoms worsened. Nobody could tell me if the medication worked anyway. It could well have been slowing things down, but from my point of view while my trouble walking was getting worse, these MS symptoms were much easier to handle than depression and chronic flu.

I decided that life was today, not what it might be in three years. The medication might help me in the future, but what was the point of that if every day between now and then was a living hell? It's here and it's now.

Forty-one

Before he was scheduled for back surgery in 2012, Philip took me through instructions should anything go wrong, the names and numbers of all the people I'd need to call to put things in train. Philip was exact, practical and unsentimental in almost everything he did. At the bottom of the second page was information about his insurance policies – housing, life and various others, then the words 'Umbrella Insurance'.

I started laughing. 'Only you!' I screeched. 'Only you!'

'What do you mean?' he asked, perplexed.

'Umbrella insurance! Who gets umbrella insurance?' I said,

laughing, and acted out a skit of him losing his umbrella and filing a claim.

Explaining that it was an insurance policy covering excess liability, he laughed heartily, repeating my words to him. 'Only you! Only you!' he howled right back.

The next morning the laughter continued in the back seat of the taxi as we drove through the empty streets to the hospital. It eased some of the foreboding we both felt.

Philip used to say old age is 'a massacre'. It was. Of course, I was in the midst of a massacre all of my own.

Eventually his needs and mine collapsed under their own weight and the 'we' that we had been ended.

Before that, though, I could arrive at Philip's apartment any time I felt defeated by the battle, take my shoes off, lie on his couch and cry. He'd put an alpaca-wool blanket over me and bring me a glass of wine. We'd talk and he'd bring me out of my despair with practical advice, jokes and anecdotes.

When we were in the country together we listened to Susan Kennedy's Big Band Hall of Fame on WMNR each Saturday night. He sang along to Frank Sinatra and the Andrews Sisters and quizzed me about the tracks. Sometimes we danced.

Forty-two

One bright afternoon, walking along 116th Street about six months after giving up on the medication, I took a spectacular fall. Senegalese men in long elegant robes were standing on the footpath selling spices and cheap suitcases held together with chains and padlocks. Distorted music blared out onto the street through bad speakers.

I was watching a little girl skipping beside her mother. Sure enough, the moment I was distracted, my foot dragged and caught the pavement. I went down hard, smashing the three wine bottles I was carrying home for a dinner party – the first I'd hosted in a very long time.

People came out of their shops. One kind man sat me in a chair, handing me paper towels for the blood. The little girl I'd been watching ran up to see if I was okay. I told her I was. She asked to see the gash under the wad of blood-soaked towels.

'You don't want to look at it. It's pretty disgusting.'

'Yes, I do,' she said so enthusiastically I almost complied with her demand.

I hobbled home deeply shaken. The illness was now really showing itself. The day before, in an act of self-regard, I had bought myself some expensive new clothes, which I was wearing when I fell. I hadn't bought clothes since before my diagnosis. These were now ruined.

The doctors had told me exercise was important. I knew it was true, but I felt so defeated I'd given up on everything. In my previous life, I'd run between six and ten miles three times a week. I did yoga. I was strong and fit. Now I was fat, my hair was falling out and I was about as out of shape as you could be.

I didn't want to go out. I didn't want to see people. I didn't want to talk or think about being sick. I didn't tell many people about my illness, only those I truly trusted, which wasn't many. As much as I loved my friends, when I was with people the subject always came up and I simply wanted to forget. I hated the question 'How are you?' It came from a good place and people asked because they cared, but what could I say? That I wanted to kill myself?

The social worker had said that patients with strong support networks do better than those without. I had a wonderful network of friends, who would have done anything for me, despite us being fairly new friends, but instead I isolated myself.

Why bother when there is not a thing in the world you can do to change what's happening to you? I had spent my life controlling things – I'd made a career of meticulously accounting for every and any possibility. I was ahead of problems before they happened and, when they did happen, I was a great fixer. But here I was in my own crisis, dealing with a body that had a mind of its own, and there was not a thing I could think to do.

But from somewhere in all that darkness came a small but significant voice, 'Pull yourself together.' It was my father's legacy taking control.

As fate would have it, I happened to be walking past a physical therapy studio two blocks from my apartment. Almost without realising what I was doing, I found myself inside, talking to the receptionist.

'Play your best hand with whatever cards you've got,' my father said. It was a good lesson.

When I asked if I could make an appointment, she inquired about my ailment.

'I have Multiple Sclerosis,' I stammered and began to cry. Saying those words to a stranger still filled me with shame.

'Okay,' she said matter-of-factly and made me an appointment for the following day.

I almost cancelled, but I dug out my old running shoes and track pants to arrive at the appointed time. Sam, the young Indian therapist, took notes as we talked. Again, I cried when I said the words to identify my disease. I explained how I'd taken a big fall and now could hardly make it around the block without my leg dragging. He explained his methods and we got to work. I was incredibly weak and out of shape. Just supporting my own body weight made my legs shake and my arms wobble.

Very early on Sam put me on the treadmill. I'd never used one before. I'd always been of the mind, why run on a treadmill when you can run outside? I found it extremely disconcerting and difficult even to walk on. I was so bad at it that Sam had to connect me up to the safety clip so I wouldn't fall off the back end of it like a slapstick Lucille Ball. After that first attempt, I was nervous to go on it again.

Sam steadily increased the intensity of my routine, working on different areas of weakness and pushing me hard. When I was lazy or feeling defeated, he told me straight that I was copping out. He made me fight when I wanted to give up. He had me doing side planks – an exercise on the floor where I lay on my side and lifted my hips off the ground. Since my right leg can't support my weight, I devised a procedure that involved bracing my feet up against Sam's stainless-steel refrigerator. Once my hips were raised off the ground, I had to hold the position and lower my free arm to the ground fifteen times.

MS has only affected the right side of my body, so while I could eventually do the routine on my left side, it was nearly impossible to get off the ground on my right. Sam always had to squat down beside me and lift me up off the ground. It was embarrassing. I hated him feeling my weight and lifting me, but he did it every time – until one day I got up all on my own. The other patients cheered and I could see that Sam was proud. I was proud. It was a huge achievement.

Sam worked with three or four patients at a time. For many months, I was the only white person there. Most of the other patients were elderly people who'd moved to Harlem from the South.

We were a motley broken crew, but we cheered each other on in our battles against our ailments. An elderly gentleman, Mr Jones, who'd had a stroke and a knee replacement, was one of my favourite work-out companions. We didn't talk a lot, but he was always happy to see me, and I him. We encouraged each other when we battled to master a new exercise and cheered when we got through a difficult one.

There was an unspoken rule in the studio that we didn't discuss our ailments. Sometimes it was obvious, but generally we respected each other's privacy. But one day Mr Jones was doing his stretches and asked me why I was there. 'You're so young,' he said.

'I've got MS,' I said on all fours, lifting my leg up with a four-pound weight around my ankle.

'I'm so sorry.'

'It's okay,' I said and kept on with my routine.

About ten minutes later, I approached him while he was resting between exercises. 'I want to thank you,' I said.

'Why? I shouldn't have asked you that question. It's none of my business.'

'I want to thank you because that's the first time I have uttered those words, "I've got MS", without crying.'

Every week I'd watched as he struggled to make himself better. Against every impediment, he was still punching, still fighting. I just had MS to contend with. I was a disgrace.

It's ironic, given my reaction to the social worker who suggested I find a support group, that I had done just that in a typically roundabout way. As far as I knew, I was the only person with MS at Sam's studio. His other patients were mostly struggling with injuries or recovering from surgery. Ailments that would get better with rehabilitation and time. I was only going to get worse over time. Even so, these people became my support group. We didn't discuss our feelings, our hopes or dreams. We simply worked at getting better. The social worker had been right: people in support groups do better.

I saw so many feats of bravery in that studio. It didn't matter how much I didn't want to turn up sometimes, I always left feeling inspired.

Harvey was a large man in his sixties whose right leg was amputated just below the hip. His young assistant pushed him in his wheelchair into the studio. Behind them she trailed a large bag the shape and size of a boxer's punching bag. I overheard Harvey explain that he hadn't used his prosthetic leg in some time, while his aide pulled out the ugly contraption from the bag.

When they tried to attach the leg to Harvey's stump, it became clear just how long the intervening period had really been. Harvey couldn't remember which straps were meant to go where and since he'd relied on his chair for such a long time, he'd gained a lot of weight. His stump no longer fit into the eggcup-shaped plastic mould, which attached to the steel rod that had a very rudimentary black shoe on the end of it.

For half an hour they struggled to get the straps in order and to fit Harvey's stump into the mould. When he stood up, his fat flesh oozed out over the edge. Finally, it looked like it was all ready and he tried to manoeuvre the leg into a step, but somehow, after the confusion of the preparation, the foot was facing backwards. I was trying not to stare, but I was transfixed.

Everything was repositioned so the foot faced forwards, but just as Harvey took his first step, a bracket underneath the cup snapped. Harvey sat back down in his chair, sweating and defeated, while Sam looked for a screwdriver to fix the bolts. In the end they all agreed that Harvey needed to go back to the hospital to have the prosthetic resized and adjusted. His assistant put the leg back in its bag and they left as they'd arrived, the leg dragging in its bag behind them.

A few weeks later they came back with a new, equally ugly but better-fitting leg. It still took four of them to get the leg on, but I watched as Harvey took his first steps and cheered as he walked slowly across the room, more or less on his own. Each of the people in that place were fighting different battles, but we were quietly united in our support for each other. I could hold on to a thumbs up from one of my fellow patients for days.

Going to Sam made me fitter, stronger and happier. My appointments with him were often the high point of the week.

I slowly began to feel better as the medications got out of my system. With the combination of stopping the drugs and working out with Sam, weight fell off. My mood lightened. I remember walking down the street one day and suddenly realising I felt cheerful. It struck me because I hadn't felt uncomplicated lightness like that for some time.

I felt that happiness again when Jack finally decided to move to New York permanently in June of 2012. I had my old purpose back. I could be a mother again. With Jack present I had to pull myself together and remember that it wasn't all about me and my woes.

I went back to my specialist to tell him I'd stopped taking the medication. He wasn't pleased but understood my reasoning. We discussed alternatives.

I was running out of medical options. There were two highly effective new drugs on the market, but both had pretty frightening side effects. The odds were slim, but a one-in-10 000 chance of permanent brain damage wasn't a risk I wanted to gamble on. My doctor thought I was taking it too seriously, but since I'd had extreme reactions to everything I'd been on so far, it didn't seem out of the question that I could be that one in the 10 000. Somebody had to be.

In the end, I ignored the nurse's urgent messages. The thought of injecting myself again made me nauseated. The thought of becoming brain dead was worse. I wouldn't do any of it.

Once, sitting in my doctor's office, while he asked questions and tapped my answers into the computer, barely looking at my face, I was reminded of the movie *The Doctor*, which is based on Edward Rosenbaum's autobiography *A Taste of My Own Medicine*. The movie version stars William Hurt as a smug surgeon, who keeps his patients at arms-length, the same as every doctor I had dealt with since my diagnosis. One day, after coughing up blood, he is diagnosed with throat cancer. Suddenly it's him walking along the fluoro-lit corridor of the oncology ward with his arse showing through the hospital gown. He's lost the power and he knows what the experience on the other side of the scalpel is like. Now it's him who is scared to death.

As my doctor tapped results into his computer, I wished he could have a taste of this.

Sam never treated me like the doctors did. He made me work and he made me fight. He helped me take control again.

I was feeling particularly strong one day and asked Sam if I could try the treadmill again. It had been six months since my first, disastrous attempt, so he set me up with the safety clip on in case I fell.

I began walking with long confident strides and then, after he left the room, I slowly started running. Soon I was running almost like I used to, with my arms and ponytail swinging. There's a mirror in front of the treadmill in the studio so patients can watch their form. I was watching mine and it wasn't too bad. I'd been told my running days were over and I had believed it. When Sam came back into the room he saw my face in the mirror and I saw his. I was crying and he was beaming. I put my head down and focused on my next steps.

All Sam's training, all my hard work, meant on days when I was feeling strong – not every day by any means, but on those days – I *could* trust my legs to do what they were meant to do. They could be where they were meant to be, even if I couldn't particularly feel them. Some days I could feel them, but on the days I couldn't, I got on the treadmill and ran from memory.

Forty-three

I'd had MS for four years when Paul LeClerc at Columbia University asked me to set up and run a literary festival in Paris. My health had stabilised on a new medication, but friends worried about the toll the necessary travel and another gruelling festival would take on my health.

I'd recently read Salman's memoir *Joseph Anton* and was reminded of the quote he cited from Joseph Conrad's *The Nigger of Narcissus*: 'I must live until I die, mustn't I?' Salman thought that when he was under the fatwa. I feel it with MS. I must live until I die.

Or as my acupuncturist so clearly put it one day, as she stuck me with pins, 'It's not how long you live, Caro. It's how well.'

Finally, after four years of anger and struggle, I had to question my fear of this condition. I had never been stopped before by anything, no matter how daunting or difficult. I had a baby at twenty-three, was a single mum at twenty-four. I had moved countries twice, this last time at forty. My life had not been sheltered and nothing much – not my lack of education, or money, or the fact that I had a kid to look after on my own – ever stopped me if I set my mind to it. Yet I had allowed myself to be utterly undone by this. I was stuck.

I had lived my life denying that my father's disability had been a big deal. I had idealised his life and let that shield me from all of his suffering.

I was an observant child. I watched quietly as people stood beside my father, speaking to him slowly and deliberately, assuming his mind was as paralysed as his body. Telling him over and over to accept his position. 'Give in to it', 'be realistic', 'be happy with what you've got'.

By the world's thinking, he should have accepted that he couldn't get a university degree because he couldn't get into the lecture halls on account of the steps. Accepted that he couldn't take a job he was qualified for because no one would push him around to meetings in his wheelchair, or because he couldn't lift his hands to push the elevator button or open the heavy doors to the entrance of the building to get inside in the first place. 'Give it up, Rich. You can't change the system.'

I had always focused on his defiance, his resilience; he had made it all look so easy. He didn't talk to us about the frustrations, the hopelessness, the anguish of being pitied. Each of us took away different lessons. But I learned to keep moving.

I had to stop thinking about the what ifs, what my future might look like if the MS meant I could no longer work. Those musings are a losing game. They're too overwhelming and get you nowhere.

I have to constantly remind myself that there is absolutely no point grinding myself into misery, wondering what might happen. Most importantly I have to remind myself I am not to blame. My father's story about helping the woman with the luggage suited him and his needs well. But I don't want to feel responsible. Blaming myself is what I had always been taught to do. I say sorry more than any other person I know. But I did not bring MS upon myself.

So when Paul called me to say he had the green light for the festival in Paris, I said yes without hesitation.

Two weeks later, with my schoolgirl French, I was on my way. For the next eight months, I flew to Paris every six weeks and generally stayed for two, except in the lead-up to the actual event, when I stayed for a month and a half.

Whenever I was in Paris, I lived in a beautiful studio apartment in Reid Hall. I made friendships that will be lifelong and came to know Montparnasse as my own. Reid Hall has a resident black cat called Yuki, which means 'snow' in Japanese, and she became my companion late at night. She'd jump on the roof and slink in through my bathroom window or meow so loudly at my front door that I had to get up and let her in.

Jack flew to Paris to help me and stayed the month of the festival. He knew instinctually how it all worked. He came in and made things happen when others had stalled on them, yet his French consisted of no more than being able to say hello and ordering a coffee. It was something to witness.

I have my father to thank for whatever professional success I've had in this business. From an early age, I had to think about whether there was a ramp at the end of the pavement. We couldn't just walk along the street, we had to know whether my father would be able to get off the footpath to cross the road. I can't put a writer on stage without having thought through and considered all the potential problems. I never wanted my father to be uncomfortable; I don't want that for anyone I work with either.

I strongly suspect that MS is a lifestyle disease, that stress is the underlying, essential link in a chain that eventuates in late-onset MS like mine. I believe you can have any number of what they think are the contributing factors – low levels of vitamin D, et cetera – but it's long and sustained stress that brings everything together to launch the body's attack on itself. I've been stressed my whole life. In fact, I think being highly stressed was my normal state.

Eventually, quite simply, stress took its inevitable toll. My body said, 'Enough.' Most doctors will dispute this, and the research into the link between stress and MS has produced contradictory and unclear results, but then again they have no real idea what *does* cause MS.

Every day we watch on as our bodies betray us and the medical profession has few, if any, answers.

Since my diagnosis, I've been the patient of at least five different neurologists. I've injected myself hundreds of times with different kinds of prescribed medications. At various moments these drugs made my hair fall out, caused me to become fat, sick, depressed, suicidal and, on occasion, all five things at once. The scars on my arms, legs, stomach and back from one injectable medication will be etched on my body forever.

In 2012, America's National Institutes of Health issued a total of 325 individual grants amounting to more than $115 million for Multiple Sclerosis research. In addition to the NIH, in the fall of 2011, the MS Society announced $45.2 million in new funding. Projects included 'explorations of new approaches to promote nervous system protection and repair; a clinical trial of a training technique to enhance cognitive function; and a study looking at how common bacteria that live in the human body might trigger immune attacks on the nervous system in MS'.

All to say, there's a lot of money being poured into MS research. And yet as everyone in the MS business reluctantly has to admit, there are no cures on the horizon and no definitive answers.

All but one of my neurologists has tried to calm me as the disease grabs me harder in its grip with the words 'this is the best possible time to have MS'. Of course that's true – no one would argue a return to earlier treatments – yet we are still very much in the dark.

My three-monthly check-ups with my specialists mostly consist of them asking me to jump on one leg, then the other. I walk heel–toe, heel–toe, along the corridor in a straight line, without stumbling or falling. I have to walk as fast as I can along a printed strip in the carpet while I am timed with a stopwatch. My arms and legs are stuck with safety pins. A tuning fork is banged on a hard surface and placed on my feet and hands to see how long I feel the vibrations. I have to touch my nose with my finger and then reach out to touch the doctor's index finger, which he moves around in front of my face.

Of course, these simple exercises reveal some deep neurological truths, but they often feel pointless. It's hard to feel any enthusiasm for my regular appointments. I know on my own, without expensive tests, whether I can feel my legs or not. I know when I can hardly drag myself out of bed in the morning or when I want to do nothing other than sleep all day.

One of the medications I was prescribed – a brand-new addition to the suite of MS drugs approved by the FDA – was originally used to treat sofas against mould. It costs $4700 a month and yet no one – not my doctor nor the drug manufacturer – could tell me how or why this drug might work to slow MS.

Until I happened upon my current specialist, Dr Erik Charlson, a miraculous human being at NYU Langone, any time I asked a doctor for more than the most rudimentary explanation of my condition, or how the medicines work, I was more often than not dismissed with a wave of annoyance. Only Dr Charlson has had any patience when I've researched alternative theories (not all of them insane) or treatments and posited them for us to discuss. Even if it's only to discover their irrelevance or wrongheadedness, I value the opportunity to talk about the mystery we're both grappling with.

Dr Charlson was the only doctor to explain the science behind why there could be no direct connection between my father's condition and mine. Of course my father's polio loomed large in my mind and I'd asked each of my doctors about it. Mostly they scoffed. Now, for the first time, someone explained how the polio virus's effect on my father's body could not have had a genetic impact on me. While my father and I might have shared genetic weaknesses that made us susceptible to such diseases, Dr Charlson assured me I wasn't predisposed to MS on account of my father's polio.

All specialists believe they are at the cutting edge of whatever research they're involved in and offering their patients the very best of what's available. Each of them is bringing all their knowledge, ability, creativity and vision to the search for better solutions. But they are only human: of course they become vested in their preferred hypotheses about the causes and cures for mysterious ailments, at the exclusion of others.

While I have the utmost respect for the dedication and personal commitment of these scientists, from where I stand the MS field looks like a feedback loop. A small number of favoured theories are admitted into the circle while all others are excluded and ridiculed.

New approaches to treatment and new perspectives on the illness are often shut out.

To come up with a cure or even just a few answers for diseases like MS or Parkinson's we don't need people working doggedly only in their silos on their specific arm of research. We need a dialogue between all those specialists and other really smart people from a number of different disciplines. Everyone knows you can't fix a city ravaged by crime just by calling in the cops.

Meanwhile, as research takes place in silos, I watch on, trying to keep my nerve as my legs get stiffer.

Forty-four

Now I am in Italy – on my first proper holiday in decades. On my own and happy in paradise.

A friend knew of this little seaside oasis and told me about it before I left for Paris. I was searching for a place to go after the festival, when I knew I'd need sunshine and rest. She showed me a picture of Marina del Cantone and I didn't need any more persuading.

In 1996, when I wrote the Italian cookbook *Fresh! Market people and their food*, it was inspired by my childhood friend Mary de Costello. I had come to deeply appreciate her Italian heritage and the amazing food her mother prepared, even though Mary shunned it, wanting to be Australian and to fit in. Years later, I feared that for Mary's generation – the children of immigrants who were so eager to assimilate, to be part of their new home – the ways of living and family recipes would be lost.

So I decided to document them. I took my tape recorder to Adelaide's many markets and talked to people who were like Mary's parents – first-generation migrants – asking them about their traditional cuisine and recipes. Mainly I chose people who had their own gardens, who grew their own produce.

My father helped me. He loved markets and he loved the Italian people from whom he and Becky bought their weekly supplies at the outdoor, dockside farmers' market. We often went together to do my interviews. Then he helped me compile the book, sitting in the sunshine in the backyard at Henley, inserting the photos I'd taken along with their corresponding stories and recipes. My friend Marisa Raniolo Wilkins, the best Italian cook I know, helped with the recipes and explained many of the traditions behind them. It was a joyful project that I'm still proud of.

So to be in Italy, the ocean lapping on the pebbled shore directly outside my hotel room, was deeply affecting. Hotel Lo Scoglio is a family-owned hotel where I ate three meals a day. Each was superb. For breakfast there were figs bursting out of their skin, which I ate with the ocean rolling in on the pebbly beach at my feet.

The father of the family, Peppino, could sense my culinary interest. One day, he explained in a combination of Italian, simple English and many descriptive hand gestures that everything served in the restaurant came from a series of family farms situated at varying altitudes up the mountain that towered above the shoreline. He asked if I'd like to see the gardens and the next day we took off in his little Fiat, up the winding roads.

There were three separate oases filled with different fruits and vegetables. In the first garden, where the bay of Sorrento sparkled below, we wandered under canopies of vines laden with fruit that intertwined with threads of red and yellow cherry tomatoes. I kept picking things along the way and every time he saw what I was doing, he inspected what I had in my hand, said 'no good', took it from me and threw it to the ground. Then he found me better samples, which he handed over with his thick leathery fingers.

In the second garden, Peppino picked a fig, broke it in half and gave it to me. He cracked a fresh walnut and carefully peeled off the brown skin, handing me the sweet white heart. He broke off celery sticks and showed me long rows of eggplants and chillies. He collected fallen apples and then threw them to two enormous stinking pigs in their pen. We walked into a beautiful dense lemon grove that felt like a sacred place, a church to lemons.

Everything was organic. 'No chemicals,' he said. There were a number of cats lying about. 'They are for catching the Mickey Mice,' he told me as he stamped his foot to scatter the cats. Before we got back in the car, he walked along the neat rows of radicchio, bending over to snap off three red, round balls, which he said he would serve me for lunch.

He still wanted to pick wild rocket and show me the church that sits on the highest peak of the three mountains that hug the secluded bay. I could see the church high above my balcony and had wondered how worshippers made it all the way up there from the village. From the beach, the church seemed perched close enough to kiss the heavens.

We sped through tiny streets and he beeped the horn whenever he saw a friend. He slowed the car to shake people's hands through the open window and to have a few words. Their beautiful faces were lined by sun and cigarettes. Old and weathered. We spun down one street that was so narrow I thought he'd scrape the sides of the car. There was a four-way intersection in the tiny alleyway that would have had a stop sign in any other place. Peppino didn't slow, just gave a little beep and sped straight through. He said he was driving slowly because I was in the car. 'If I go, I will go happy,' I thought.

We drove up and up. Before we left the hotel I'd explained to Peppino's daughter, Antonia, that I had a bad leg so she could let him know that I wasn't going to be good for long trekking.

'Do you want to go up?' he asked when we got to the base of the long path to the church. 'We can try. It's up to you. If it's no good,' he slapped his leg, 'we come back.'

'Okay,' I said, thinking I'd never make it all the way.

'We'll go piano, piano,' he said, which seemed like one of the most beautiful sentences anyone had ever said to me.

We did indeed walk piano, piano, stopping every now and then for Peppino to pick wild mint, which he crushed in his fingers and placed under my nose. The scent was sweet, and stronger than the tiny sprig suggested. I suspect Peppino stopped for wild offerings along the way as a thoughtful way of allowing me to rest.

When we arrived at the top of the path, we looked back over Capri, out to the blue edge of the world. As we turned to walk to the other side of the peak, a British tourist with two long hiking sticks told us the cathedral was closed.

'Nothing is closed up here,' I said to Peppino with a sweep of my arm. 'I don't need to be inside. This is the cathedral.' The smile he gave made me certain that he understood exactly what I had said.

We got back to the hotel and he disappeared into the kitchen to deliver a bag of his pickings to his son, Tomasso, who was the chef. Antonia came out to report her father was taking care of my lunch.

She showed me to a table far out on the deck and brought me a glass of local wine, then a salad of cherry tomatoes, the radicchio from the garden and the wild rocket her father had just picked on our way down the mountain. The salad was followed by a whole grilled sea bass expertly filleted at my table, then drizzled in olive oil and fresh lemon juice from the grove we'd just walked through.

All the while, the sea pounded on the pebbled shore and the sun's rays danced on the water. I thought about what Philip had said the day I crawled up the road by his house on my hands and knees. It's here and it's now.

This had been a truly memorable morning. The sound of the waves lapping against the wooden posts underneath reminded me of hot days, sitting on the pier next to my brother, our lines cast out, my skinny legs hanging out over the edge, waiting for a fish to bite. I sat on the deck relishing the sunshine, as my father always had, with my eyes set on the horizon.

Afterword

For the sake of my father's four children and numerous grandchildren – some of whom he'd yet to meet – on 16 March 2004, as part of his preparation for death, my father began a series of tape recordings in which he was interviewed by Susan Lang, an artist he'd first exhibited in the early seventies, when she was about twenty-one.

My father bought the very first painting she ever sold, so he'd had some significance in her life, and she was delighted to see the painting still hanging in the house when she arrived to begin the interviews. Susan and my father had not particularly kept up in the intervening three decades, but she sat with him over eleven days, prompting him with questions and occasionally asking for clarification or more information, as he told the story of his life.

I have not been able to bring myself to listen to the nine tapes they made in that time, but I have made extensive use of the transcript of those interviews, which ended on 27 March, just two months before his death on 24 May 2004.

Acknowledgements

Diving into Glass had a very long gestation. Over its fifteen years of development, the book had numerous titles, changes in focus and was, for a while, even presented as a work of fiction. So it is no surprise that there is a long list of people who have helped me throughout this journey.

I would like to sincerely thank Sophia Beckett, Lisa Swanson, Jill Brack, Christina Mahle, Elizabeth Brack, Kris McIntyre, Beowulf Sheehan, Sam Douglas, Jane Rosenman, Dorothy Blackmun, Peter Kayafas, Amanda Stead, Jane Allen, Rhonda Sherman, Peter Pearce, Gretel Killeen, Trudy Armstrong, Jodie Bennett, Jane Palfreyman,

Irene Skolnick, Ben Ball, Vyvian and Peter Wilson, Edwina Johnson, Judy Cotton, Bob Evans, Marisa Raniolo Wilkins, and Antonia, Peppino, Santina, Mario, Tommaso and everyone at Lo Scoglio, Marina del Cantone.

I am grateful to my friends at Narrative 4 who first listened to my story atop a mountain in Colorado and gave me the courage to tell it more broadly: Colum McCann, Lisa Consiglio, Tobias Wolff, Firoozeh Dumas, Andrew Sean Greer, Terry Tempest Williams, Assaf Gavron, Ron Rash, Gregory Khalil, William Loizeaux, Terry Cooper, Luís Alberto Urrea, Cindy Urrea, Darrell Bourque, David Wroblewski, Reza Aslan, Ishmael Beah, Rob Spillman and Randall Kenan.

I am indebted to my agent, Gregory Messina, who has stuck with me through thick and thin long after it was reasonably fair to ask him to do so.

Importantly, I would like to thank Nikki Christer, Meredith Curnow, Louisa Maggio, Bella Arnott-Hoare and Johannes Jakob at Penguin Random House for their guidance, great care, kindness and faith. Johannes, special thanks for your editorial prowess and smarts – I could not have done this on my own and working through these pages with you has been a privilege.

Lastly, but most importantly, I would like to thank my family.

Crowdfunding Donors

In 2015, inspired by Jane McGonigal's *SuperBetter*, which is all about enlisting a team to battle life's big fights, I decided to call on the support of my friends. I was wrestling with the book and what I wanted to say and knew I needed an editor to help me make sense of the story I was trying to write. What happened when my work colleagues – Jill Brack and Esra Ar – encouraged and helped me launch my fundraising campaign was one of the most humbling and life-affirming experiences to witness. The incredible generosity and spirit with which each of the remarkable human beings listed below – some of whom I didn't know, others who I had lost contact with and hadn't been in touch with for decades – enabled me to enlist the services of the editor, Sam Douglas, who helped me find my way again. I am eternally grateful to each of you.

Bec Allen; Jane Allen; Esra Ar; Lotte Beckett; Simeon Beckett; Sophia Beckett; Dorothy Blackmun; Jessica Block; Jill and Regi Brack; Liz Brack; Giovanna Calvino; Kevin Chong; Lisa Consiglio; Brigid Costello; Pip Cummings; Laura Dalrymple; Humberto de Andrade Soares; Petrina Dorrington; Jo Duffy; Anne-Louise Falson; Neil Gaiman; Steven Galloway; Assaf Gavron; Kathleen Gilbert; Jacqui, Mark and Oscar; Sebastian Job; Edwina Johnson; Peter Kayafas; Gregory Khalil; Gretel Killeen; Tricia And Jonathan Koff; Rob Kovell; John Laxon; Frankie Lee; Lisa, Trevi and Thomas; Jane Lydon; Christina Mahle and Peter DiCaprio; Daina McDonald; Kris McIntyre; Katie McMurray; Rosemary Milsom; Charlotte Morgan; Epiphany Morgan; Ezekiel 'Zeke' Morgan; Sam Mostyn; Laszlo Jakab Orsos; Fiona Pak-Poy; Fiona Pearce; Peter Pearce; Rich & Kate; Elissa Schappell; Sheila Shaver and Jeremy Beckett; Juliet Sheen; Rob Spillman; Lisa Swanson; Peter and Vyvian Wilson; Wolfe family; Lila Azam Zanganeh.